Accession no.
36187015

KU-453-788

ASSESSMENT
and LEARNING

Education at SAGE

SAGE is a leading international publisher of journals, books, and electronic media for academic, educational, and professional markets.

Our education publishing includes:

- accessible and comprehensive texts for aspiring education professionals and practitioners looking to further their careers through continuing professional development

- inspirational advice and guidance for the classroom

- authoritative state of the art reference from the leading authors in the field

Find out more at: **www.sagepub.co.uk/education**

SECOND EDITION

LIS - LIBRARY

Date	Fund
18/9/15	Snr-xe

Order No.

2057442

University of Chester

ASSESSMENT and LEARNING

Edited by **JOHN GARDNER**

Los Angeles | London | New Delhi
Singapore | Washington DC

Editorial arrangement, Introduction and
Chapter 1 © John Gardner 2012
Chapter 2 © Paul Black and Dylan Wiliam
2012
Chapter 3 © David Pedder and Mary James
2012
Chapter 4 © Siobhan Leahy and Dylan
Wiliam 2012
Chapter 5 © Richard Daugherty, Paul
Black, Kathryn Ecclestone, Mary James
and Paul E. Newton 2012
Chapter 6 © Wynne Harlen 2012
Chapter 7 © John Gardner 2012

Chapter 8 © Louise Hayward 2012
Chapter 9 © Kathryn Ecclestone 2012
Chapter 10 © Judy Sebba 2012
Chapter 11 © Wynne Harlen 2012
Chapter 12 © Mary James with Jenny
Lewis 2012
Chapter 13 © Paul Black and Dylan
Wiliam 2012
Chapter 14 © Gordon Stobart 2012
Chapter 15 © Paul Black and Dylan
Wiliam 2012
Chapter 16 © Paul E. Newton 2012
Chapter 17 © John Gardner 2012

First edition published 2006
Second edition first published 2012

Apart from any fair dealing for the purposes of research or private study, or criticism or
review, as permitted under the Copyright, Designs and Patents Act, 1988, this publication may be reproduced, stored or transmitted in any form, or by any means, only with
the prior permission in writing of the publishers, or in the case of reprographic reproduction, in accordance with the terms of licences issued by the Copyright Licensing Agency.
Enquiries concerning reproduction outside those terms should be sent to the publishers.

SAGE Publications Ltd
1 Oliver's Yard
55 City Road
London EC1Y 1SP

SAGE Publications Inc.
2455 Teller Road
Thousand Oaks, California 91320

SAGE Publications India Pvt Ltd
B 1/I 1 Mohan Cooperative Industrial Area
Mathura Road
New Delhi 110 044

SAGE Publications Asia-Pacific Pte Ltd
3 Church Street
#10-04 Samsung Hub
Singapore 049483

Library of Congress Control Number: 2011927013

British Library Cataloguing in Publication data

A catalogue record for this book is available from the British Library

ISBN 978-0-85702-382-7
ISBN 978-0-85702-383-4 (pbk)

Typeset by C&M Digitals (P) Ltd, Chennai, India
Printed and bound by CPI Group (UK) Ltd, Croydon, CR0 4YY
Printed on paper from sustainable resources

Contents

About the Editor and Contributors

Editor

John Gardner, AcSS is Deputy Principal and Professor of Education at the University of Stirling. He has over 120 academic publications and his most recent assessment book is: *Developing Teacher Assessment* (McGraw-Hill/Open University, 2010). He is a visiting professor at the University of Oxford's Centre for Educational Assessment, a fellow of the British Computer Society and a fellow of the Chartered Institute of Educational Assessors. In 2009–2011 he was President of the British Educational Research Association.

Contributors

Paul Black is Professor Emeritus of Science Education at King's College London. He has made many contributions in both curriculum development and in assessment research. He has served on advisory groups of the USA National Research Council and as visiting professor at Stanford University. His work on formative assessment with Dylan Wiliam and colleagues at King's has had widespread impact.

Richard Daugherty is Director of the Oxford University Centre for Educational Assessment (OUCEA) and Honorary Professor at Cardiff University. His recent research has focused on education policy, especially policies on the school curriculum and on student assessment. From 1992 until 2010 he was a member of the Assessment Reform Group. Richard is a member of the Academy for the Social Sciences and was awarded the OBE in 2005.

Kathryn Ecclestone is Professor of Education and Social Inclusion at the University of Birmingham. Before working in higher education, she worked in further and adult education. Kathryn is a consultant to the National Board of Education in Finland on reforms to assessment and evaluation in Finnish vocational education. She is also a member of EdExcel/Pearson's expert group on assessment, is on the editorial boards of Studies in the Education of Adults and is book review editor for *Assessment in Education*.

Wynne Harlen has held positions as Professor of Science Education and head of the department of education at the University of Liverpool and Director of the Scottish Council for Research in Education. She was deputy director of the Assessment of Performance Unit and chair of the Science Expert Group of the OECD PISA project. She was a founder member of the British Educational Research Association and of the Assessment Reform Group. Her publications include 25 research reports, over 160 journal articles, contributions to 38 books and 30 books of which she is author or co-author.

Louise Hayward is Professor of Educational Assessment and Innovation in the University of Glasgow and was a member of the Assessment Reform Group from 2006–10. She was a founding member of the Assessment is for Learning programme in Scotland. Until 2010 she served on the Board of LTScotland and chaired its Advisory Council (the body charged to offer independent advice to Ministers). Currently, she is a member of the Board of the newly founded Education Scotland.

Mary James, AcSS, is Professor and Associate Director of Research at the University of Cambridge Faculty of Education, and is President of the British Educational Research Association. She was a member of the Assessment Reform Group from 1992. She was Deputy Director of the ESRC's Teaching and Learning Research Programme and director of the TLRP project – 'Learning How to Learn' – which researched the conditions in schools needed to promote assessment for learning in classrooms.

Siobhan Leahy: after many years teaching in inner-city schools in Birmingham and London, Siobhan Leahy was the founding headteacher of Oaklands School in Bethnal Green, principal of Orton Longueville School in Peterborough, and, from 2007 until her retirement in 2010, headteacher of Edmonton County School, Enfield.

From 2003 to 2006 she was a Senior Research Associate at Educational Testing Service, Princeton, New Jersey.

Jenny Lewis is a teacher at Recreation Road Infant School in Norwich. She has been using Mantle of the Expert (MoE) as a main pedagogy in her classroom for eight years and has been working to develop an assessment system that fits in with this way of learning. Jenny also runs workshops at MoE conferences and trains and supports teachers in Norfolk and further afield.

Paul E. Newton is the Director of the Cambridge Assessment Network Division, within Cambridge Assessment. Much of his research has focused on issues related to the design and evaluation of large-scale assessment systems. He has published papers on a range of assessment topics, including: comparability theory; purposes; validity; and the public understanding of measurement inaccuracy. Paul is a fellow of the Association for Educational Assessment – Europe.

David Pedder is Professor of Education at the University of Leicester. He was principal investigator of a large scale national project for the Training and Development Agency: 'Schools and Continuing Professional Development in England: the State of the Nation' and was senior research associate for the TLRP Learning How to Learn project. He has extensive teaching experience working in schools and classrooms in Japan and West Papua and many years' experience supporting teachers' learning in a range of contexts in West Papua and in the UK.

Judy Sebba is Professor of Education and Director of Research and Knowledge Exchange at the School of Education and Social Work at the University of Sussex. Her research focuses on assessment, personalized learning, pedagogy, teacher development and using research in policy and practice. She is a member of the Academy of Social Sciences and previously worked for six years in the Department of Education and Employment as an adviser on research strategy.

Gordon Stobart is Emeritus Professor of Education at the Institute of Education, University of London. He taught in secondary schools and worked as an educational psychologist before working as an assessment specialist in exam boards and government agencies. He was a founder member of the Assessment Reform Group (ARG) and his current work focuses on formative assessment and on the development of expert performance.

Dylan Wiliam is Emeritus Professor of Educational Assessment at the Institute of Education, University of London. In a varied career, he has taught in inner-city schools, trained teachers, run a large-scale testing programme, and served a number of roles in university administration, including Dean and Provost. From 2003 to 2006 he was Senior Research Director at Educational Testing Service, Princeton, New Jersey.

Chapter 1

Assessment and Learning: Introduction

John Gardner

On first inspection, the title of this book arguably places learning, one of the most fundamental processes in a person's lifecourse, secondary to one of the most contrived processes, the assessment of that learning. Our intention, however, is quite the opposite. As members of the Assessment Reform Group (ARG) we have accumulated over 21 years of collective research into assessment policy and practice, and many more years as individuals. As with the first edition, this second edition of *Assessment and Learning* is a book that unapologetically places learning at the centre of our concerns while unambiguously underscoring the importance of assessment in that learning.

The Assessment Reform Group was a research and lobbying group based in the UK and though it is natural for us to turn to our own contexts to illustrate analyses of assessment practice, the key aspiration throughout the group's existence has been to collate and use research from around the globe to develop a better understanding of how assessment can significantly contribute to learning. The reader will therefore find a liberal sprinkling of research-informed insights from a wide variety of international contexts. Here and there, throughout the book, we refer to various types of learning contexts in these countries but it is fair to say that, with the notable exception of Kathryn Ecclestone's Chapter 9, we draw heavily on the compulsory phases of education (roughly 4–16 years in most countries) to contextualize the practice of assessment for and, in some cases, of learning. It is also fair to say that it is in this context that the majority of research and experimentation has been recorded. We recognize that it is beyond the capacity of any one book to cover the huge span of educational endeavour in a world in which lifelong learning is the name of the game but we hope that the concepts and processes we illuminate throughout the chapters, such as learner engagement, feedback, motivation and pedagogic style, are key to any learning environment facilitated by teaching or instruction. Translating them to other learning contexts such as work-based learning, adult and community education or post-compulsory education, is not straight-forward but the principles and practices will be relevant.

In most developed countries, the pursuit of reliable and valid means of assessing people's learning generates high volumes of published discourse and, not infrequently, dissent; the documentation on the various assessment policies, practices and theories could conceivably fill whole libraries. Some of the discourse and much of the dissent relate to whether the use to which assessment is put is valid, or, to put it more mundanely, useful to the learners themselves or to other audi-ences. Our pursuit is somewhat different. We would argue that learn-ing should take centre stage and we address the role that assessment should play in this. Assessment is our focus but learning is the goal – and the implication for this edition as with the first is that in much of what follows it is assessment *for* learning that dominates the writing with assessment *of* learning given its secondary but still important place.

Two phrases, 'formative assessment' and 'assessment for learning', are used throughout all of the chapters that follow. The older phrase, 'formative assessment', can be traced back to Scriven's (1967) con-cepts of formative and summative evaluation, distinguished at the time solely on the basis of when the evaluation in question is carried out. While timing is merely one of the distinctions today, formative assessment remains a widely used concept in education. However, it is sometimes used to describe a process in which frequent ad hoc assessments, in the classroom or in formal assessment contexts such as practical skills work, are carried out over time and collated specifi-cally to provide a final (summative) assessment of learning. Such assessments potentially do not contribute to the students' learning. The second phrase, 'assessment for learning', came into use in the late 1980s and early 1990s (the chronological sequence and provenance is set out in detail in Siobhan Leahy and Dylan Wiliam's Chapter 4) and may therefore be considered a somewhat 'newer' concept.

In truth, though, assessment for learning comprises the same time-honoured practices as formative assessment, that is, what good teach-ers do and have always done (AAIA, 2005) when using assessment to assist students to take the next steps in their learning. In contrast to the term 'formative assessment', however, assessment for learning is arguably less likely to be used to describe the summative use of multi-ple assessments of learning. The words focus squarely on the essence of our pursuit: the promotion of assessment to support learning and this is neatly contra-distinct from assessment *of* learning. In the final analysis there is little of substance to distinguish the two terms 'formative assessment' and 'assessment for learning', but for the wider educational and policy-making audiences we feel that the latter is more accessible than the more technical term, 'formative assessment'. That said, we are content to use both phrases interchangeably, when there is no ambiguity in the type of assessment process being described.

In order to ensure we remain consistent in how we describe the type of process that assessment for learning is, we have defined it to be: 'the process of seeking and interpreting evidence for use by learners and their teachers, to identify where the learners are in their learning, where they need to go and how best to get there' (ARG, 2002).

Unpacking this deceptively simple definition, in terms of classroom practice, reveals a complex weave of activities involving pedagogic style, student–teacher interaction, self-reflection (teacher and student), motivation and a variety of assessment processes. For example, teachers need to plan the learning environment and activities, students need to engage in the assessment of their learning and teachers need to assess the extent of the students' understanding as they are learning. They then need to challenge and support these students to enable them to reach the next stage in their learning progress. An analysis of such a complex learning approach could never be exhaustive but we have tried to make it accessible through a previous publication entitled *Assessment for Learning: 10 Principles*. These principles are mentioned in various places in the chapters that follow and are summarized below:

Assessment for learning

- Is part of effective planning;
- Focuses on how students learn;
- Is central to classroom practice;
- Is a key professional skill;
- Is sensitive and constructive;
- Fosters motivation;
- Promotes understanding of goals and criteria;
- Helps learners know how to improve;
- Develops the capacity for self-assessment;
- Recognizes all educational achievement. (ARG, 2002)

All of these qualities, which we attribute collectively to assessment for learning, appear in various guises throughout the book – in their practice, in the theories underlying them and in the educational policies that relate to them.

Purposes and practice; impact; theory; and validity and reliability

Under these generic headings the structure of the book proceeds in four parts, which in turn address the purposes and practice of assessment (Part 1), its impact in a variety of contexts including its impact on learners (Part 2), its theoretical underpinnings (Part 3), and the enduring issues of validity and reliability (Part 4).

Part 1 – Purposes and Practice – represents a significant enhancement of the book with three new chapters. The first chapter (Chapter 2) by Paul Black and Dylan Wiliam draws as before on empirical evidence from several projects to portray how the findings from formative assessment research may be translated to classroom practice. In addition to significant changes to pedagogy, the chapter demonstrates that a full espousal of assessment for learning creates inevitable changes in teachers' and learners' understanding and attitudes to learning itself. Dave Pedder and Mary James pick up the story in Chapter 3 as they did in the first edition. This chapter draws on another project, Learning How to Learn, to tackle how such changes can be promoted and supported through teachers' professional learning. Central to the findings is the observation that very often, in an assessment for learning context, there is little to distinguish between the processes of learning for students and teachers. Chapter 4 is a new chapter from Siobhan Leahy and Dylan Wiliam that proposes up to 80% increases in students' speed of learning when formative assessment practices are truly integrated 'minute-by-minute and day-by-day' into teachers' classroom activities.

Chapter 5 is also new and draws on ARG's Assessment of Significant Learning Outcomes, the ASLO project. Richard Daugherty and colleagues present case study evidence that takes the analysis of the relationship between curriculum and assessment beyond the simple notion of explicit outcomes of assessment being in some way aligned to, or congruent with, a pre-specified curriculum. Rather than thinking in terms of aligning assessment more closely to curriculum, they argue that the construction of learning outcomes is better understood as a complex, non-linear, interacting system that embraces curriculum, pedagogy and assessment.

In Chapter 6 Wynne Harlen explores whether it is feasible for evidence gathered for one purpose to be used for another, focusing specifically on formative and summative assessments. Proposing a spectrum of possibilities that allows an overlap of purposes in its middle region, the chapter highlights the pitfalls of blithely advocating dual usage of the same information and suggests the conditions under which its integrity may be preserved.The final chapter in the section, Chapter 7 by John Gardner, tackles the thorny issue of what is considered to be quality in assessment practice. This chapter draws on the Analysis and Review of Innovations in Assessment project (ARIA) to identify key principles for quality assessment and then uses a selection of these to discuss the central aim for all assessment, the challenges of assessing complex learning, assessment and social inequality, and the public understanding of assessment.

Part 2 – Impact – focuses on the impact of assessments in several areas: on learners themselves, in vocational education and across several international contexts. Chapter 8 is a new chapter by Louise Hayward, in which she reflects on what we might learn from listening to learners. The chapter also identifies the process of working with learners, to explore the world as they experience it, as a research priority for the future development of assessment for learning. In Chapter 9, Kathryn Ecclestone probes trends in UK vocational education assessment that have resulted in what she terms the 'Holy Grail of crystal clarity'. These trends are skilfully unpacked as she identifies the pressing need to explore educational questions about the sort of person our current learning and assessment culture is creating, and the forms of knowledge, skills and dispositions that assessment fosters, overlooks or discourages. Judy Sebba's Chapter 10 acknowledges the problems inherent in any attempt to compare practices across cultures but points to the commonalities of understanding and practice across several nations. Wynne Harlen's Chapter 11 concludes the section by addressing a key element of formative assessment's armoury: promoting learners' motivation. Drawing on research from around the world, she argues that some summative assessment practices may have a negative impact on learners, while steps that ameliorate the worst effects, by developing and sustaining learner motivation, are often based on the principles of assessment for learning.

Part 3 – Theory – begins with a revamped chapter from Mary James (Chapter 12), which no longer reviews a history of learning theories (as in the first edition) but instead focuses on the problems and possibilities of developing assessment practice that is congruent with socio-cultural learning theory. This 'third generation' learning theory is neatly exemplified from a classroom perspective in a contribution from Jenny Lewis. Paul Black and Dylan Wiliam return in Chapter 13 with a fully revised and updated chapter offering a clear rationale for formative assessment, insights into its theoretical basis and a theoretical framing of formative assessment activities designed to suggest ways they may be evaluated and further improved.

Part 4 – Validity and Reliability – presents three authoritative chapters on these central themes of assessment practice. Gordon Stobart's Chapter 14 picks up the validity issue and concludes that there is a simple test for the validity of any assessment for learning process: did learning take place as a consequence? He poses a consequential validity argument and focuses on all aspects of the cultural and learning context, the quality of classroom interaction, the teacher's and learners' clarity about what is being learned and the effectiveness of feedback. Paul Black and Dylan Wiliam's Chapter 15 is a significant updating of their first edition chapter, and carries on a well-informed and well-argued debate about the perceived reliability of national and other external (to the school) testing. They conclude with the hard-hitting statement that trust in test scores is clearly not justified and is a serious issue when decisions on a student's future may be based on this misguided trust. The final chapter in this section, Chapter 16, is a new one from Paul Newton, which returns to the overarching keystone in assessment practice: validity. Taking a 'purposes' approach, the chapter warns the unwary about inappropriate (invalid) uses of assessments and points to the need for a sophisticated conception of validity to ensure assessment results are 'recycled' responsibly.

Chapter 17 from John Gardner rounds up the book with a concluding discussion on its main messages.

A note on the Assessment Reform Group

From its establishment in 1988, as the then Assessment Policy Task Group of the British Educational Research Association (BERA), the Assessment Reform Group occasionally changed in personnel but doggedly pursued the agenda of improving assessment in all of its forms. The founding members were Patricia Broadfoot, Bryan Dockrell, Caroline Gipps, Wynne Harlen and Desmond Nuttall, and its first task was to consider the implications of the 1988 Education Reform Act. Following Bryan Dockrell's retirement, Mary James and Richard Daugherty joined the group in 1992 and, in 1994, after the untimely death of Desmond Nuttall the previous year, Gordon Stobart and John Gardner also joined.

The membership then remained more or less unchanged until Caroline Gipps and Patricia Broadfoot moved on, in 2000 and 2002 respectively. Very able replacements were on hand and when the group finally wound up in 2010, it included Jo-Anne Baird, Paul Black, Kathryn Ecclestone, Louise Hayward and Paul Newton. Judy Sebba and Dylan Wiliam had also been members in the interim period before external commitments took over their time. In this edition we are very pleased to welcome them back along with guest contributors: Dave Pedder, Siobhan Leahy and Jenny Lewis.

From 1997, when BERA ceased to sponsor policy task groups, the ARG worked as an independent group with funding primarily from the Nuffield Foundation. The Foundation generously supported a variety of our activities including group meetings, regional seminars and the dissemination of our work. This funding was crucial to our success and we would be very remiss if we did not take the opportunity here to acknowledge our grateful appreciation of both BERA's and, in more recent times, the Foundation's support.

On that note, this introduction to the second edition would be seriously deficient if acknowledgement of our sources and influences was not formally recorded. Over the period of its existence, the group worked with many people including teachers, academics and curriculum and assessment agency personnel from around the world, local authority advisers and district superintendents, government officials, politicians and, most importantly, students in a variety of national and local contexts. There are too many to name and it would be inappropriate to single out specific people. However, the content of this book has been influenced by them all and we humbly record our thanks to everyone with whom we have had the privilege to work.

Postscript

In March 2008 members of the ARG, using funds from their publications, spent 24 hours 'away from it all' at Ross Priory on the shores of Loch Lomond. The aim was to take stock of past work, particularly on formative assessment, to consider implications of current assessment policy and to decide the future for the Group. The decision was made to wind up the Group in 2010 – 21 years after it began. More than half of the group is now retired, though all of them continue to be active in assessment research. On 8 June 2010, Cambridge Assessment hosted an event to say 'thank you and farewell' to the ARG on the occasion of our retirement. Held at Downing College, Cambridge, it provided an opportunity to reflect on the contribution that the Group has made to assessment policy and practice, both in the UK and beyond. With a view to the future, members of the Group offered reflections on what makes for successful assessment reform, encouraging a broader debate on the topic. Materials from the event, including a write-up of proceedings by education journalist Warwick Mansell and photos from the occasion, can be found at http://www.assessnet.org.uk/arg/.

References

AAIA (2005) *Managing Assessment for Learning*. Birmingham: Association for Achievement and Improvement through Assessment.

ARG (2002) *Assessment for Learning: 10 Principles* Assessment Reform Group. www.assessment-reform-group.org

Scriven, M. (1967) 'The methodology of evaluation', in R. W. Tyler (ed.), *Perspectives of Curriculum Evaluation*. Chicago: Rand McNally. pp. 39–83.

Part 1

Purposes and Practice

Chapter **2**

Assessment for Learning in the Classroom

Paul Black and Dylan Wiliam

Introduction

Assessment in education must, first and foremost, serve the purpose of supporting learning. So it is fitting to start a study of assessment with an exploration of the meaning and practices of assessment that serve this purpose most directly. This chapter is the story of a development that started with a review of what research had to say about formative assessment. The background to this review, and the main features of its findings, are first described. Its results led to development work with teachers to explore how ideas taken from the research could be turned into practice. A description of this work is followed by reflections on outcomes and implications. Finally, we will discuss the dissemination of the project's findings and its wider impact.

The research review

The background

Studies over many years have shown that formative assessment is an important aspect of teachers' classroom work and that attention to improving its practice can enhance the learners' achievements. Harry Black, a researcher in Scotland, who was unique at the time in working with teachers to develop formative assessment, introduced his account of the subject by pointing out that formative assessment has always been part of the practice of teachers, quoting in evidence a letter written by the Principal of Greenwich Hospital School (quoted in Chadwick, 1864), and calling attention to its neglect in the following trenchant terms:

> Consider the amount of time, energy and money spent by both individual teachers, and schools in general, on setting and marking continuous assessment tests, end of session examinations and mock O' levels. Reflect on the money spent by examination boards and the number of assessment specialists employed by them. Read, if you can find a sabbatical term, the literature on the technology of assessment for reporting and certification. Compare these in turn with the complete lack of support normally given to teachers in devising and applying procedures to pinpoint their students' learning problems, with the virtual absence of outside agencies to develop formative assessment instruments and procedures, and the limited literature on the topic. (Black, 1986: 7)

Linn, writing three years later, made a different and prophetic point about what might be involved:

> the design of tests useful for the instructional decisions made in the classroom requires an integration of testing and instruction. It also requires a clear conception of the curriculum, the goals, and the process of instruction. And it requires a theory of instruction and learning and a much better understanding of the cognitive processes of learners. (Linn, 1989: 5)

These extracts should not be misunderstood: it is clear from Harry Black's work that his terms 'procedures' and 'instruments' were not references to conventional summative tests, and it should also be clear that Linn's 'tests useful for ... instructional decisions' was not a reference to such tests either. However, despite such insights in the writing of several authors, formative assessment was not regarded as a more than marginal component by many involved in public debates on education, even when the report of the government's Task Group on Assessment and Testing (TGAT; National Curriculum Task Group, 1988) made teachers' formative assessment a central plank for its proposals.

Yet there was accumulating in the research literature on formative assessment practices a formidable body of evidence that could support claims for its importance. Early reviews by Natriello (1987), Crooks (1988) and Black (1993) drew attention to this evidence, but these were neither sufficiently comprehensive in scope, nor targeted directly at making the argument that formative assessment was a powerful way to raise standards. The Assessment Reform Group, however, whose main concern was consideration of research evidence as a basis for formation of assessment policy, judged that further exploration of formative assessment was essential and in 1996 obtained funding from the Nuffield Foundation to support a review of research. The Group then invited the two of us to carry out this review, and because of our long-standing interest in formative assessment, we were happy to agree to undertake the task.

The review

Our survey of the research literature involved checking through many books, through the issues of over 160 journals published between 1988 and 1997, and studying earlier reviews of research (Crooks, 1988; Natriello, 1987). This process yielded about 580 articles or chapters to study. Out of this we prepared a lengthy review that cited 250 of these sources. The review was published (Black and Wiliam, 1998a) together with comments on our work by experts from five different countries. As this work progressed, we developed a new view of the issues relevant to the field; a view that we set out in six sections.

A first section surveyed the evidence. We looked for studies that showed quantitative evidence of learning gains by comparing data for an experimental group with similar data from a control group. We reported on about 30 such studies, all of which showed that innovations which included strengthening the practice of formative assessment produced significant, and often substantial, learning gains. They ranged over ages (from 5-year-olds to university undergraduates), across several school subjects, and over several countries.

The fact that such gains had been achieved by a variety of methods that had, as a common feature, enhanced formative assessment indicated that it is this feature that accounted, at least in part, for the successes. However, it did not follow that it would be an easy matter to achieve such gains on a wide scale in normal classrooms, in part because the research reports lacked enough detail about the practical use of the methods, detail that would be essential if replication were envisaged. More significantly, successful implementation of such innovations is dependent on the social and educational context of their development, so that they cannot merely be implemented in the same way if they are to be successful in a different context.

A second section covered research into current practices of teachers. The picture that emerged was that, for the vast majority of teachers, formative assessment was not a well-developed aspect of practice.

In relation to *effective learning* it seemed that teachers' questions and tests encouraged rote and superficial learning, even where teachers said that they wanted to develop understanding. There was also evidence of the *negative impact* of a focus on comparing students with one another, so emphasizing competition rather than personal improvement. Furthermore, teachers' feedback to students often seemed to serve social and managerial functions, often at the expense of the learning functions.

A third section focused on research into the involvement of students in formative assessment. Students' beliefs about the goals of learning, about the risks involved in responding in various ways, and about what learning work should be like, were all shown to affect their motivation. Other research explored the different ways in which positive action could be taken, covering such topics as study methods, study skills, and peer- and self-assessment.

A fourth section looked at ideas that could be gleaned from the research about strategies that might be productive for teachers. One feature that emerged was the potential of the learning task, as designed by a teacher, for exploring students' learning. Another was the importance of the classroom discourse, as steered by teachers' questions and by their handling of students' responses.

A fifth section shifted attention to research into comprehensive systems of teaching and learning in which formative assessment played a part. One example was mastery learning programmes. In these it was notable that students were given feedback on their current achievement against some expected level of achievement (i.e. the 'mastery' level); that such feedback was given promptly; and that students were given the opportunity to discuss with their peers how to remedy any weaknesses.

A sixth section explored in more detail the literature on feedback. The review of empirical evidence by Kluger and DeNisi (1996) showed that feedback can have positive effects only if the feedback is used as a guide to improvement, whilst the conceptual analysis of the concept of feedback by Ramaprasad (1983) and the development of this by Sadler (1989) emphasized that learners must understand both the 'reference level' (i.e. the goal of their learning) and the actual level of their understanding. Another important message came from the research on attribution theory (for example by Vispoel and Austin [1995] and by Dweck [2000]) that teachers must aim to inculcate in their students the idea that success is due to internal, unstable, specific factors such as effort, rather than on stable general factors such as ability (internal) or whether one is positively regarded by the teacher (external).

Four key themes emerged from the research we reviewed. First, formative work involves new ways to enhance feedback between those taught and the teacher, ways which require new modes of pedagogy and significant changes in classroom practice. Second, underlying the various approaches are assumptions about what makes for effective learning – in particular that students have to be actively involved. Third, for assessment to function formatively, the results have to be used to adjust teaching and learning – so a significant aspect of any programme will be the ways in which teachers do this. Fourth, the ways in which assessment can affect the motivation and self-esteem of students, and the benefits of engaging students in self-assessment, both deserve careful attention.

The structure of the six sections outlined above did not emerge automatically: as our work progressed, so we had to find ways of organizing the field, and making new conceptual links in order to be able to combine the various findings into as coherent a picture as possible. We believe that our review generated a momentum for work in this field by providing a new framework that would be difficult to create in any other way.

Moving into action

Setting up a project

Given that our review had shown that innovations in formative assessment could raise standards of student achievement substantially, it was natural to think about ways to help schools secure these benefits. However, even if a recipe for practice could have been derived from the variety of research studies, our own experience of teachers' professional development had taught us that the implementation of innovative practices in classrooms could not be a straightforward matter of proclaiming a recipe for teachers to follow. We believed that new ideas about teaching and learning could only be made to work in particular contexts, in our case that of teachers in (initially) secondary schools in the UK, if teachers were able to transform or 'morph' them (Ginsburg, 2001) and so create new practical knowledge relevant to their work.

We obtained funding from the UK's Nuffield Foundation (and later also from the National Science Foundation in the USA), for a two-year development project. To find schools and teachers to work with, we talked with assessment specialists from two local education authorities (usually called school districts in the USA, and local authorities, or just LAs in England). The two were chosen because we knew that they would understand and support our aims, and visits to their respective districts (Oxfordshire and Medway) could reasonably be managed in a day.

In each local authority, three schools teaching students from 11 to 18 years of age were then chosen by the LA specialists. The initial choice was made by the specialists, although we had requested that schools that were either in serious difficulties or unusually successful would not be chosen. The schools agreed to collaborate with us and each school identified two science and two mathematics teachers. In the second year of the project we added two teachers of English, from each of the same schools, and one additional mathematics and science teacher, so that in all 48 teachers were involved. The LA specialists were involved with the work throughout. The project was called the King's College Medway Oxford Formative Assessment Project (KMOFAP) to highlight our close collaboration with these partners (Black and Wiliam, 2003).

Because the teachers within the schools were chosen by the schools themselves (sometimes with advice from the LA specialists), the teachers varied considerably in their experience, qualifications and expertise. Some were newly qualified, others were heads of the subject departments, one was close to retirement, and one apparently was identified because the head teacher of the school thought she 'needed some INSET'. However the majority were experienced and well qualified. Before the start of the project's work, we and the LA specialist visited each school in order to explain the aims and the requirements to the head teacher. We chose to work with secondary mathematics and science because we were specialists in those two subjects at this level and believed that the nature of the subject matter was important. English teachers were brought in when a colleague specializing in English was able to join the team.

We advised the teachers to focus on a few, and eventually just one, focal class to try out the innovations that they chose to work at, with a caveat that they might do well to avoid those age groups (13–14 and 15–16-year-olds), for which statutory national tests might inhibit their freedom to experiment. In the event, some ignored this advice, so that the classes involved ranged over ages 11 to 16. Whilst support from each school's senior management was promised in principle, it varied in practice; moreover, within the school subject faculty or department, some had stronger support from subject colleagues than others, and in fact the collegial support that would be essential in an endeavour of this kind was largely provided by the meetings, once every five weeks, when the project teachers all spent a day together with the staff at King's. There was evidence of interest and support from other school colleagues – several productive ideas were injected into the group from this type of source, and it was soon clear that the ideas in the project were influencing teachers more widely, to the extent that in some cases it was difficult to find suitable 'control' classes for comparison of their test performance with those of pupils in the focal classes of the project.

The practices developed

These practices will be described here under four headings: oral feedback in *classroom questioning* (more recently re-labelled as *dialogue*), *feedback through marking, peer- and self-assessment,* and the *formative use of summative tests.* The account given will be brief – more detailed accounts have been published elsewhere (Black et al., 2003). These practices were defined and developed in the course of the project, the process being one in which we drew, from the research findings, a variety of ideas for which there was evidence of potential value, and then teachers selected from these and developed them in their own ways. The four themes discussed below were an outcome of the project, for while they were related to our inputs, we could not have predicted at the outset that a set of themes would emerge in the way that they did.

For *classroom dialogue* the aim was to improve the interactive feedback that is central to formative assessment. After hearing an account of research on wait-time (e.g., Rowe, 1974) teachers were motivated to allow a longer time after asking a question so that students would have time to think out responses, and so that all could be expected to become actively involved in question and answer discussions, and to make longer replies. Increased participation of students also required that all answers, right or wrong, be taken seriously, the aim being to develop thoughtful improvement rather to evoke the expected answers. A consequence of such changes was that teachers learnt more about the pre-knowledge of their students, and about any gaps and misconceptions in that knowledge, so that their next 'moves' could address the learners' real needs.

As they tried to develop this approach, teachers realized that more effort had to be spent in framing questions that would evoke, and so help to explore, critical indicators of students' understanding. They also had to listen carefully to students and then formulate meaningful responses and challenges that would help them to extend that understanding.

The task of developing an interactive style of classroom dialogue required a radical change in teaching style from many teachers, one that they found challenging. Some were well over a year into the project before such change was achieved. Subsequent work with other schools has shown that it is this aspect of formative work that teachers are least likely to implement successfully.

To address *feedback through marking,* teachers were first given an account of research studies that established that, while students' learning can be advanced by feedback through comments, the giving of marks or grades has a negative effect because students ignore comments when marks are also given (Butler, 1988). These results surprised and worried the teachers, because of concern about the effect of returning students' work with comments but no marks. However, potential conflicts with school policy were resolved as the teachers discovered that providing comments rather than grades gave both students and their parents advice on how to improve. It also set up a new focus on the issue of how to move learning forward rather than on trying to interpret a mark or grade. To make the most of the learning opportunity created by feedback on written work, procedures that required students to follow up comments had to be planned as part of the overall learning process.

One consequence of this change was that teachers had to think more carefully in framing comments on written work in order to give each student guidance on how to improve. As the skills of formulating and using such feedback were developed, it became clearer that the quality of the tasks set for written homework or class work was critical: as for oral questions, tasks had to be designed to encourage students to develop and express key features of their understanding.

For *peer- and self-assessment,* the starting point was Sadler's (1989) argument that self-assessment is essential to learning because students can only achieve a learning goal if they understand that goal and can assess what they need to do to reach it. Thus the criteria for evaluating any learning achievements must be made transparent to students to enable them to have a clear overview both of the aims of their work and of what it means to complete it successfully. In so far as they do so they begin to develop an overview of that work so that they can manage and control it: in other words, they develop their capacity for meta-cognitive thinking. A notable example of the success of such work is the research of White and Frederiksen (1998).

In practice, peer-assessment turned out to be an important stimulus to self-assessment. It is uniquely valuable because the interchange will be in language that students themselves would naturally use, because students learn by taking the roles of teachers and examiners of others (Sadler, 1998), and because students appear to find it easier to make sense of criteria for their work if they examine other students' work alongside their own. A typical exercise would be on the marking of homework. Students were asked to label their work with 'traffic lights' as an indicator of their confidence in their learning (i.e. using red or amber if they were totally or partially unsure of their success, and green where they were confident). Then those who had used amber or green would work in mixed groups to appraise and help with one another's work, whilst the teacher would pay special attention to those who had chosen red.

Teachers developed three ways of making *formative use of summative tests*. One way was to ask students, in preparation for a test, to 'traffic light' a list of key words or of the topics on which the test would be set, an exercise which would stimulate them to reflect on where they felt their learning was secure and where they needed to concentrate their efforts. One reason for doing this was that teachers had realized that many students had never thought about developing a strategy for preparing for a test such as formulating a strategic appraisal of their learning.

A second way was to mark one another's test papers in peer groups, in the way outlined above for the marking of homework. This could be particularly challenging when they were expected to invent their own marking rubric, for to do this they had to think about the purpose of a question and about the criteria of quality to apply to responses. After peer marking, teachers could reserve their time for discussion of the questions that gave particular difficulty.

A further idea was introduced from research studies that have shown that students trained to prepare for examinations by generating and then answering their own questions out-performed comparable groups who prepared in conventional ways (Foos et al., 1994; King, 1992). Preparation of test questions calls for, and so develops, an overview of the topic.

The teachers' work on summative assessments challenged our expectations that, for the context in which they worked, formative and summative assessments are so different in their purpose that they have to be kept apart. The finding that emerged was quite different – that summative tests should be, and should be seen to be, a positive part of, and therefore integrated into, the learning process. If they could be actively involved in the test process, students might see that they can be beneficiaries rather than victims of testing, because tests can help them improve their learning. However, this synergy could not be achieved in the case of high-stakes tests set and marked externally; for these, as currently designed and administered, formative use would not be possible; it can be achieved in the case of summative tests designed and used for internal use in a school (see Black et al., 2010).

Reflections on the outcome

It was clear that the new ideas that had emerged between the teachers and ourselves involved far more than the mere addition of a few tactical tricks. Some reflection was needed to tease out the more fundamental issues that seemed to be raised.

A focus on learning

One of the most surprising things that happened during the early project meetings was that the participating teachers asked us to run a session on learning theories. In retrospect, perhaps, we should not have been so surprised. Whilst teachers could work out after the event whether or not any feedback had had the desired effect, what they needed was to be able to give their students feedback that they knew in advance was going to be useful. To do that they needed to build up models of how students learn.

As a result, the teachers came to take greater care in selecting tasks, questions, and other prompts, to ensure that the responses made by students actually 'put on the table' the ideas that they bring to a learning task. The key to effective learning is to then find ways to help students restructure their knowledge to build in new and more powerful ideas. In the KMOFAP classrooms, as the teachers came to listen more attentively to the students' responses, they began to appreciate more fully that learning is not a process of passive reception of knowledge, but one in which the learners are active in creating their own understandings. These ideas reflect some of the main principles of the constructivist view of learning – to start where the student is and to involve the students actively in the process, and to understand that because students are active in the construction of their own knowledge, what they construct may be very different from what the teacher intended.

Students also changed, coming to understand what counted as good work through a focus on the criteria and on their exemplification. Sometimes this was done through focused whole-class discussion around a particular example; at other times it was achieved through students using criteria to assess the work of their peers. The activities, by encouraging students to review their work in the light of the goals and criteria, were helping them to develop meta-cognitive approaches to learning.

Finally, the involvement of students both in whole-class dialogue and in peer-group discussions, as part of a broader shift in the classroom culture (to which all four activities contributed), created a richer community of learners where the social learning of students would become more salient and effective.

A learning environment and changes of role

Reflection on the experiences described above led to more profound thinking by participants about their role as teachers and about the need to 'engineer' learning environments in order to involve students more actively in learning tasks. The emphasis had to be on the students doing more of the thinking and making that thinking public. As one teacher said:

> There was a definite transition at some point, from focusing on what I was putting into the process, to what the students were contributing. It became obvious that one way to make a significant sustainable change was to get the students doing more of the thinking. I then began to search for ways to make the learning process more transparent to the students. Indeed, I now spend my time looking for ways to get students to take responsibility for their learning and at the same time making the learning more collaborative. Tom, Riverside School. (Black et al., 2002)

This teacher had changed his role from being a presenter of content to being a leader of an exploration and development of ideas in which all students were involved. One of the striking features of the project was the way in which, in the early stages, many spoke about the new approach as 'scary', because they felt that they were losing control of their classes. Towards the end of the project, they described this same process not as a loss of control, but as one of sharing responsibility for the class's learning with the class – exactly the same process, but viewed from two very different perspectives.

The learning environment envisaged requires a classroom culture that may well be unfamiliar and disconcerting for both teachers and students. The effect of the innovations implemented by our teachers was to change the rules, usually implicit, that govern the behaviours that are expected and seen as legitimate by teachers and by students. As Perrenoud (1991: 92) put it: 'Every teacher who wants to practise formative assessment must reconstruct the teaching contract so as to counteract the habits acquired by his pupils'.

For the students, they have to change from behaving as passive recipients of the knowledge offered to becoming active learners who could take responsibility for their own learning. These students became more aware of when they were learning, and when they were not. One class, who were subsequently taught by a teacher not emphasizing assessment for learning, surprised that teacher by complaining: 'Look, we've told you we don't understand this. Why are you going on to the next topic?'

Another way of thinking about what happened in the project is that the role expectations – that is, what teachers and students thought that being a teacher or being a student required you to do – had been altered. Whilst it can seem daunting to undertake such changes, they do not have to happen suddenly. Changes with the KMOFAP teachers came slowly, typically over two years rather than one, and steadily, as experience developed and confidence grew in the use of the various strategies for enriching feedback and interaction.

A collection of individual and group discussion data near the end of the project did expose one unresolved problem – the tension between the formative approach and summative demands. Some, but not all, teachers were confident that the new work would yield better test result than 'teaching to the test'. However, for their in-school summative tests, many felt impelled to use questions from the key stage 3 and GCSE tests despite doubts about the validity of these in relation to the improved pupil learning achieved in the project. The general picture was that, despite developing the formative use of their summative tests, teachers felt that they could not reconcile the external test and accountability pressures with their investment in improved formative assessment.

Research and practice

Explaining success: the focus of the project

We were surprised that the project was so successful in promoting quite radical changes in the practices of almost all of the teachers involved, and wondered whether lessons could be learned from it about the notoriously difficult problem of turning research into practice. One relevant factor is that the ideas that the project set before the teachers had an intrinsic acceptability to them. We were talking about improving learning in the classroom, which was central to their professional identities, as opposed to bureaucratic measures such as predicting test levels. One feature of our review was that most of it was concerned with such issues as students' perceptions, peer- and self-assessment, and the role of feedback in a pedagogy focused on learning. Thus it helped to take the emphasis in formative assessment studies away from *systems,* with its emphasis on the formative-summative interface, and re-locate it on classroom *processes.* Acceptability was also enhanced by our policy of emphasizing that it was up to each teacher to make his or her own choice between the different formative practices; so teachers developed their own personal portfolios, adding to or dropping components as experience and the experiences of their colleagues led them to change.

Linked to the previous factor is that in our choice to concentrate on the classroom processes, we had decided to live with the external constraints operating at the formative–summative interface: the legislated attempts to change the *system*, in the 1980s and 1990s in England, were set aside. Whilst it might have been merely prudent to not try to tilt at windmills, the more fundamental strength was that it was at the level chosen – learning processes in classrooms – that formative work stakes its claim for attention. Furthermore, given that any change has to work out in teachers' practical action, this is where reform should always have started.

Another factor that appears to have been important is the credibility that we brought as researchers to the process. In their project diaries, several of the teachers commented that it was our espousal of these ideas, as much as the ideas themselves, that persuaded them to engage with the project. Part of that credibility is that we chose to work with teachers in the three subjects, English, mathematics and science, when, in each of these, one or two members of the team had expertise and reputations in the subject community. Thus, when specific issues, such as 'Is this an appropriate question for exploring students' ideas about the concept of photosynthesis?' arose, we could discuss them seriously.

Explaining success: the process strategy

The way in which teachers were involved was also important. They all met with the researchers for a whole day every five weeks, over a period of two years. In addition, two researchers were able to visit the schools, observe the teachers in their classrooms, give them feedback, collect interview data on their perceptions, and elicit ideas about issues for discussion in the whole-day meetings. The detailed reports of our findings (Black et al., 2002, 2003) are based on records of these meetings, on the observations and records of visits to classrooms by the King's team, on interviews with and writing by the teachers themselves, on feedback from the LA specialists who held their own discussions with their teachers, and on a few discussions with student groups. As the project developed, the King's team played a smaller part as the teachers took over the agenda and used the opportunity for their own peer learning.

In our development model, we attended to both the *content* and the *process* of teacher development (Reeves et al., 2001). We attended to the *process* of professional development through an acknowledgement that teachers need time, freedom, and support from colleagues, in order to reflect critically upon and to develop their practice (Lee and Wiliam 2000), whilst offering also practical strategies and techniques about how to begin the process. By themselves, however, these are not enough. Teachers also need concrete ideas about the directions in which they can productively take their practice, and thus there is a need for work on the professional development of teachers to pay specific attention to subject-specific dimensions of teacher learning (Wilson and Berne, 1999).

One of the key assumptions of the project was that if the promise of formative assessment was to be realized, a research design in which teachers are asked to test out, and perhaps modify, a scheme worked out for them by researchers would not be appropriate. We presented them with a collection of ideas culled from research findings rather than with a structured scheme. We argued that a process of supported development was an essential next step. In such a process, the teachers in their classrooms had to work out the answers to many of the practical questions that the research evidence that we presented could not answer. The issues had to be reformulated in collaboration with them, where possible in relation to fundamental insights, and certainly in terms that could make sense to their peers in ordinary classrooms.

The key feature of the INSET sessions was the development of action plans. Since we were aware from other studies that effective implementation of formative assessment requires teachers to renegotiate the 'learning contract' that they had evolved with their students (Brousseau, 1984; Perrenoud, 1991), we decided that implementing formative assessment would best be done at the beginning of a new school year. For the first six months of the project (January 1999 to July 1999), therefore, we encouraged the teachers to experiment with some of the strategies and techniques suggested by the research, such as rich questioning, comment-only marking, sharing criteria with learners, and student peer- and self-assessment. Each teacher was then asked to draw up an action plan of the practices they wished to develop and to identify a single focal class with whom these strategies would be introduced at the start of the new school year in September 1999. Details of these plans can be found in Black et al. (2003). As the teachers explored the relevance of formative assessment for their own practice, they transformed ideas from the research and from other teachers into new ideas, strategies and techniques, and these were in turn communicated to teachers, creating a 'snowball' effect. As we have introduced these ideas to more and more teachers outside the project, we have become better at communicating the key ideas (see Chapter 3 for further exploration of this issue).

Through our work with teachers, we have come to understand more clearly how the task of applying research to practice is much more than a simple process of 'translating' the findings of researchers into the classroom. The teachers in our project were engaged in a process of knowledge creation, albeit of a distinct kind and possibly relevant only in the settings in which they work (Hargreaves, 1999). We stressed this feature of our approach with the teachers right from the outset of the project. We discovered later that some of them did not, at that stage, believe us: they thought that we knew exactly what we wanted them to do but wanted them to discover it for themselves. As they came to know us better, they realized that, at the level of everyday classroom practice, we really did not know what to do. The arguments in this section are addressed only to the specific question with which it started – why did this project work – with the intent of thereby illuminating the vexed issues of the relationship between research and practice. They cannot claim to address the question of whether an innovation with similar aims would succeed in different circumstances. Any attempt to answer such a question would have to relate the context and particular features of our work to the context and features of any new situation, bearing in mind that any such innovation will start from where our work finished and not from where we started.

Dissemination and impact

Publicity

Publicity designed to make a case for formative assessment started, alongside the publication of the research review, in 1998. Although we tried to adhere closely to the traditional standards of scholarship in the social sciences when conducting and writing our review, we did not do so when exploring the policy implications in a booklet, entitled *Inside the Black Box* (Black and Wiliam, 1998b) that we published, and publicized widely, alongside the academic review. This raised a great deal of interest and created some momentum for our project and for subsequent dissemination. While the standards of evidence we adopted in conducting the review might be characterized as those of 'academic rationality', the standard for *Inside the Black Box* was much closer to that of 'reasonableness' as advocated by Stephen Toulmin for social inquiry (Toulmin, 2001). In some respects, *Inside the Black Box* represented our opinions and prejudices as much as anything else, although we would like to think that these are supported by evidence, and are consistent with the 50 years of experience in this field that we had between us. It is also important to note that the success of *Inside the Black Box* – it has to date sold about 50,000 copies – has been as much due to its rhetorical force as to its basis in evidence, whilst the version published in a USA teacher journal has been the most frequently quoted article in that journal. This would make many academics uneasy – for it appears to blur the line between fact and value, but as Flyvbjerg (2001) argues, social enquiry has failed precisely because it has focused on analytic rationality rather than value-rationality (see also Wiliam, 2003).

The quantitative evidence that formative assessment does raise standards of achievement was a powerful motivator for the teachers at the start of the project. One aspect of the KMOFAP project was that the King's team worked with each teacher to collect data on the gains in test performance of the students involved in the innovation, and comparable data for similar classes who were not involved (Wiliam et al., 2004). The project did not introduce any tests of its own but rather relied on achievement data used from the tests that the schools used for all students, whether or not they were involved in the project. The analysis of these data showed an overall and significant gain in achievement outcomes. Thus the evidence from the research review can now be supplemented by evidence of enhanced performance on the UK national and on schools' own examinations. This evidence was incorporated, with an account of the practical lessons learnt in the KMOFAP project, in a second small booklet, *Working Inside the Black Box* (Black et al., 2002), which has also been widely successful with over 50,000 copies sold to date, whilst a detailed account of the project's work (Black et al., 2003) has also been very well received. Further booklets on specific aspects of formative assessment have also been produced[1] and other publicity for formative assessment, further research results and practical advice, notably from the Assessment Reform Group (ARG: 1999, 2001, 2002; Mansell et al., 2009) have added to the impact.

Dissemination

Following this project, members of the King's team have responded to numerous invitations to talk to other groups: over three years they have made over 500 such contributions. These have ranged across all subjects, across primary, secondary and post-compulsory phases. In addition, there has been sustained work with four groups of primary schools. The King's team has also been involved as advisers to large-scale development ventures, in several local government districts in the UK, and with education ministries in Scotland and in Jersey.

The Education Department of the Scottish Executive, which has full legislative powers in education in Scotland, has taken up the work as one of several strands of its Assessment is for Learning Development Programme. This project, entitled Support for Professional Practice in Formative Assessment, involved four groups of eight or nine schools, including both secondary and primary. They were supported by one development officer and staff from two university faculties, and also by contributions from the King's project staff. The work started in May 2002, and an evaluation project, conducted by the Institute of Education, University of London completed its work in summer 2004. The evaluation report (Hallam et al., 2004) reported the following findings for the impact on pupils:

- a substantial increase in perceptions of pupils' engagement with learning, with particular notable impact on lower attainers, and shy and disengaged pupils in a special school for pupils with complex learning needs;
- better motivation, more positive attitudes to learning, and, for many, enhanced confidence;
- some improvements in behaviour and more cooperation in class in teamwork and in learning;
- dramatic improvements in pupils' learning skills, in learning about their strengths and weaknesses and about what they needed to do to make progress, so encouraging them to take more responsibility for their learning. ⟍reflection

For the teachers, they reported greater awareness of the needs of individual pupils, and improvement in their motivation, confidence and enjoyment of their work. They believed that their capacity for self-evaluation, reflection and continuous improvement had been enhanced. A positive impact on their schools as a whole was also reported, and a similar benefit for parents was reported by the primary schools. *motivation*

Just as these features reflected the experience of the KMOFAP project (which was not independently evaluated), so did most of the points which were judged to contribute to its success. These included the provision of time out of class for teachers to plan, prepare, reflect and evaluate, the action research elements of the project, and the commitment of each school's head teacher and senior management team.

The evaluation also revealed several challenges. One was that some staff found that the initiative called for a fundamental change in their pedagogy, which they found stressful, and for more priority in developing differentiation in implementation of the strategies. The need to meet demands of external accountability was also a cause for concern, with teachers reporting tension between the demands of summative assessment and the implementation of new formative practices. Again, in all of these features there was close correspondence with the KMOFAP experience.

One problem with the dissemination is that the phrase 'Assessment for Learning' has been attached as a headline label to programmes and publications which do not justify this title, or at the very least, have an idiosyncratic interpretation of the phrase. The most frequent misunderstanding has been to equate this work with frequent summative testing, even to the extent of publicizing highly atomized tests so that pupils' progress towards myriad component targets can be subject to regular checks. A less evident misinterpretation is based on a belief that a short training day, followed up by bulky documentation setting out in detail what teachers should do, will produce the required changes. It will not – the changes needed run too deep for such an approach to work.

Future issues

Many questions arise from this work that await further research inquiry. Some will be taken further in subsequent chapters of this book. The need to co-ordinate all of the above issues in a comprehensive theoretical framework linking assessment in classrooms to issues of pedagogy and curriculum will be tackled in Chapter 13. The tensions and possible synergies between teachers' own assessments and the assessment results and methods required by society will be explored further in Chapter 15.

A further issue is that of the assumptions about learning underlying the curriculum and pedagogy. The beliefs of teachers about learning, about their roles as assessors and about the 'abilities' and prospects of their students, will affect their interpretations of their students' learning work, and will thereby determine the quality of their formative assessment. This will be taken further in Chapters 12 and 13. A parallel inquiry is also needed into the perceptions and beliefs held by students about themselves as learners, and into their experience of the changes that follow from innovations in formative assessment: exploration of this issue is a current aim of the ESRC-funded project: Learning How to Learn: in Classrooms, Schools and Networks.

Light will also be cast by that project on the problem of the generalizability of the findings from KMOFAP and from the Scottish initiative. The experience so far of schools basing their own innovations on the existing findings of results from research and from recently developed practice is that a sustained commitment over at least two years is needed, that evaluation and feedback have to be built in to any plan, and that any teachers involved need strong support, both from colleagues and from their school leadership. The more recent Learning How to Learn project, a collaboration between Cambridge, King's College and the Open University, has implemented interventions based in part on the findings of our project: this work is reported in Chapter 3, and issues of the leadership of such changes feature in Chapter 4.

Other issues that might repay further exploration are:

- the surprising feature that the research in this field has paid virtually no attention to issues relating to race, class and gender;
- the effect on practice of the content knowledge, and the pedagogical content knowledge, that teachers deploy in particular school subjects: issues for enquiry would be the way in which these resources underlie each teacher's composition and presentation of the learning work, and the interpretative frameworks that he or she uses in responding to the evidence provided by feedback from students;
- the need to pursue in more detail the many issues about pedagogy that are entailed in formative assessment work, notably the deployment in this context of the results of the numerous studies of classroom dialogue (see e.g. Alexander, 2008), and the findings of research and development work aimed at improving the quality of peer-group work (Blatchford et al., 2006; Mercer et al., 2004);
- the nature of the social setting in the classroom, as influenced both by the divisions of responsibility between learners and teachers in formative assessment, and by the constraints of the wider school system;
- the need to extend work of this nature to other groups, notably pupils in infant and junior school and students in post-16, tertiary and non-statutory assessment settings (Chapter 9).

More generally, this work raises questions about the 'application' of research to practice, and the links between this and the professional development of teachers (Black and Wiliam, 2003). Researching how teachers take on research, adapt it, and make it their own is much more difficult than researching the effects of different curricula, of class sizes, or of the contribution of classroom assistants. Furthermore, the criteria applied in judging the practical value of research aligned to development can easily be made too stringent. If, as we believe is reasonable, an approach in which 'the balance of probabilities' rather than 'beyond reasonable doubt' was adopted as the burden of proof, then this type of educational research would be accepted as having much to say. Thus we take issue with the stance of some policy makers who appear to want large-scale research conducted to the highest standards of analytic rationality, but also insist that the associated findings are also relevant to policy. It may often be the case that these two goals are, in fact, incompatible. To put it another way, when policy without evidence meets development with some evidence, development should prevail.

This chapter is based on a story. We claim that it is an important story, in that the success of the project that it describes helped to give impetus to the wider adoption of formative assessment practices and to recognition of their potential. The significance for this book is that the practices developed with the teachers helped to put classroom flesh on the conceptual bones of the idea of assessment for learning. Given that serving learning is the first and most important of the purposes of assessment, this is an appropriate starting point for the comprehensive picture of assessment that is developed through the subsequent chapters.

Note

1   In addition to *Inside the Black Box* and *Working Inside the Black Box*, there are a further eight booklets exploring aspects of assessment for learning in primary schools, and in specific subjects in secondary schools (currently Design and Technology, English, Geography, ICT, Mathematics, Modern Foreign Languages, and Science). Further details can be found at http://shop.gl-assessment.co.uk/home.php?cat=383.

References

Alexander, R. (2008) *Towards Dialogic Teaching: Rethinking Classroom Talk* (4th edn). York, UK: Dialogos.

Assessment Reform Group (ARG) (1999) *Assessment for Learning: Beyond the Black Box*. Cambridge, UK: University of Cambridge School of Education.

Assessment Reform Group (ARG) (2002a) *Assessment for Learning: 10 Principles*. Cambridge, UK: University of Cambridge Faculty of Education.

Assessment Reform Group (ARG) (2002b) *Testing, Motivation and Learning*. Cambridge, UK: University of Cambridge Faculty of Education.

Black, H. (1986) 'Assessment for learning', in D.L. Nuttall (ed.), *Assessing Educational Achievement*. London: Falmer Press. pp. 7–18.

Black, P. J. (1993) 'Formative and summative assessment by teachers', *Studies in Science Education*, 21(1): 49–97.

Black, P. and Wiliam, D. (1998a) 'Assessment and classroom learning', *Assessment in Education: Principles, Policy and Practice*, 5(1): 7–73.

Black, P. and Wiliam, D. (1998b) *Inside the Black Box: Raising Standards through Classroom Assessment*. London, UK: King's College London School of Education.

Black, P. and Wiliam, D. (2003) 'In praise of educational research: formative assessment', *British Educational Research Journal*, 29(5): 623–37.

Black, P., Harrison, C., Lee, C., Marshall, B. and Wiliam, D. (2002) *Working Inside the Black Box: Assessment for Learning in the Classroom*. London, UK: GL Assessment.

Black, P., Harrison, C., Lee, C., Marshall, B. and Wiliam, D. (2003) *Assessment for Learning: Putting it into Practice*. Buckingham, UK: Open University Press.

Black, P., Harrison, C., Hodgen, J., Marshall, M. and Serret, N. (2010) 'Validity in teachers' summative assessments', *Assessment in Education* 17(2): 215–32.

Blatchford, P., Baines, E., Bassett, P., Chowne, A. and Rubie-Davies, C. (2006) 'The effect of a new approach to group work on pupil–pupil and teacher–pupil interactions', *Journal of Educational Psychology*, 98(4): 750–65.

Brousseau, G. (1984) 'The crucial role of the didactical contract in the analysis and construction of situations in teaching and learning mathematics' (G. Seib, trans.), in H.-G. Steiner (ed.), *Theory of Mathematics Education: ICME 5 Topic Area and Miniconference* (Vol. 54). Bielefeld, Germany: Institut für Didaktik der Mathematik der Universität Bielefeld. pp. 110–19.

Butler, R. (1988) 'Enhancing and undermining intrinsic motivation: the effects of task-involving and ego-involving evaluation on interest and performance', *British Journal of Educational Psychology*, 58: 1–14.

Chadwick, E. B. (1864) 'Statistics of educational results', *Museum: a Quarterly Magazine of Education, Literature, and Science*, 3: 479–84.

Crooks, T. J. (1988) 'The impact of classroom evaluation practices on students', *Review of Educational Research*, 58(4): 438–81.

Dweck, C. S. (2000) *Self-theories: Their Role in Motivation, Personality and Development*. Philadelphia, PA: Psychology Press.

Flyvbjerg, B. (2001) *Making Social Science Matter: Why Social Inquiry Fails and How it can Succeed Again*. Cambridge, UK: Cambridge University Press.

Foos, P.W., Mora, J.J. and Tkacz, S. (1994) 'Student study techniques and the generation effect', *Journal of Educational Psychology*, 86(4): 567–76.

Ginsburg, H.P. (2001) *The Mellon Literacy Project: What Does it Teach Us about Educational Research, Practice, and Sustainability?* New York, NY: Russell Sage Foundation.

Hallam, S., Kirton, A., Peffers, J., Robertson, P. and Stobart, G. (2004) *Evaluation of Project 1 of the Assessment is for Learning Development Programme: Support for Professional Practice in Formative Assessment. Final Report*. London, UK: Institute of Education, University of London.

Hargreaves, D.H. (1999) 'The knowledge-creating school', *British Journal of Educational Studies*, 47(2): 122–44.

King, A. (1992) 'Facilitating elaborative learning through guided student-generated questioning', *Educational Psychologist*, 27(1): 111–26.

Kluger, A.N. and DeNisi, A. (1996) 'The effects of feedback interventions on performance: a historical review, a meta-analysis, and a preliminary feedback intervention theory', *Psychological Bulletin*, 119(2): 254–84.

Lee, C. and Wiliam, D. (2005) 'Studying changes in the practice of two teachers developing assessment for learning', *Teacher Development: an International Journal of Teachers' Professional Development*, 9(2): 265–83.

Linn, R.L. (1989) 'Current perspectives and future directions', in R.L. Linn (ed.), *Educational Measurement* (3rd edn). Washington, DC: American Council on Education/Macmillan. pp. 1–10.

Mansell, W., James, M. and Assessment Reform Group (2009) *Assessment in Schools: Fit for Purpose?* London, UK: Economic and Social Research Council Teaching and Learning Research Programme.

Mercer, N., Dawes, L., Wegerif, R. and Sams, C. (2004) 'Reasoning as a scientist: ways of helping children to use language to learn science', *British Educational Research Journal*, 30(3): 359–77.

National Curriculum Task Group on Assessment and Testing (1988) *A Report.* London, UK: Department of Education and Science.

Natriello, G. (1987) 'The impact of evaluation processes on students', *Educational Psychologist*, 22(2): 155–75.

Perrenoud, P. (1991) 'Towards a pragmatic approach to formative evaluation', in P. Weston (ed.), *Assessment of Pupil Achievement* (Vol. Part A: 25). Amsterdam, Netherlands: Swets & Zeitlinger. pp. 79–101.

Ramaprasad, A. (1983) 'On the definition of feedback', *Behavioural Science*, 28(1): 4–13.

Reeves, J., McCall, J. and MacGilchrist, B. (2001) 'Change leadership: planning, conceptualization and perception', in J. MacBeath and P. Mortimore (eds), *Improving School Effectiveness.* Buckingham, UK: Open University Press. pp. 122–37.

Rowe, M.B. (1974) 'Wait time and rewards as instructional variables, their influence on language, logic and fate control', *Journal of Research in Science Teaching*, 11: 81–94.

Sadler, D.R. (1989) 'Formative assessment and the design of instructional systems', *Instructional Science*, 18: 119–44.

Sadler, D.R. (1998) 'Formative assessment: revisting the territory', *Assessment in Education: Principles, Policy and Practice,* 5(1): 77–84.

Toulmin, S. (2001) *Return to Reason.* Cambridge, MA: Harvard University Press.

Vispoel, W.P. and Austin, J.R. (1995) 'Success and failure in junior high school: a critical incident approach to understanding students' attributional beliefs', *American Educational Research Journal*, 32(2): 377–412.

White, B.Y. and Frederiksen, J.R. (1998) 'Inquiry, modeling, and metacognition: making science accessible to all students', *Cognition and Instruction*, 16(1): 3–118.

Wiliam, D. (2003) 'The impact of educational research on mathematics education', in A. Bishop, M.A. Clements, C. Keitel, J. Kilpatrick and F.K.S. Leung (eds), *Second International Handbook of Mathematics Education.* Dordrecht, Netherlands: Kluwer Academic Publishers. pp. 468–88.

Wiliam, D., Lee, C., Harrison, C. and Black, P. J. (2004) 'Teachers developing assessment for learning: impact on student achievement', *Assessment in Education: Principle, Policy and Practice*, 11(1): 49–65.

Wilson, S.M. and Berne, J. (1999) 'Teacher learning and the acquisition of professional knowledge: an examination of research on contemporary professional development', in A. Iran-Nejad and P. D. Pearson (eds), *Review of Research in Education*, 24. Washington, DC: American Educational Research Association. pp. 173–209.

Chapter 3

Professional Learning as a Condition for Assessment for Learning

David Pedder and Mary James

Assessment for learning: practices, values, agency and accountability

When teachers and students use assessment information for supporting improvements in learning, they are fulfilling the educational purposes of assessment. The classroom strategies teachers and students develop and use to support learning are commonly referred to as formative assessment or assessment for learning. Five general strategies for promoting assessment for learning in classroom lessons have been identified (e.g. Wiliam and Thompson, 2007): (a) clarifying and understanding learning intentions and sharing criteria for success; (b) promoting and supporting effective classroom discussions and developing activities and tasks that elicit evidence of learning; (c) providing feedback that moves learners forward; (d) activating students as pedagogic resources for one another; and (e) activating students as the owners of their own learning. More specific practices and techniques have been developed in relation to the five broad strategies in different lessons (see Leahy and Wiliam, Chapter 4, this volume).

Using and developing assessment for learning practices and values in schools and classrooms has been found to be effective not only for raising students' attainments on standardized tests (Black and Wiliam, 1998; Black et al., 2003; Clymer and Wiliam, 2006), but also for supporting the development of learning how to learn (James et al., 2007):

a set of practices that can be developed by students to help them to learn autonomously (Black et al., 2006; James and McCormick, 2009). Nevertheless, large scale research concluded that for the majority of teachers, incorporating assessment for learning practices into classroom lessons in a way that were consistent with their values was far from easy.

The Learning How to Learn (LHTL) project involved large-scale research and development with 40 schools, over 1,000 teachers and 4,000 students using survey, observation and interview methods to examine the use by teachers and students of assessment for learning strategies for promoting Learning How to Learn (James and McCormick, 2009; James et al., 2007). From analysis of large-scale teacher survey data from this project, three dimensions of teachers' classroom assessment practices were identified and these are summarized in Table 3.1.

Measures of the value teachers placed on different classroom assessment practices were compared with their reported levels of practices. The LHTL project data shows that teachers tend to place the highest value on 'making learning explicit' and these high values were in line with similarly high levels of reported practice. However, the majority of teachers in the project (about 80%) struggled to bring practice into line with values with regard to 'promoting learning autonomy' and 'performance orientation'. Levels of reported practice for 'promoting learning autonomy' were significantly behind their values whereas levels of practice reported for 'performance orientation' were significantly ahead of their values.

These survey findings are reflected in the interview and classroom observation evidence from the same project reported by Marshall and Drummond (2006). They report genuine difficulties faced by teachers as they attempted to transform classroom cultures through the use of assessment for learning (AfL) strategies aimed at promoting learning autonomy. They found only about a fifth of the lessons they observed

Table 3.1 Dimensions of teachers' classroom assessment[1]

Promoting learning autonomy	Widening scope for students to take on greater autonomy over their learning objectives and the assessment of their own and one another's learning
Making learning explicit	Eliciting, clarifying and responding to evidence of learning; working with students to develop a positive learning orientation
Performance orientation	A concern to help students comply with performance goals prescribed by the curriculum through closed questioning and the use of marks and grades

captured the spirit of AfL – assessment practices with an explicit orientation to the promotion of learning autonomy. Many teachers felt constrained by a policy context that encouraged rushed curriculum coverage, teaching to the test, and a tick-box culture. What is clear from analysis of these different LHTL data sets is that in attempting to develop classroom assessment practices, teachers struggle to realize their values in practice with regard to both the 'promotion of learning autonomy' and 'performance orientation'.

And yet the promotion of autonomous learning is a key principle underlying AfL purposes and practices. When teachers develop deep understanding of such principles and find practical ways of realizing the potential of assessment for learning for promoting learning autonomy, they reflect the 'spirit' of AfL (Marshall and Drummond, 2006). Teaching to the 'spirit' of AfL enables the renewal and growth of learning as a set of achievements that belong both individually and collectively to teachers and students. Engendered in the spirit of AfL is the sense of agency and ownership among teachers and students connected to the choices they make for their own and one another's learning.

Predominantly, in classrooms and schools where AfL is successfully and authentically promoted, students and teachers are accountable to themselves and those in their milieu for their learning and the relationships that underscore that learning. Teachers and students, as agents, take responsibility for their actions and choices *with one another*. Fulfilling the potential of AfL then is a collective responsibility because the learning practices that develop through genuine and deep engagement with AfL principles – autonomous, intentional learning – are realized and developed not in isolation but in interaction with others and on the basis of choices, judgements and interpretations that are made collectively, for example in peer-assessment or through collective negotiation of criteria for success. This shared accountability for one another's learning together with the transactional and interactive nature of AfL strategies are what give AfL its social character. But when considering and planning to support such patterns of collective endeavour and accountability, focus on the individual learner can be lost. An individual's learning is something that fulfils the life of an individual agent and thus it is easy to forget that learners are not only accountable to one another but also to themselves as individuals. Therefore, incorporating AfL into the life of classrooms and schools is not only a collective responsibility shared by groups of teachers and students. It is also the responsibility of each student and teacher as individual learners.

Incorporating AfL into routine classroom practice: more than a question of changing behaviour

In light of this argument, promoting the authentic spirit of AfL can never be reduced to a set of practices understood as techniques that can be straightforwardly implemented in classroom lessons. Changes in practice go beyond changes in surface behaviours. Processes of incorporating assessment for learning into everyday practice at school and in class involve facing up to two main difficulties and challenges connected with: (a) the nature of the classroom as a place in which teaching, learning and assessment take place; and (b) transformations in teachers' and students' roles and how they are conceived by teachers and students. We turn to consider these challenges now.

The classroom environment

The classroom is a complex environment that shapes a great deal of teaching, learning and assessment and is one source of challenge for all school teachers and students. McIntyre (2000) refers to the complexity of classrooms in terms of six main features of the demands made on teachers during classroom lessons: their multi-dimensionality, simultaneity, immediacy, unpredictability, publicness and historical embeddedness. He goes on to suggest that the sustained high quality oral and/or written interactions involved in effective assessment for learning 'so adds to the complexity of classroom teaching as to make it a quite impracticable option for teachers' (McIntyre, 2000: 98). McIntyre goes on to ask how far advice and guidance to teachers from researchers such as Black and Wiliam (1998) and Torrance and Pryor (1998) about using assessment for learning in classrooms 'takes sufficient account of the complexity of classroom life, and of the sophisticated ways in which expert teachers have learned to work effectively in classrooms through rigorous prioritisation, simplification and intuitive decision-making' (McIntyre, 2000: 99). Fairly low uptake of assessment for learning practices was reported as part of the large-scale LHTL project (James et al., 2007). Decisions by teachers not to build regular high quality formative interactions with individuals or small groups into their classroom lessons might well be understood in terms of constraints of the classroom as an environment for teaching and learning.

However, over the past 10 years, researchers have been designing research and development projects on the assumption that, despite such complexities, teachers can build assessment for learning into

their routine classroom practices so long as they are supported appropriately in doing so. These researchers believe that the integration of
AfL within normal everyday classroom practice is possible because all
aspects of student activities during classroom lessons carry some
potential for informing teachers and students about current levels of
understanding. When AfL strategies are successfully integrated into
routine classroom practices, the boundaries between teaching, learning and assessment become blurred. As James (1998: 172) argues, 'the
aspiration is that assessment should become fully integrated with
teaching and learning, and therefore part of the educational process
rather than a "bolt-on activity"'. And since then, research and development projects such as those undertaken by Black et al. (2003),
James et al. (2007), Thompson and Wiliam (2008), and Wiliam
(2007) have supported groups of teachers and schools in using and
improving assessment for learning as part of their everyday practice
in the complex environments of their classrooms.

The transformation of teachers' and students' classroom roles

A second and related source of complexity and professional challenge
teachers face when attempting to build AfL into everyday classroom
practice concerns transformations in classroom roles and in the conception of these roles by both teachers and students. Asking teachers
to incorporate AfL into their practice is not a straightforward matter,
any more than it is for students. It involves transformations in classroom processes, and this entails change not only in what teachers and
students do but also in how they relate. It involves behaviour imbued
with deeper understanding and values. These understandings and
values are informed by norms associated with particular conceptions
of appropriate roles for teachers and for students.

A central feature of AfL is that students are actively supported by
their teachers in taking increased responsibility for their own and
one another's learning. This increased responsibility is encouraged
when learning itself becomes established as an explicit and critical
focus of classroom talk, for example when discussing with students
what to try next in order to improve, or when considering with students what learning objectives will be most appropriate and useful,
or when supporting students to clarify understandings of assessment
criteria. As learning becomes more explicit and visible, students and
teachers are helped to become more conscious of the 'how' and 'why'
of learning as an invaluable support for developing more effective
strategies and increasing agency, autonomy, accountability and
informed choice in learning.

Transforming roles and relationships is a necessary condition for the development of assessment for learning as a genuine endeavour involving teachers and students collectively and individually as agents advancing the quality of learning – both teachers' and students'. Perhaps the importance of teachers' learning finds clearest expression in one of the Assessment Reform Group's (ARG, 2002) 10 principles:

> Assessment for learning should be regarded as a key professional skill for teachers. Teachers require the professional knowledge and skills to: plan for assessment; observe learning; analyse and interpret evidence of learning; give feedback to learners and support learners in self assessment. Teachers should be supported in developing these skills through initial and continuing professional development.

In other words, teachers as well as students go to school in order to learn. To make this a reality, new understandings and perspectives are developed among teachers and students about themselves and each other and, therefore, about the nature of learning and teaching. Furthermore, new attitudes to and practices of learning and teaching, shaped by explicit and critically reflective modes of participation and relationships, are acquired and developed.

What makes assessment for learning both exciting and challenging is that, to be truly effective, it requires teachers and students to change the way they think about their classroom roles and the norms that influence their behaviour. In its fullest expression, assessment for learning gives explicit roles to learners, not just to teachers, for instigating teaching and learning. Thus students are not merely the objects of their teacher's behaviour, they are animators of their own effective teaching and learning processes. This has its clearest embodiment in processes of peer- and self-assessment when students: (i) individually or collaboratively, develop the motivation to reflect on their previous learning and identify objectives for new learning; (ii) when they analyze and evaluate problems they or their peers are experiencing and structure a way forward; and (iii) when, through self-regulation, they act to bring about improvement. In other words, they become autonomous, and intentional learners.

Summary: the challenges teachers face in building AfL into classroom practice

This shift in emphasis in the roles, relationships and perspectives of teachers and students is not trivial and further complicates the work of teachers in an already complex classroom environment. Teachers are challenged to change the ways they see their role: from prescribing what tasks students do to 'a kind of orchestration of the learning itself' (James et al., 2007: 217). Similarly there is a perspective shift involved for students as they are challenged to take on a more assertive role in initiating classroom teaching and learning. Students are not merely the objects of their teacher's behaviour, but co-constructors and animators of collective teaching and learning processes. As such, building AfL into classroom routines challenges teachers and students to establish conditions of trust and norms of participation that are conducive to the kind of power-sharing that supports students to have more of a say over decisions that influence the conditions of their classroom learning.

If teachers are to sustain support for high quality student learning through their use of AfL strategies, and to constructively engage with these challenges of encouraging development of the authentic spirit of AfL, then teachers need to be prepared to change not merely at the level of observable classroom behaviour, but also in terms of the values and principles that underpin new kinds of relationships with and expectations of their students, and in terms of new power dynamics which provide more scope for students to influence the conditions and processes of their learning.

Thus changes are needed in teachers' role conceptions of their students and of students' role conceptions of their teachers. This, together with the complexity of classrooms as places in which to teach, learn and assess, represents a set of significant professional challenges and cultural shifts for both teachers and students. For such transformational change to occur, teachers need to continue learning and to be encouraged and supported to do so by their schools within a wider institutional culture and commitment to teachers' professional learning (Pedder, 2006, 2010; Pedder and MacBeath, 2008; Pedder et al., 2005). Hence teachers' professional learning is a key condition for establishing and embedding AfL in classrooms.

The importance of teachers' professional learning as a condition for developing effective classroom assessment for learning

What kinds of professional learning are most conducive to the development of assessment for learning approaches in classrooms? This is a question examined as part of the LHTL project (James et al., 2007). Four dimensions of teachers' professional learning practices

Table 3.2 Dimensions of teachers' professional learning[2]

Inquiry	Using and responding to different sources of evidence; carrying out joint research and evaluation with colleagues
Building social capital	Learning, working, supporting and talking with one another
Critical and responsive learning	Reflection, self evaluation, experimentation and responding to feedback
Valuing learning	Valuing their own and their students' learning

were identified through analysis of the LHTL survey data (Pedder et al., 2005) and these are summarized in table 3.2. (see Appendix 2 for the specific practices listed under each dimension of teachers' learning).

The most striking finding from analysis of the LHTL survey data was the importance of the 'inquiry' group of teacher learning practices. This group of practices reflects a range of research-informed, classroom-based approaches to collaborative teacher learning, and it is these that were most directly and powerfully associated with 'promoting learning autonomy' and 'making learning explicit' dimensions of classroom assessment (Pedder, 2006). This association suggests that teachers' uses of, and responses to, different sources of evidence (from more formal research and their own inquiries) together with their collaboration with colleagues in joint research and evaluation activities, are important for the development of assessment for learning practices that lead to autonomous and intentional learning among their students.

Collaborative classroom-focused inquiry can take many forms. Teachers can visit one another's lessons and have focused conversations about what was observed to have taken place and how practice can be further refined. Teachers can consult their students about what they do that is helpful or not for supporting their students' learning (e.g. Rudduck and McIntyre, 2007). Research Study Lessons or Lesson Study represents a more formal approach to collaborative professional learning pioneered in Japan and developed in England by Dudley (2006). Thompson and Wiliam (2008) report the centrality of teacher learning communities as opportunities for knowledge creation and transfer of AfL expertise and for sustained reflective practice (see Leahy and Wiliam, Chapter 4, this volume).

A collaborative classroom inquiry orientation helps teachers develop subject content knowledge and find ways of applying it appropriately as they realize broad AfL strategies as specific and increasingly refined practices in particular subject and classroom contexts. Thompson and Wiliam (2008) argue that well-developed content knowledge is a necessary precondition if teachers are to ask good questions, interpret the responses of their students, provide richly formative feedback that focuses on what students can do to improve, and adapt their teaching to developments as they unfold in lessons, based on the information they are gathering about their students' understanding of particular content.

Similar findings related to the importance of classroom-based professional learning in specific subject and classroom contexts have been replicated in a number of other research and development studies, such as the King's Medway Oxfordshire Formative Assessment project in the UK (e.g. Black et al., 2003); Classroom Assessment as a Basis for Teacher Change project in the Netherlands and the USA (e.g. Dekker and Feijs, 2005), the Assessment is for Learning project in Scotland (e.g. Hutchinson and Hayward, 2005), the Keeping Learning on Track™ programme in USA (e.g. Thompson and Wiliam, 2008); and a number of case studies involving Canada, Denmark, England, Finland, Italy, New Zealand, Australia and Scotland as part of the OECD study of formative assessment (e.g. Sebba, 2006).

Given the importance of collaborative, classroom-based professional learning and inquiry for fostering effective assessment for learning, it is vital that teachers sustain such learning at the centre of their professional classroom practice.

Conclusions

If 'promoting learning autonomy' is the ultimate goal but the greatest challenge, as the LHTL evidence suggests it is, and if 'inquiry' approaches to teacher learning are productive in this respect, then more emphasis needs to be placed on providing opportunities and encouragement to teachers to engage with and use research relevant to their classroom interests, and recognizing the value of, and supporting, teachers' collaborative inquiries into their own practices. The LHTL research suggests that classroom-based teacher research and inquiry is not only an important strand of teachers' continuing learning, as Stenhouse (1975) argued, but also an important factor in helping students develop intentionality and autonomy in their learning.

The explanation for this might be quite simple, yet profound. If teachers are prepared and committed to engage in the risky business of problematizing their own practice, seeking evidence to evaluate in order to judge where change is needed, and then to act on their decisions, they are thus engaging in assessment for learning with respect to their own professional learning. Helping students to do the same with respect to their learning becomes less challenging because teachers are familiar with the principles and processes through inquiry into their own practices. In other words, they are well on the way to conceptualizing, developing and valuing expanded roles for themselves and their students in teaching and learning.

Thus we have argued that assessment for learning practices are underpinned most strongly by teachers' learning in the contexts of their classrooms with a clear focus on change in teacher and learner roles and practices and on interactions between assessment, curriculum and pedagogy. This implies that programmes of professional development, whether school-based or course-based, should be focused on classrooms and classroom practice.

Notes

1   See Appendix 1 for the individual practices grouped with each dimension.
2   See Appendix 2 for the individual practices grouped with each dimension.

References

Assessment Reform Group (ARG) (2002) *Assessment for Learning: 10 Principles*. Cambridge, UK: University of Cambridge, Faculty of Education.
Black, P. and Wiliam, D. (1998) 'Assessment and classroom learning', *Assessment in Education: Principles, Policy and Practice*, 5: 7–75.
Black, P., Harrison, C., Lee, C., Marshall, B. and Wiliam, D. (2003) *Assessment for Learning: Putting it into Practice*. Maidenhead: Open University Press.
Black, P., McCormick, R., James, M. and Pedder, D. (2006) 'Learning how to learn and assessment for learning: a theoretical inquiry', *Research Papers in Education*, 21(2): 119–32.
Clymer, J.B. and Wiliam, D. (2006) 'Improving the way we grade science', *Educational Leadership*, 48(7): 71–6.
Dekker, T. and Feijs, E. (2005) 'Scaling up strategies for change: change in formative assessment practices', *Assessment in Education: Principles, Policy and Practice*, 12: 237–54.
Dudley, P. (2006) *Network Leadership in Action: Getting Started with Networked Research Lesson Study*. Nottingham: National College of School Leadership.
Hutchinson, C. and Hayward, L. (2005) 'The journey so far: assessment for learning in Scotland', *The Curriculum Journal*, 16: 225–48.

James, M. (1998) *Using Assessment for School Improvement.* Oxford: Heinemann.

James, M. and McCormick, R. (2009) 'Teachers learning how to learn', *Teaching and Teacher Education*, 25(7): 973–82.

James, M. and Pedder, D. (2006) 'Beyond method: assessment and learning practices and values', *The Curriculum Journal*, 17(2): 109–38.

James, M., McCormick, R., Black, P., Carmichael, P., Drummond, M-J., Fox, A., MacBeath, J., Marshall, B., Pedder, D., Procter, R., Swaffield, S., Swann, J. and Wiliam, D. (2007) *Improving Learning How to Learn: Classrooms, Schools and Networks.* London: Routledge.

Leahy, S. and Wiliam, D. (2011) 'From teachers to schools: scaling up professional development for formative assessment', in J. Gardner (ed.), *Assessment and Learning* (2nd edn). London: Sage Publications.

Marshall, B. and Drummond, M-J. (2006) 'How teachers engage with assessment for learning: lessons from the classroom', *Research Papers in Education*, 21: 133–49.

McIntyre, D. (2000) 'Has classroom teaching served its day?', in B. Moon., M. Ben-Peretz and S. Brown. (eds), *The Routledge International Companion to Education.* London: Routledge. pp. 83–108.

Pedder, D. (2006) 'Organisational conditions that foster successful classroom promotion of learning how to learn', *Research Papers in Education* 21: 171–200.

Pedder, D. (2010) 'School policies and practices to support effective classroom assessment for learning', in P. Peterson, E. Baker and B. McGaw (eds), *International Encyclopedia of Education,* Vol 3. Oxford: Elsevier. pp. 464–71.

Pedder, D. and MacBeath, J. (2008) 'Organisational learning approaches to school leadership and management: teachers' values and perceptions of practice', *School Effectiveness and School Improvement,* 19: 207–24.

Pedder, D., James, M. and MacBeath, J. (2005) 'How teachers value and practise professional learning', *Research Papers in Education* 20: 209–43.

Rudduck, J. and McIntyre, D. (2007) *Improving Learning through Consulting Pupils.* London: Routledge.

Sebba, J. (2006) 'Policy and practice in assessment for learning: the experience of selected OECD countries', in J. Gardner (ed.), *Assessment for Learning: Theory, Policy and Practice.* London: Sage. pp. 185–96.

Stenhouse, L. (1975) *An Introduction to Curriculum Research and Development.* London: Heinemann Educational Books.

Thompson, M. and Wiliam, D. (2008) 'Tight but loose: a conceptual framework for scaling up school reforms', in E.C. Wylie (ed.), *Tight but Loose: Scaling Up Teacher Professional Development in Diverse Contexts,* Vol. RR-08-29. Princeton, NJ: Educational Testing Service. pp. 1–44.

Torrance, H. and Pryor, J. (1998) *Investigating Formative Assessment: Teaching, Learning and Assessment in the Classroom.* Buckingham: Open University Press.

Wiliam, D. (2007) 'Keeping learning on track: classroom assessment and the regulation of learning', in F.K. Lester (ed.) *Second Handbook of Research on Mathematics Teaching and Learning.* Greenwich, CT: Information Age Publishing. pp. 1051–98.

Wiliam, D. and Thompson, M. (2007) 'Integrating assessment with instruction: what will it take to make it work?', in C.A. Dwyer (ed.), *The Future of Assessment: Shaping Teaching and Learning.* Mahwah, NJ: Lawrence Erlbaum Associates. pp. 53–82.

Appendix 1

Dimensions of classroom assessment
(see James and Pedder, 2006 for further details)

1: 'Making Learning Explicit'
eliciting, clarifying and responding to evidence of learning; working with students to develop a positive learning orientation

Item No	Item Text
1.	Assessment provides me with useful evidence of students' understandings which they use to plan subsequent lessons.
10.	Students are told how well they have done in relation to their own previous performance.
11.	Students' learning objectives are discussed with students in ways they understand.
14.	I identify students' strengths and advise them on how to develop them further.
15.	Students are helped to find ways of addressing problems they have in their learning.
16.	Students are encouraged to view mistakes as valuable learning opportunities.
18.	I use questions mainly to elicit reasons and explanations from students.
20.	Students' errors are valued for the insights they reveal about how students are thinking.
21.	Students are helped to understand the learning purposes of each lesson or series of lessons.
27.	Student effort is seen as important when assessing their learning.

2: 'Promoting Learning Autonomy'
widening scope for students to take on greater autonomy over their learning objectives and the assessment of their own and each other's work

Item No	Item Text
6.	Students are given opportunities to decide their own learning objectives.
13.	I provide guidance to help students assess their own work.
19.	I provide guidance to help students to assess one another's work.
24.	I provide guidance to help students assess their own learning.
29.	Students are given opportunities to assess one another's work.

3: 'Performance Orientation'
a concern to help students comply with performance goals prescribed by the curriculum, through closed questioning, and measured by marks and grades

Item No	Item Text
2.	The next lesson is determined more by the prescribed curriculum than by how well students did in the last lesson.
3.	The main emphasis in my assessments is on whether students know, understand or can do prescribed elements of the curriculum.
7.	I use questions mainly to elicit factual knowledge from my students.
8.	I consider the most worthwhile assessment to be assessment that is undertaken by the teacher.
12.	Assessment of students' work consists primarily of marks and grades.

LIBRARY, UNIVERSITY OF CHESTER

Appendix 2

Dimensions of teachers' learning
(see Pedder et al., 2005 for further details)

1: 'Inquiry'
using and responding to different sources of evidence; carrying out joint research and evaluation with colleagues

Item No	Item Text
2.	Staff draw on good practice from other schools as a means to further their own professional development.
3.	Staff read research reports as one source of useful ideas for improving their practice.
4.	Staff use the web as one source of useful ideas for improving their practice.
5.	Students are consulted about how they learn most effectively.
6.	Staff relate what works in their own practice to research findings.
12.	Staff modify their practice in the light of published research evidence.
15.	Staff carry out joint research/evaluation with one or more colleagues as a way of improving practice.

2: 'Building Social Capital'
learning, working, supporting and talking with each other

Item No	Item Text
16.	Staff regularly collaborate to plan their teaching.
19.	If staff have a problem with their teaching they usually turn to colleagues for help.

20.	Teachers suggest ideas or approaches for colleagues to try out in class.
21.	Teachers make collective agreements to test out new ideas.
22.	Teachers discuss openly with colleagues what and how they are learning.
23.	Staff frequently use informal opportunities to discuss how students learn.
24.	Staff offer one another reassurance and support.

3: 'Critical and Responsive Learning'
reflection, self-evaluation, experimentation and by responding to feedback

Item No	Item Text
7.	Staff are able to see how practices that work in one context might be adapted to other contexts.
9.	Staff reflect on their practice as a way of identifying professional learning needs.
10.	Staff experiment with their practice as a conscious strategy for improving classroom teaching and learning.
11.	Staff modify their practice in the light of feedback from their students.
13.	Staff modify their practice in the light of evidence from self-evaluations of their classroom practice.
14.	Staff modify their practice in the light of evidence from evaluations of their classroom practice by managers or other colleagues.

4: 'Valuing Learning'
Valuing their own and their students' learning

Item No	Item Text
1.	Staff as well as students learn in this school.
25.	Staff believe that all students are capable of learning.
26.	Students in this school enjoy learning.
27.	Student success is regularly celebrated.

Chapter 4

From Teachers to Schools: Scaling Up Professional Development for Formative Assessment[1]

Siobhan Leahy and Dylan Wiliam

Introduction

The surgeon Atul Gawande has pointed out that the advances in highly demanding aspects of medical practice such as surgery have been greater than in apparently 'easier' areas such as basic hygiene. He quotes the example of washing hands after contact with patients, where the compliance rate in many hospitals is below 50%, even though it is widely accepted that a compliance rate of over 95% is required to control the spread of resistant forms of staphylococcus aureus such as vancomycin-resistant Staphylococcus aureus (VRSA) and methicillinin-resistant Staphylococcus aureus (MRSA) (Gawande, 2007: 15).

The problem is not ignorance, nor wilful disobedience. A strict procedure is specified for hand washing, but, as Gawande points out:

> Almost no one adheres to this procedure. It seems impossible. On morning rounds, our residents check in on twenty patients in an hour. The nurses in our intensive care units typically have a similar number of contacts with patients requiring hand washing in between. Even if you get the whole cleansing process down to a minute per patient, that's still a third of staff time spent just washing hands. Such frequent hand washing can also irritate the skin, which can produce dermatitis, which itself increases bacterial counts. (2007: 18)

An analysis of the practice of teachers would appear to share many features of that of clinicians. The work moves at a fast pace, so that there is little time for reflective thought, and as a result, the workplace behaviours are driven by habit as much as anything else. This would not matter too much if those habits were the most effective ways of engendering student learning, but there is ample evidence that a significant proportion of teacher practices are sub-optimal, and that substantial improvements in student achievement would be possible with changes in teachers' classroom practices. In this chapter, we describe our efforts to develop ways of supporting changes in teachers' classroom practice through a focus on formative assessment, with a particular focus on finding ways of doing so that could, in principle, be implemented at scale – for example across 300,000 classrooms in England, or across 2 million classrooms in the United States. In the following two sections, we briefly summarize the research that has led us to focus on formative assessment as the most powerful lever for moving teacher practice in ways that are likely to benefit students, and why we have adopted teacher learning communities as the mechanism for supporting teachers in making these changes in their practice. In subsequent sections we describe the creation of a professional development product that would assist the creation of school-based teacher learning communities to support teachers in taking forward their own formative assessment practices, and we conclude with a case study of the implementation of the product in one urban school district in London.

The case for formative assessment

The evidence that formative assessment is a powerful lever for improving outcomes for learners has been steadily accumulating over the last quarter of a century. Over that time, at least 15 substantial reviews of research, synthesizing several thousand research studies, have documented the impact of classroom assessment practices on students (Fuchs and Fuchs 1986; Natriello, 1987; Crooks, 1988; Bangert-Drowns et al., 1991; Dempster, 1991, 1992; Elshout-Mohr, 1994; Kluger and DeNisi, 1996; Black and Wiliam, 1998; Nyquist, 2003; Brookhart, 2004, 2007; Allal and Lopez, 2005; Köller, 2005; Hattie and Timperley, 2007; Wiliam, 2007; Shute, 2008).

While many of these reviews have documented the negative effects of some assessment practices, they also show that, used appropriately, assessment has considerable potential for enhancing student achievement. Drawing on the early work of Scriven (1967) and Bloom (1969), it has become common to describe the use of assessment to improve student learning as 'formative assessment' although more recently the phrase 'assessment for learning' has also become common. In the United States, the term 'assessment for learning' is often mistakenly attributed to Rick Stiggins (2002), although Stiggins himself has always attributed the term to authors in the United Kingdom. In fact, the earliest use of this term in this sense appears to be a chapter written by Harry Black (1986). The term was brought to a wider audience by a paper given at the annual conference of the Association for Supervision and Curriculum Development (James, 1992) in New Orleans, USA, while three years later, the phrase was used as the title of a book (Sutton, 1995). However, the first use of the term 'assessment for learning' in contrast to the term 'assessment of learning' appears to be Gipps and Stobart (1997), where these two terms are the titles of the second and first chapters respectively. The distinction was brought to a wider audience by the Assessment Reform Group in 1999 in a guide for policy makers (Broadfoot et al., 1999).

Wiliam (2009) summarizes some of the definitions for formative assessment (and assessment for learning) that have been proposed over the years, and suggests that these are all subsumed within the definition that is adopted by Black and Wiliam (2009):

> Practice in a classroom is formative to the extent that evidence about student achievement is elicited, interpreted, and used by teachers, learners, or their peers, to make decisions about the next steps in instruction that are likely to be better, or better founded, than the decisions they would have taken in the absence of the evidence that was elicited. (2009: 9)

In commenting on this definition, Black and Wiliam emphasize that the focus of the definition on *decisions* represents a compromise between basing the definition on intent (which would be a loose definition, admitting almost any data collection activity as formative) and basing it on outcomes (which would be a highly restrictive definition, due to the unpredictable nature of learning). The second point they make is that while these decisions are regularly made by the teacher, it is also the case that the learners themselves, and their peers, may also be involved in making these decisions. Indeed, ultimately, as the work of Monique Boekaerts suggests (see also Chapter 13, this volume), unless the learners themselves choose growth in learning over personal well-being, little learning is likely to take place (Boekaerts, 2006). The third point is that the definition is probabilistic, again due to the unpredictable nature of learning, and the fourth point is that formative assessment need not alter instruction to be formative – it may simply confirm that the proposed course of action is indeed the most appropriate.

The general finding is that across a range of different school subjects, in different countries, and for learners of different ages, the use of formative assessment appears to be associated with considerable improvements in the rate of learning. Estimating how big these gains might be is difficult because most of the reviews appear to ignore the fact that outcome measures differ in their sensitivity to instruction (Wiliam, 2009), but it seems reasonable to conclude that use of formative assessment can increase the rate of student learning by somewhere between 50 and 100%. This suggests that formative assessment is likely to be one of the most effective ways – and perhaps the most effective way – of increasing student achievement (Wiliam and Thompson [2007] for example, estimate that it would be 20 times more cost-effective than typical class-size reduction programmes).

The substantial evidence regarding the potential cost-effectiveness of formative assessment as a lever for school improvement has, predictably, attracted considerable attention, and a number of test publishers have produced what they call 'formative assessment systems' or 'benchmark assessments'. These include the *MAP* produced by the Northwest Evaluation Association (NWEA), the *Focus on Standards*™/ *Instructional Data Management System*™ produced by ETS, *Homeroom*™ produced by Princeton Review, *Benchmark Tracker*™/*SkillWriter*™ and *Stanford Learning First*™ by Harcourt Assessment, and *Prosper*™ produced by Pearson Assessments, as well as a host of other similar systems. Typically, these systems provide for assessment of student progress at regular intervals (generally every four to nine weeks) and provide reports that identify students, or particular aspects of the curriculum, that require special attention.

While some of the publishers of these products simply appropriate the existing literature on formative assessment as evidence of their efficacy, others have undertaken original research on the impact of these formative assessment systems. ETS, as the owner of 'Focus on Standards™,' has undertaken investigations of the impact of adoption of this programme and found that while it could have significant impact in particular settings (for example when the alignment of curriculum to standards was poor) the general impact appears to be limited (Goe and Bridgeman, 2006).

In terms of the definition proposed by Black and Wiliam discussed above, such systems may be formative, in the sense that they may provide evidence about student achievement that could be used to make better decisions about instruction than would have been possible without that evidence. However, since few if any of the studies synthesized in the 15 reviews mentioned earlier dealt with such 'long-cycle' formative assessment, one cannot conclude on the basis of the existing research that these periodic assessments are likely to have significant impact on student achievement. Formal systems for testing students on a regular basis may have a role to play in the effective monitoring of student progress – indeed, some means of tracking student progress over the medium term, and taking action to address any problems identified, would seem to be an essential component of any comprehensive assessment system. But it is disingenuous at least, and possibly mendacious, to claim that the research literature provides evidence of the effectiveness of such systems. Quite simply, it does not (Popham, 2006; Shepard, 2007). That is not to say that such evidence will not be forthcoming in the future – it may well be – but little such evidence has been assembled to date.

The same can be said for what are called 'common formative assessments' or 'interim assessments,' defined by DuFour et al. (2005) as:

> an assessment typically created collaboratively by a team of teachers responsible for the same grade level or course. Common formative assessments are frequently administered throughout the year to identify (1) individual students who need additional time and support for learning, (2) the teaching strategies most effective in helping students acquire the intended knowledge and skills, (3) program concerns – areas in which students generally are having difficulty achieving the intended standard – and (4) improvement goals for individual teachers and the team. (2005: 214)

Again, while such assessments clearly have a valuable role to play in aligning instruction to standards, as a focus for professional dialogue, and for supporting good management and supervision, the evidence on the impact of such 'medium-cycle' formative assessments on student achievement is weak, although a recent study by Saunders et al. (2009) did find that regular teacher learning teams produce an effect size of around 0.16 standard deviations for student achievement[2].

In contrast, there is strong evidence that what Wiliam and Thompson (2007) term 'short-cycle' formative assessments can have a profound impact on student achievement. Yeh (2006) summarizes a number of studies that show that what he calls 'rapid formative assessment' (assessments conducted from two to five times per week) can significantly improve student learning. On an even shorter timescale Black et al. (2003) describe how they supported a group of 24 mathematics and science teachers in developing their use of 'in-the-moment' formative assessment and found that even when measured through externally-set, externally-scored, state-mandated standardized assessments, the gains in student achievement were substantial, equivalent to an increase of the rate of student learning of around 70% (Wiliam, et al., 2004). Other similar interventions have produced similar effects (Hayes, 2003; Clymer and Wiliam, 2006/2007).

It therefore seems reasonably clear that the effects that the literature shows are possible, are indeed achievable in real classrooms, even where outcomes are measured using externally-mandated, standardized tests. What is much less clear is how to achieve these effects at scale – across 300,000 classrooms in England, or across 2 million classrooms in the United States.

Designing for scale

In designing ways of supporting the implementation of formative assessment across a large number of classrooms, we and our colleagues at the Educational Testing Service adopted as a design constraint the idea of 'in-principle scalability'. By this we meant that the intervention need not be scalable at the outset, but any aspect of the intervention that could not, under any reasonable set of assumptions, be implemented at scale, was ruled out.

A second constraint was a commitment to a single model for the whole school. One of the most surprising findings in our work with schools over the past 20 or so years is how 'Balkanized' the arrangements for teacher professional development are, especially in secondary schools. It is quite common to find the mathematics teachers engaged in one set of professional development activities, the science teachers another, and the social studies teachers doing something else entirely. Quite apart from the fact that this is difficult and confusing for the students, these differences in approach make it far more difficult to generate a coherent dialogue around the school about teaching and learning. However, while we were committed to a single model for the whole school, we realized we had also to honour the specificities of age and school subject. Teaching five-year-olds is not the same as teaching 10-year-olds, and teaching mathematics is not the same as teaching history.

We were also aware that any model of effective, scalable teacher professional development would need to pull off a delicate balancing act between two conflicting requirements. The first was the need to ensure that the model was sufficiently flexible to allow the model to be adapted to the local circumstances of the intervention, not just to allow it to succeed, but also so that it could capitalize upon any affordances present in the local context that would enhance the intervention. The second was to ensure that the model was sufficiently rigid to ensure that any modifications that did take place preserved sufficient fidelity to the original design to provide a reasonable assurance that the intervention would not undergo a 'lethal muta-tion' (Haertel, cited in Brown and Campione, 1996).

To address this issue, we explicitly adopted a framework entitled 'tight but loose':

> The Tight but Loose formulation combines an obsessive adher-ence to central design principles (the 'tight' part) with accommo-dations to the needs, resources, constraints, and particularities that occur in any school or district (the 'loose' part), *but only where these do not conflict with the theory of action of the intervention.* (Thompson and Wiliam, 2008:35, emphasis in original)

A fuller account of the application of the 'Tight but Loose' frame-work to the design of a professional development programme for supporting teachers in their use of formative assessment can be found in Thompson and Wiliam (2008). Of particular relevance here is that our design work was guided by a number of principles that previous work had suggested were important in supporting teachers in the development of their practice of formative assessment in par-ticular: choice, flexibility, small steps, accountability and support (Wiliam, 2006).

Choice

It is often assumed that to improve, teachers should work to develop the weakest aspects of their practice, and for some teach-ers, these aspects may indeed be so weak that they should be the priority for professional development. But for most teachers, our experience has been that the greatest benefits to students come from teachers becoming even more expert in their strengths. In early work on formative assessment with teachers in England (Black et al., 2003), one of the teachers, Derek (this, like the names of all teachers, schools and districts mentioned in this chapter, is a pseudonym) was already quite skilled at conducting whole-class discussion sessions, but he was interested in improving this prac-tice further. A colleague of his at the same school, Philip, has a much more 'low-key' presence in the classroom, and was much more interested in helping students develop skills of self-assessment and peer-assessment. Both Derek and Philip are now extraordinar-ily skilled practitioners – amongst the best we have seen – but to make Philip work on questioning, or to make Derek work on peer-assessment and self-assessment would, we feel, be unlikely to benefit their students as much as supporting each teacher to become excellent in their own way. Furthermore, we have found that when teachers themselves make the decision about what it is that they wish to prioritize for their own professional development, they are more likely to 'make it work'. In traditional 'top-down' models of teacher professional development, teachers are given ideas to try out in their own classrooms, but often respond by blaming the professional developer for the failure of new methods in the classroom (e.g. 'I tried what you told me to do and it didn't work'). However, when the choice about the aspects of practice to develop is made by the teacher, then the responsibility for ensuring effective implementation is shared.

Flexibility

Teachers need the flexibility to be able to modify or 'morph' the formative assessment techniques with which they are presented to fit their own classroom context (Ginsburg, 2001). The danger in this is that a teacher may so modify an idea that it is no longer effective (an example of the 'lethal mutation' described above). What is needed, therefore, is a way of allowing teachers flexibility, while at the same time constraining the use of that flexibility so that modifications to the original ideas do not unduly weaken their effectiveness. Our solution to this was a clarification of the distinction between the *strategies* and the *techniques* of formative assessment. To define the strategies of formative assessment, we began by identifying three key processes involved in formative assessment:

- identifying where the learners are in their learning;
- identifying where they are going;
- identifying what steps need to be taken to get there.

Considering the role of the teacher, the learners and their peers in these processes yielded nine cells, which can be collapsed into the five 'key strategies' of formative assessment as shown in Figure 4.1 (Wiliam and Thompson, 2007).

Each of these five 'key strategies' provides a focal point for a range of related aspects of practice for teachers. In other words, they provide a starting point for a consideration of a number of wider issues in teaching, such as curriculum, psychology, and pedagogy.

For each of these five key strategies, a number of specific classroom routines, termed 'techniques', were identified. The techniques take

	Where the learner is going	Where the learner is right now	How to get there
Teacher	Clarifying learning intentions and sharing and criteria for success (1)	Engineering effective classroom discussions, activities and tasks that elicit evidence of learning (2)	Providing feedback that moves learners forward (3)
Peer	Understanding and sharing learning intentions and criteria for success (1)	Activating students as instructional resources for one another (4)	
Learner	Understanding learning intentions and criteria for success (1)	Activating students as the owners of their own learning (5)	

Figure 4.1 Aspects of formative assessment

the form of 'validated practices' that are consistent with the research on formative assessment and teachers are free to adopt whichever of these techniques they wish (thus providing choice – see above). By anchoring the techniques to (at least) one of the five key strategies, we provided a means by which teachers could modify the techniques, but still provide a reasonable assurance of fidelity to the original research.

Small steps

In implementing any professional development model, we have to accept that teacher learning is slow. In particular, for changes in practice as opposed to knowledge to be lasting, they must be integrated into a teacher's existing routines, and this takes time. Many of those involved in professional development are familiar with the experience of encouraging teachers to try out new ideas, and seeing them being enacted when they visit teachers' classrooms, only to learn shortly afterwards that the teachers have reverted to their former practices.

Some authors have attributed such reversion to resistance on the part of teachers, caused by each teacher's adherence to a series of professional habits, that to a very real extent, represent a core part of each teacher's professional identity. This may be part of the reason for the slowness of teacher change, but it seems to us that a far more significant cause of the failure of many changes in classroom practice to 'stick' is due to the fact that high-level performance in a domain as complex as teaching requires automatizing a large proportion of the things that teachers do. For learner drivers, shifting gear, using the turn indicator and steering all at the same time seem impossibly complicated – and undertaken consciously, they are. Experienced drivers have practised these activities so many times that they become automatic and thus take up little of the available resources for cognitive processing. However, as anyone who tries to change the way they drive – for example in order to reduce the extent to which they 'ride the clutch' – has discovered, these automatic procedures are extremely hard to change.

Teaching is even more extreme than driving in this respect, because every teacher comes to the profession with a series of 'scripts' of how classrooms should operate 'hard-wired' into their minds from their time as a student. These scripts, such as requiring students to raise their hands if they have an answer to a teacher's question, seem natural, but of course they are learned, and maladaptive (Wiliam, 2005).

Moreover, many of the changes in practice associated with implementing formative assessment are not just difficult to change because they are habituated – they also contradict widely distributed and strongly held beliefs about, for example, the value of grades for motivating students. Even when teachers are convinced of the value of approaches such as 'comment-only marking' they are often dissuaded from trying them out by more senior colleagues who dismiss innovations as fads advocated by ivory tower academics who don't know what real teaching is. That is why, even if we are in a hurry to help teachers improve their practice, we should 'hasten slowly'.

Support and accountability

The last two principles – support and accountability – can be thought of as two sides of the same coin. Indeed, elsewhere, we have described them as a single feature of effective learning environments for teachers: supportive accountability (Ciofalo and Leahy, 2006). The central idea is the creation of structures that, while making teachers accountable for developing their practice, also provide the support for them to do this.

Clearly, creating this 'supportive accountability' could be done in a number of ways. One way would be to assign each teacher a coach, but this would be expensive, and it is by no means clear that an adequate supply of coaches would be available. The requirements of 'in-principle scalability' led to the rejection of a coaching-based model, and instead, focused on the idea of building-based teacher learning communities.

Supporting formative assessment with teacher learning communities (TLCs)

Between 2003 and 2006, working with other colleagues at Educational Testing Service, we developed and piloted a number of models for supporting teachers (for extended accounts of these early developments, see Thompson and Goe, 2008; Wylie et al., 2008, 2009). One of our earliest models involved one of us (SL) meeting every two or three weeks with groups of four to six high school mathematics teachers to discuss the changes they were attempting to make in their practice. As a result of this work, it became clear that a two-week cycle did not allow enough time for the teachers involved to plan and implement changes in their practice in time for reporting back at the next meeting. In contrast, implementations that involved meetings that occurred at intervals of six weeks or more appeared to lose momentum. This led to the adoption of a monthly cycle of meetings that has persisted in all our implementations to the present day. In work with literally hundreds of schools in dozens of districts over the last five years, we have not come across any evidence that suggests that intervals between meetings of approximately four weeks is not an optimum, at least in respect of changes in practice related to formative assessment.

Originally we had assumed that schools would be able to find two hours for each of the monthly meetings, and while this was clearly possible in some districts, in others it was not, so we looked carefully at ways of reducing the length of the monthly meeting. After experimentation with different lengths of meetings (including meetings as short as 60 minutes), we concluded that 75 minutes should be an absolute minimum.

Our experiences with meetings with small numbers of participants had also led us to conclude that the minimum number of participants needed for a meeting to be effective was around eight. Meetings with fewer than eight participants often required significant input from the group's leader or facilitator, particularly when occasional absences due to illness and other factors reduced the size of the group further. While such intensive support from the facilitator might provide an effective learning environment for those attending, such a model would be unlikely to be scalable.

On the other hand, where the group was much larger than 12, there was not enough time to hear back from each member of the group. In interviews, many participants in teacher learning communities have told us that it was the fact that they knew that they would be required to give their colleagues an account of what they had been doing that made them prioritize working on changing their classroom practice over all the pressing concerns of a teacher's life (Ciofalo and Leahy, 2006).

As well as design guidelines for the size of group and frequency of meetings, we also explored the extent to which it was necessary for teachers to share particular assignments (e.g. early grades or subject specialisms in secondary schools). It has been our experience that teachers greatly value meeting in mixed-subject groups, in order to get ideas from teachers of different subjects or different ages. However, we had also observed many instances of a teacher rejecting suggestions from other members of the group with a claim that the suggested idea would not work for her or his own subject specialism. In order to balance these tensions, we have explored models where the teachers do not all come from the same subject specialism, but, in order to provide some disciplinary support, we ensure that for each teacher in the group, there was at least one other with the same age or subject specialism. To date, however, we do not have any data that suggests that any particular method of constituting a group is better than another, although we are aware that the scope for deep conversations about subject matter is likely to be limited where the group is made up of individuals with different subject specialisms (Grossman et al., 2000).

One final design feature of the monthly meetings of the teacher learning communities was related to their structure. As a result of Shulman's work on the 'signature pedagogies' of the professions (Shulman, 2005), we realized that there could be considerable benefits of adopting a standard structure for these monthly meetings, but that, in most approaches to teacher professional development, novelty was often regarded as paramount, in order to keep things 'fresh'. In such situations, the result is often that the structure of the learning takes precedence over the content of the learning, and much time is spent on learning about the structure of the learning, rather than the learning itself. In order to 'background' the structure of the learning, so that the learning itself could be foregrounded, we decided to arrange each meeting around the same six activities, that would occur in the same sequence in each monthly meeting. The fact that each meeting follows the same structure means that participants come to the meeting knowing the roles they are to play, both in terms of reporting back on their own experiences, and providing support to others.

Introduction (5 minutes)

Agendas for the meeting are circulated and the learning intentions for the meeting are presented.

Starter activity (5 minutes)

Participants engage in an activity to help them focus on their own learning.

Feedback (25 minutes)

Each teacher gives a brief report on what they committed to try out during the 'personal action planning' section at the previous meeting, while the rest of the group listen appreciatively and then offer support to the individual in taking their plan forward.

New learning about formative assessment (20 minutes)

In order to provide an element of novelty into each meeting of the teacher learning community (TLC), and to provide a steady stream of new ideas, each meeting includes an activity that introduces some new ideas about formative assessment. This might be a task, a video to watch and discuss, or a 'book study' in which teachers will discuss a book chapter relevant to formative assessment that they have read over the past month.

Personal action planning (15 minutes)

The penultimate activity of each session involves each of the participants planning in detail what they hope to accomplish before the next meeting. This may include trying out new ideas or it may simply be to consolidate techniques with which they have already experimented. This is also a good time for participants to plan any peer observations that they want to undertake. It is our experience that if the participants leave the meeting without a definite date and time to observe one another, the peer observation is much less likely to take place (Maher and Wiliam, 2007).

Summary of learning (5 minutes)

In the last five minutes of the meeting, the group discusses whether they have achieved the learning intentions they set themselves. If they have not, there is time for the group to decide what to do about it.

From principles to products

The research on formative assessment and the design principles for the teacher learning summarized above create a very clear vision of what should be happening in classrooms, and what kinds of teacher professional development might help move teachers towards such practice. However, this clarity only takes one so far in the design of products that might be distributed at scale.

Since 2005, ETS has been involved in extensive piloting and trialing of a product called 'Keeping Learning on Track™' (KLT) and this was made available to schools in 2009 (now marketed in the USA by Northwest Evaluation Associates). Early versions of KLT involved a four-day training programme (two days for all participants and two further days for TLC leaders), and the materials to support the training and the monthly TLC meetings ran to several hundred pages, providing detailed guidance to TLC leaders on which items on the agenda to omit if time was running short. While such extensive support materials might be necessary for some schools, there is a danger that such detail conveys the idea that the person leading the TLC needs to be an 'expert' in formative assessment. One of the key drivers motivating the five principles identified above was that each teacher is a professional, making plans for her or his own personal professional development, and getting the support of like-minded professionals in carrying out those plans.

Therefore, since 2007, we (the two authors of the current chapter) have been involved in developing a 'minimal' set of materials for supporting schools in supporting teachers in developing their own practice of formative assessment.

'Embedding Formative Assessment' (Leahy and Wiliam, 2009, 2010) is a set of resources containing sufficient materials for a school to run two-year professional development programmes for its teachers. Pack 1 includes the materials needed to run a one-day workshop on formative assessment (PowerPoint slides and a complete transcript for the workshop), seven 10-minute video clips of one of us (DW) presenting the research basis of, and some techniques for, formative assessment, and materials for running nine monthly follow-up meetings of the TLC. The materials for supporting the nine monthly meetings run to 75 pages in total, including agendas, handouts, and notes for the group leader. Pack 2 contains the materials for the second year of the programme, and includes further video presentations of key issues in teacher professional development, together with clips of classroom practice exemplifying the techniques described in the pack, and interviews with students and teachers. As the materials for the monthly meetings were developed, they were circulated to about 60 other schools that had expressed an interest in trying them out. Further materials were sent only to those schools that had provided feedback on the materials they had received.

Perhaps the most interesting finding from this early phase of development was that many schools appropriated elements of the programme to support their existing plans. Despite having attended presentations where the research basis for formative assessment was discussed at some length, and where it was shown that there was little or no research to support other innovations in learning that were attracting interest at the time (e.g. 'brain gym' or learning styles), many schools reported that they liked the idea of teacher learning communities, but had decided to use them to support teachers in whatever was the school's current priority for professional development (e.g. differentiated teaching, mobile learning, personalization, learning styles). Of course, this appropriation of resources is hardly surprising, impossible to prevent, and may be very positive in its outcomes, but what was surprising was that most of those who had transformed the innovation beyond recognition appeared to believe that they were implementing the materials *as intended*.

Evaluation of both Keeping Learning on Track™ and Embedding Formative Assessment are both at early stages, but the challenges of implementing effective professional development at scale are manifest in both programmes. In the remainder of this chapter, we discuss briefly a case study of the implementation of Embedding Formative Assessment in a municipality in England. While some of the details are unique to the English education system, the major problems appear to be exactly the same as are encountered in other rich countries.

A case study in one district

Cannington is a local authority (school district) in Greater London, covering an area of approximately 10 square miles, and serving a diverse population of approximately 200,000 residents, with three times as many of its residents from minority ethnic communities as in the country as a whole.

In July 2007, a charitable foundation made available some funds for the establishment of a research project designed to raise student achievement in mathematics, science and modern foreign languages – subjects that supervisory staff in Cannington had identified as priorities for development. Although the Embedding Formative Assessment materials had been intended for whole-school use, the opportunity to examine their use in subject-specific learning communities across an entire school district was considered to be too important to pass up.

In November 2007, a presentation was made to a meeting of the principals of the secondary schools in Cannington, proposing the establishment of three teacher learning communities in each secondary school, one focusing on mathematics, one focusing on science and the third, on modern foreign languages, to provide support for teachers in their development of classroom formative assessment practices. Members of the project team attended meetings of the Cannington principals over the subsequent months to provide updates on progress, and in July 2008, a series of three training events was held – one for each school subject – for teachers in the participating schools. The number of teachers from each school attending each of the events is shown in Table 4.1.

The training day consisted of a brief summary of the research on formative assessment, an overview of the five 'key strategies' of formative assessment, an introduction to approximately 30 different techniques that teachers might use to implement formative assessment in their classrooms, and details on the creation of the three subject-specific school-based teacher learning communities that would be established to provide ongoing support in each school. The training session also provided guidance on the role of the leader of each of the three teacher learning communities to be established in each school.

The reactions of the teachers to the training was extremely positive, and at the end of the training day, the participants from six of the nine schools appeared to have a firm plan for implementation. One school (Ashtree) had decided to delay participation in the project for a year, and Hazeltree School had earlier that month decided to create mixed-subject, rather than subject-specific teacher learning communities, as they felt that this was more in keeping with the professional development work that had already taken place at the school. However, since the funding had been provided specifically for supporting the teachers of mathematics, science and modern foreign languages, it was agreed that this would in effect mean that Hazeltree would be withdrawing from the project, although they continued to receive all materials necessary for supporting teacher

Table 4.1 Numbers of teachers attending each training event

| School | Number of teachers attending training event for: | | |
	Mathematics	Science	Modern languages
Ashtree School	1	1	0
Cedar Lodge School	5	1	3
Hawthorne School	4	10	5
Hazeltree School	7	12	2
Larchtree School	1	0	0
Mallow School	6	7	3
Poplar School	11	3	1
Spruce School	7	8	5
Willowtree School	2	5	2
Totals	44	47	21

learning communities. Larchtree School had only sent a single teacher (to the mathematics session), but the teacher concerned appeared confident that she would be able to 'cascade' the training to other teachers in the mathematics department, and possibly also to the other subjects.

While it was not possible for each teacher of mathematics, science and modern foreign languages in each school to attend the one-day workshop, all teachers of these subjects in the secondary schools in Cannington were provided with a short (30-page) booklet outlining the major principles of formative assessment, together with specific applications in their subject (Black and Harrison, 2002; Hodgen and Wiliam, 2006; Jones and Wiliam, 2007).

In order to provide a simple channel of communication between the teachers in the school and the project, six expert facilitators (two for each subject specialism) were appointed. Their major role was not to 'drive' the implementation of the programme in the schools, but rather to respond to requests from TLC leaders and administrators within the school on the use of the materials. Each facilitator kept a log of their contacts with teachers at the school, which provided the main source of evidence on the extent to which the TLCs were functioning as intended.

Given the involvement of the principals of the school at each step of the process up to this point, and their investment in releasing significant numbers of teachers to attend the initial workshops, we expected the teacher learning communities would be established quickly, but for a variety of reasons, adoption was extremely patchy.

At the end of seven months, logs provided by the facilitators were coded by two different raters, with each rater being asked to rate the progress made by each teacher learning community on a scale from 1 (little or no progress) to 4 (good progress). When the ratings generated independently were compared, in no case did the ratings differ by more than one point, and agreed ratings of the two raters are shown in Table 4.2.

Two features of this table are particularly worth noting. First the greatest progress appears to have been made in Modern Foreign Languages, which (we hope coincidentally!) is the subject with the least-well attended initial session. Second, with the exception of Spruce School, there does not appear to be any tendency for the best-progressing TLCs to be in the same school.

In the schools that were participating in the project, only 9 of the 21 possible TLCs were making reasonable progress (defined as a rating of 3 or 4 in Table 4.2). A more careful analysis of the facilitator logs indicates that the major cause of the poor progress made by the 12 TLCs making slow or no progress (a rating of 2 or 1 in Table 4.2) was that the teachers had not been given time to meet

Table 4.2   Extent of progress of teacher learning communities in each school

School	Progress		
	Mathematics	Science	Modern Languages
Ashtree School*	–	–	–
Cedar Lodge School	1	1	2
Hawthorne School	2	2	4
Hazeltree School*	–	–	–
Larchtree School	4	1	1
Mallow School	3	1	2
Poplar School	1	3	3
Spruce School	4	3	3
Willowtree School	1	1	4
Average	2.3	1.8	2.8

*Did not participate in project (Ashtree deferred for a year; Hazeltree implemented a different model).

(this was also the case for some of the more successful TLCs, who had decided to commit their own personal time to these meetings because of their interest in, and commitment to, the project). Where time within their contracted hours had been made available for members of TLCs to meet, the TLCs were going well, with considerable enthusiasm for the meetings, and, in particular, the teachers appeared to value the opportunity to talk about practice in a structured way.

The difficulty that TLCs had in finding time to meet is, at first sight, rather surprising. While none of the schools in Cannington is on the list of approximately 600 schools in England designated by the government as 'National Challenge' schools for their failure to achieve the key benchmark of 30% of their students achieving proficiency (grade C or above) in English, mathematics, and three other subjects in the national school-leaving examination for 16-year-olds, there is considerable pressure to improve results. Public transport links in Cannington are good; students can easily travel from one side of the municipality to the other, so parents have a great deal of choice of secondary schools, and this choice is at least informed, if not driven, by examination results at age 16. All the principals say that improving academic outcomes, as measured by success on national examinations taken at ages 16 and 18, is one of their top priorities, and yet despite the research evidence suggesting that formative assessment could make more difference to these academic outcomes than anything else, it appears as if it was difficult for the principals and other school administrators to prioritize the development of formative assessment.

It is even more surprising when one considers that the principals had made a commitment to the programme six months before its commencement, had been kept fully informed of the resource requirements necessary for the monthly meetings, and had made a considerable investment in the project by committing an average of 12 teacher days so that teachers could attend the introductory workshop.

However, the principals of the secondary schools in Cannington remain committed to – and in fact quite positive about – the project, and each of them is looking forward to a 'relaunch' of the Embedding Formative Assessment programme across the whole school next year, using those who have been involved in the TLCs this year as leaders next year.

Conclusions

The research evidence suggests that when formative assessment practices are integrated into the minute-to-minute and day-by-day classroom activities of teachers, substantial increases in student achievement – of the order of a 70 to 80% increase in the speed of learning – are possible, even when outcomes are measured with externally-mandated standardized tests. Indeed, the currently available evidence suggests that there is nothing else that is remotely affordable that is likely to have such a large effect. And while there was clear evidence about how teachers could be supported in developing their use of formative assessment, and that it was feasible in both the US and UK context, how to do so at scale was less clear. In this chapter, we have described the development of two products – Keeping Learning on Track™ and Embedding Formative Assessment – that appear to be effective ways of supporting teachers in their development of formative assessment, even when delivered with little support beyond the resources that can be supplied on a CD-ROM. These resources were designed to be scalable, and to be implemented with minimal additional resources from the school, and within a time allocation that is well within what is routinely spent in schools on administration and bureaucracy. We believe, therefore, that we have made two important steps: clarifying what should be the priority for teacher professional development, and what form that professional development should take.

What we have been surprised to learn, however, is that the third step – actually getting schools to prioritize professional development – appears to be more difficult than either of the first two, and this will be a priority for our future work.

Notes

1   An earlier version of this chapter was presented at a symposium entitled
     'From Advocacy to Adoption – Getting Formative Assessment into More
     Classrooms' at the annual meeting of the American Education Research
     Association, April 2009, San Diego, CA, organized by the AERA Classroom
     Assessment Special Interest Group.
2   The effect size quoted by Saunders et al. was 0.79 standard deviations cumu-
     latively over three years, but this was a school effect size. Since the correlation
     between school quality and student progress is around 0.2 standard devia-
     tions, this equates to an effect of 0.16 standard deviations at the student
     level.

References

Allal, L. and Lopez, L.M. (2005) 'Formative assessment of learning: a review of
    publications in French', in J. Looney (ed.), *Formative Assessment: Improving
    Learning in Secondary Classrooms*. Paris, France: Organisation for Economic
    Cooperation and Development. pp. 241–64.
Bangert-Drowns, R.L., Kulik, C-L.C., Kulik, J.A., and Morgan, M. (1991) 'The
    instructional effect of feedback in test-like events', *Review of Educational
    Research*, 61(2): 213–38.
Black, H. (1986) 'Assessment for learning', in D. Nuttall (ed.), *Assessing
    Educational Achievement*. London, UK: Falmer. pp. 7–18.
Black, P. and Harrison, C. (2002) *Science Inside the Black Box: Assessment for
    Learning in the Science Classroom*. London, UK: King's College London
    Department of Education and Professional Studies.
Black, P.J. and Wiliam, D. (1998) 'Assessment and classroom learning', *Assessment
    in Education: Principles, Policy and Practice*, 5(1): 7–73.
Black, P.J. and Wiliam, D. (2009) 'Developing the theory of formative assess-
    ment'. *Educational Assessment, Evaluation and Accountability*, 21(1): 5–31.
Black, P., Harrison, C., Lee, C., Marshall, B. and Wiliam, D. (2003) *Assessment
    for Learning: Putting it into Practice*. Buckingham, UK: Open University
    Press.
Bloom, B.S. (1969) 'Some theoretical issues relating to educational evaluation',
    in R.W. Tyler (ed.), *Educational Evaluation: New Roles, New Means: The 68th
    Yearbook of the National Society for the Study of Education (Part II)*, Vol. 68(2),
    Chicago, IL: University of Chicago Press. pp. 26–50.
Boekaerts, M. (2006) 'Self-regulation and effort investment', in K.A. Renninger
    and I.E. Sigel (eds), *Handbook of Child Psychology, Volume 4: Child Psychology in
    Practice* (6th edn). New York, NY: Wiley. pp. 345–77.
Broadfoot, P.M., Daugherty, R., Gardner, J., Gipps, C.V., Harlen, W., James, M.
    and Stobart, G. (1999) *Assessment for Learning: Beyond the Black Box*. Cambridge,
    UK: University of Cambridge School of Education.
Brookhart, S.M. (2004) 'Classroom assessment: tensions and intersections in
    theory and practice', *Teachers College Record*, 106(3): 429–58.
Brookhart, S.M. (2007) 'Expanding views about formative classroom assessment: a
    review of the literature', in J.H. McMillan (ed.), *Formative Classroom Assessment:
    Theory into Practice*. New York, NY: Teachers College Press. pp. 43–62.

Brown, A.L. and Campione, J.C. (1996) 'Psychological theory and the design of innovative learning environments: on procedures, principles, and systems', in L. Schauble and R. Glaser (eds), *Innovations in Learning: New Environments for Education*. Hillsdale, NJ: Lawrence Erlbaum Associates. pp. 291–2.

Ciofalo, J. and Leahy, S. (2006) 'Personal action plans: helping to adapt and modify techniques', paper presented at the annual meeting of the American Educational Research Association, San Francisco, CA.

Clymer, J.B. and Wiliam, D. (2006/2007) 'Improving the way we grade science', *Educational Leadership*, 64(4): 36–42.

Crooks, T.J. (1988) 'The impact of classroom evaluation practices on students', *Review of Educational Research*, 58(4): 438–81.

Dempster, F.N. (1991) 'Synthesis of research on reviews and tests', *Educational Leadership*, 48(7): 71–6.

Dempster, F.N. (1992) 'Using tests to promote learning: a neglected classroom resource', *Journal of Research and Development in Education*, 25(4): 213–17.

DuFour, R., DuFour, R., Eaker, R. and Many, T. (2005) *Learning by Doing: A Handbook for Professional Learning Communities at Work*. Bloomington, IL: Solution Tree.

Elshout-Mohr, M. (1994) 'Feedback in self-instruction', *European Education*, 26(2): 58–73.

Fuchs, L.S. and Fuchs, D. (1986) 'Effects of systematic formative evaluation – a meta-analysis', *Exceptional Children*, 53(3): 199–208.

Gawande, A. (2007) *Better: A Surgeon's Notes on Performance*. London, UK: Profile Books.

Ginsburg, H.P. (2001) *The Mellon Literacy Project: What does it Teach Us about Educational Research, Practice, and Sustainability?* New York, NY: Russell Sage Foundation.

Gipps, C.V. and Stobart, G. (1997) *Assessment: A Teacher's Guide to the Issues* (3rd edn). London, UK: Hodder and Stoughton.

Goe, L. and Bridgeman, B. (2006) 'Effects of focus on standards on academic performance', unpublished report, Princeton, NJ, Educational Testing Service.

Grossman, P., Wineburg, S. and Woolworth, S. (2000) *What Makes Teacher Community Different from a Gathering of Teachers?* Seattle, WA: University of Washington Center for the Study of Teaching and Policy.

Hattie, J. and Timperley, H. (2007) 'The power of feedback', *Review of Educational Research*, 77(1): 81–112.

Hayes, V.P. (2003) 'Using pupil self-evaluation within the formative assessment paradigm as a pedagogical tool', unpublished EdD thesis, University of London.

Hodgen, J. and Wiliam, D. (2006) *Mathematics Inside the Black Box: Assessment for Learning in the Mathematics Classroom*. London, UK: NFER-Nelson.

James, M. (1992) 'Assessment for learning', paper presented at the Annual Conference of the Association for Supervision and Curriculum Development (assembly session on 'Critique of Reforms in Assessment and Testing in Britain') held at New Orleans, LA. Cambridge, UK: University of Cambridge Institute of Education.

Jones, J. and Wiliam, D. (2007) *Modern Foreign Languages Inside the Black Box: Assessment for Learning in the Modern Foreign Languages Classroom*. London, UK: Granada.

Kluger, A.N. and DeNisi, A. (1996) 'The effects of feedback interventions on performance: a historical review, a meta-analysis, and a preliminary feedback intervention theory', *Psychological Bulletin*, 119(2): 254–84.

Köller, O. (2005) 'Formative assessment in classrooms: a review of the empirical German literature', in J. Looney (ed.), *Formative Assessment: Improving Learning in Secondary Classrooms*. Paris, France: Organisation for Economic Cooperation and Development. pp. 265–79.

Leahy, S. and Wiliam, D. (2009) *Embedding Assessment for Learning – a Professional Development Pack*. London, UK: Specialist Schools and Academies Trust. Available at: https://www.schoolsnetwork.org.uk/pages/default.aspx

Leahy, S. and Wiliam, D. (2010) *Embedding Assessment for Learning* – Pack 2. London, UK: Specialist Schools and Academies Trust. Available at: https://www.schoolsnetwork.org.uk/pages/default.aspx

Maher, J. and Wiliam, D. (2007) 'Keeping learning on track in new teacher induction', paper presented at the Symposium entitled 'Tight but Loose: Scaling Up Teacher Professional Development in Diverse Contexts' at the annual conference of the American Educational Research Association held at Chicago, IL.

Natriello, G. (1987) 'The impact of evaluation processes on students', *Educational Psychologist*, 22(2): 155–75.

Nyquist, J.B. (2003) 'The benefits of reconstructing feedback as a larger system of formative assessment: a meta-analysis', unpublished MSc, Vanderbilt University.

Popham, W.J. (2006) 'Phony formative assessments: buyer beware!', *Educational Leadership*, 64(3): 86–7.

Saunders, W.M., Goldenberg, C.N. and Gallimore, R. (2009) 'Increasing achievement by focusing grade level teams on improving classroom learning: a prospective, quasi-experimental study of title 1 schools', *American Educational Research Journal*, 46(4): 1006–33.

Scriven, M. (1967) 'The methodology of evaluation', in R.W. Tyler, R.M. Gagné and M. Scriven (eds), *Perspectives of Curriculum Evaluation* (Vol. 1). Chicago, IL: Rand McNally. pp. 39–83.

Shepard, L.A. (2007) 'Formative assessment: caveat emptor', in C.A. Dwyer (ed.), *The Future of Assessment: Shaping Teaching and Learning*. Mahwah, NJ: Lawrence Erlbaum Associates. pp. 279–303.

Shulman, L.S. (2005) The signature pedagogies of the professions of law, medicine, engineering, and the clergy: potential lessons for the education of teachers. Retrieved April 1, 2011 from www.taylorprograms.com/images/Shulman_signature_pedagogies.pdf

Shute, V.J. (2008) 'Focus on formative feedback', *Review of Educational Research*, 78(1): 153–89.

Stiggins, R.J. (2002) 'Assessment crisis: the absence of assessment for learning', *Phi Delta Kappan*, 83(10): 758–65.

Sutton, R. (1995) *Assessment for Learning*. Salford, UK: RS Publications.

Thompson, M. and Goe, L. (2008) *Models of Effective and Scalable Teacher Professional Development* (Research report RR-09-07). Princeton, NJ: Educational Testing Service.

Thompson, M. and Wiliam, D. (2008) 'Tight but loose: a conceptual framework for scaling up school reforms', in E. C. Wylie (ed.), *Tight but Loose: Scaling Up Teacher Professional Development in Diverse Contexts* (Research report RR-08-29). Princeton, NJ: Educational Testing Service. pp. 1–44.

Wiliam, D. (2005) 'Measuring "intelligence": what can we learn and how can we move forward?', paper presented at the annual meeting of the American Educational Research Association held at Montreal, Canada.

Wiliam, D. (2006) 'Assessment: learning communities can use it to engineer a bridge connecting teaching and learning', *Journal of Staff Development*, 27(1): 16–20.

Wiliam, D. (2007) 'Keeping learning on track: classroom assessment and the regulation of learning', in F.K. Lester Jr (ed.), *Second Handbook of Mathematics Teaching and Learning*. Greenwich, CT: Information Age Publishing. pp. 1053–98.

Wiliam, D. (2009) 'An integrative summary of the research literature and implications for a new theory of formative assessment', in H.L. Andrade and G.J. Cizek (eds), *Handbook of Formative Assessment*. New York, NY: Taylor & Francis.

Wiliam, D. and Thompson, M. (2007) 'Integrating assessment with instruction: what will it take to make it work?', in C. A. Dwyer (ed.), *The Future of Assessment: Shaping Teaching and Learning*. Mahwah, NJ: Lawrence Erlbaum Associates. pp. 52–82.

Wiliam, D., Lee, C., Harrison, C. and Black, P.J. (2004) 'Teachers developing assessment for learning: impact on student achievement', *Assessment in Education: Principles, Policy and Practice*, 11(1): 49–65.

Wylie, E.C., Lyon, C.J. and Goe, L. (2009) *Teacher Professional Development Focused on Formative Assessment: Changing Teachers, Changing Schools* (Vol. RR-09-10). Princeton, NJ: Educational Testing Service.

Wylie, E.C., Lyon, C.J., and Mavronikolas, E. (2008) *Effective and Scalable Teacher Professional Development: A Report of the Formative Research and Development* (Vol. RR-08-65). Princeton, NJ: Educational Testing Service.

Yeh, S.S. (2006) *Raising Student Achievement through Rapid Assessment and Test Reform*. New York, NY: Teachers College Press.

Chapter 5

Alternative Perspectives on Learning Outcomes: Challenges for Assessment

Richard Daugherty, Paul Black, Kathryn Ecclestone, Mary James and Paul E. Newton

Introduction

The nature and quality of the outcomes of learning are central to any discussion of the learner's experience, from whichever perspective that experience is considered. For those outcomes to be assessed it is also necessary to articulate in some way the constructs on which such judgements are based. For the assessments of outcomes to be valid the inferences drawn from the evidence of learning should be demonstrably aligned to the learning outcomes.

The project that is reported in this chapter, 'Assessment of Significant Learning Outcomes' (ASLO), is a seminar series funded by the Teaching and Learning Research Programme (TLRP) of the Economic and Social Research Council (ESRC). It has its origins in two features of debates about the alignment between the outcomes that are assessed and the programmes of learning to which those assessments purport to relate. The first of these is the challenge, all too familiar to practitioners and policy makers as well as to academics, of maximizing the validity of assessments. The second, less frequently acknowledged, is the way in which the debates about alignment are conceptualized in different ways across different educational contexts. Within the UK, discussion of how the procedures for assessing learning outcomes are aligned takes on a somewhat different character in each of the four constituent countries and a fundamentally different form when the focus is on the school curriculum than when, say, workplace learning is the context under consideration.

With the latter consideration in mind five case studies were chosen to illuminate the differences in the way alignment is conceptualized:

- a school subject: mathematics education in England;
- Learning to Learn: an EC project to develop indicators;
- workplace learning in the UK;
- higher education in the UK;
- vocational education in England.

The aim of each of the context-specific seminars[1] in the ASLO series was to clarify the terms in which the alignment of assessment procedures to learning outcomes is discussed. This necessarily involved exploring how, and by whom, control over programmes of learning is exercised in each context as well as how those who are engaged in the discussions perceive and express the issues involved. The main aim was to identify insights that may have implications beyond the context from which they emerged rather than to develop an overarching conceptual framework that could be applicable to any context.

The roots of the ASLO project can be found in the work of the Assessment Reform Group (ARG) and in TLRP's Learning Outcomes Thematic Group (LOTG). Since its inception as a response to the policy changes in curriculum and assessment brought in by the Education Reform Act 1988, the ARG has reviewed the implications for policy and practice of research on assessment. It has taken a particular interest in the relationship between assessment and pedagogy (Gardner, 2006) and between assessment and curriculum, especially through its work on enhancing quality in assessment (Harlen, 1994). In recent years the assessment/pedagogy interaction has been a prominent focus of the Group's work (for example ARG, 2002).

Validity is the natural starting point for the assessment dimension of the project, drawing on the work of Crooks et al. (1996), Stobart (2008) and others. There are recurring themes concerning the technical aspects of validity that can be traced across diverse contexts. Some contributors to the validity debate (Lissitz and Samuelson, 2007) have made the case for a focus on the content and process of the assessment itself. Others (Messick, 1989, 1995) argue that consideration of the consequences of assessment is also necessary because construct validity is undermined if inappropriate inferences are drawn from the assessment evidence.

Whatever position is taken in that debate any discussion of validity will require an answer to the question: 'Valid in relation to what?'

A rational consideration of valid assessment procedures presupposes that the curriculum is expressed clearly enough for the alignment of the one to the other to be feasible. This in turn assumes that the constructs of interest are already established, agreed and expressed in unambiguous terms. In practice, the desired outcomes of learning are often strongly contested and there is a multiplicity of ways, at every level from programme design through to the individual student and her/his teacher, of expressing the anticipated outcomes of learning.

The TLRP's remit has been to sponsor research 'with the potential to improve outcomes for learners'. In 2004, a grounded analysis by the Programme's Learning Outcomes Thematic Group (LOTG) of the outcomes mentioned in the first 30 TLRP projects to be funded, led it to propose seven categories of outcome:

- *Attainment* – often school curriculum based or measures of basic competence in the workplace;
- *Understanding* – of ideas, concepts, processes;
- *Cognitive and creative* – imaginative construction of meaning, arts or performance;
- *Using* – how to practise, manipulate, behave, engage in processes or systems;
- *Higher-order learning* – advanced thinking, reasoning, metacognition;
- *Dispositions* – attitudes, perceptions, motivations;
- *Membership, inclusion, self-worth* – affinity towards/readiness to contribute to the group where learning takes place.

(James and Brown, 2005, 10–11)

Research questions

The linking of these two distinct strands of academic debate began with the setting out of three research questions the ASLO project intended to address:

- What are the significant learning outcomes that are not being assessed in a system that relies wholly on test-based assessment procedures?
- What are the indicators of student performance which have been/could be developed in relation to such learning outcomes?
- What are the assessment procedures that do not rely on testing but do give/could give dependable measures of student performance in relation to those indicators?

Framing the research questions in such terms is indicative of the project team's initial concerns about the limited range of outcomes that are seen to be prioritized in contexts that rely on tests and examinations as the only sources of evidence about students' learning. All three questions imply that deficiencies in the alignment of indicators of students' learning are attributable to the narrow range of outcomes that it is feasible to measure if assessment systems make use only of tests or examinations as sources of evidence of learning.

As the seminar series developed, other dimensions of the alignment of assessment to learning outcomes were identified. The first of these was that a discourse within which 'learning outcomes' are explicit is apparent only in certain of the contexts under review and in only two of the five contexts is the term itself in widespread use. In one of these contexts – indicators of 'learning to learn' across the countries of the European Union (EU) – learning outcomes are central to a political debate the terms of which were established in 2000 by the European Council's setting of the so-called 'Lisbon Objectives' for education and training. In the other – higher education in the UK – learning outcomes are part of the discourse about learning developed by the organization overseeing higher education institutions (HEIs), the Quality Assurance Agency. In that context, where responsibility for defining outcomes is devolved to individual institutions, outcomes are being articulated and codified not at a whole system level but by the teaching staff responsible for the multiplicity of course units that are brought together in degree programmes.

A second, related dimension that emerged during the course of the seminar series was the way in which the role that assessment is seen to have in each context colours the debate in that context about alignment. Not only is the extent to which the term 'learning outcomes' has currency variable across the five contexts but it is also clear, more broadly, that the very nature of 'curriculum' and 'assessment' is seen in fundamentally different ways in each context. In the workplace learning context, 'curriculum' itself is not a term in common usage; 'assessment' relates to becoming qualified for the workplace. In the National Curriculum in England, 'curriculum' has been interpreted by policy makers as what must be taught in all state-funded schools; 'assessment' is coloured by the extent to which data on student performance is aggregated and used as an indicator of the quality of schooling. In the vocational education context, the definition of what is learned in terms of what will be formally assessed has taken root to such an extent that in many vocational programmes 'curriculum' and 'assessment' are indistinguishable because all learning activities are assessed.

The discussion that follows relates therefore only in part to the project's initial three research questions. It reflects also a growing awareness as the seminar series proceeded that rethinking the alignment of assessment to curriculum calls for a more fundamental questioning of the terms in which debates about alignment (or, more commonly, misalignment) are conducted. To echo one of the conclusions of the TLRP's Learning Outcomes Thematic Group:

> The first challenge would be to convince stakeholders that the existing models no longer serve us well; the second would be to convince them that alternatives are available or feasible to develop. Alternatives would also need to be succinct, robust and communicable ... (James and Brown, 2005: 20).

Emerging themes

In the course of the ASLO project seminar series a number of themes emerged as offering insights into some, if not all, of the contexts under review. What follows here is a brief discussion of each of those themes, illustrated as appropriate by reference to the relevant contexts.

The reader who is interested in a specific context can refer to reports of each seminar on the project's website at: http://www.tlrp. org/themes/seminar/daugherty/index.html. A conference paper by the project team (Daugherty et al., 2007) also includes an overview of the issues that arose in each of the first four context-specific seminars.

Construct definition

How, and by whom, the constructs involved are defined, interpreted and made real, in terms of curriculum, pedagogy and assessment practices, has emerged as a major issue in each of the case study contexts. 'Construct validity' has long been a central concern in the field of assessment without the constructs themselves necessarily being critically explored or closely defined. Even if the constructs have been considered at the levels of assessment theory and qualification design, they may not be applied in the day-to-day practice of assessors. At the other end of the curriculum/assessment relationship the constructs informing the design of programmes of learning have often been strongly contested. For example, in school mathematics diverse traditions, interest groups and constituencies are involved, leading to strongly differentiated views about desirable learning outcomes.

Only in two of the project's case studies, school mathematics and learning to learn indicators, was a particular learning domain in focus but uncertainties about learning domains and the associated constructs were also apparent in the three sector-focused studies. For example, none of the participants in the discussion of vocational education was confident that 'business studies' had been adequately defined, either by those designing such programmes as a basis for national qualifications or by teachers of business studies.

This suggests a need to clarify the constructs within a domain that informs the development both of the programmes of learning and of the related assessments. That requires much more than reference to, say, a domain of 'school mathematics' as distinct from, say, 'academic mathematics'. It calls for answers to the question 'school mathematics for what?' and yet, even amongst those who advocate a greater emphasis on 'functional mathematics', there is no consensus on the constructs underpinning that concept. If learning mathematics in school is to contribute to using what has been learned to solve everyday 'real life' problems, how mathematics is constructed for that purpose, and the ways in which learning outcomes are assessed, will differ fundamentally from a mathematics curriculum with different priorities.

In relation to workplace learning, how knowledge is represented, and the ways in which learners' capabilities are then assessed, offers a contrast to the construct dilemmas in school subjects. The types of professional learning that have been studied by Eraut (2007) all depend to some extent on the novice professional acquiring a formalized knowledge base. But, crucially, the informal, day-to-day and tacit nature of necessary knowledge is just as important to effective performance, or 'capability'. Judgement of those learning outcomes needs to take place in situations that are as close as possible to the 'real-life' workplace context. Whereas the hoped-for subsequent applicability of learning mathematics in school may or may not figure in 'school mathematics', the learner's ability to deploy his/her knowledge in a real-life situation is central to any conceivable version of, say, 'nurse education and training'. In workplace contexts, as Eraut has argued, learning is better understood as 'complex performances developed over time', with formative and summative assessments as 'windows on the learning trajectories of individuals'.

The language used to define programmes of learning and the way formal specifications are translated into student experiences differ in each of the five contexts. The 'subject benchmarks' for higher education, developed under the auspices of the QAA and interpreted at the levels of institutions and course units, are quite different in form and substance from the statutory regulations for school subjects in England, though the latter are, of course, also mediated and modified in schools and in classrooms.

A central question in all the contexts investigated is who exercises control over the design of programmes, their implementation and the assessment of outcomes. In two of the case studies, school mathematics in England and the Learning to Learn indicators project, organizations of the state have been prominent. In the other three, workplace learning, higher education and vocational education, a variable degree of control of curriculum and assessment is being exerted by such organizations. In all five contexts, a diverse array of expertise, interest groups and government agencies dabble in the specification and assessment of learning outcomes, thus contributing to incoherence and exacerbating the alignment/congruence problem.

Progression

Progression is a key concern in the design and implementation of learning programmes, and in particular for the implementation of assessment for learning. However, its relevance to summative assessment depends on the structure of the assessment system. If the only high-stakes summative test is a terminal one, then the desired final outcomes are laid down, the test constructors have to reflect these in as valid a way as they can, and the teachers discern, from study of a syllabus and of examples of the test instruments and procedures, how best to focus their work.

Progression will also be an issue where the focus is on formative assessment. For example, prior to the introduction of the national curriculum in England, secondary teachers would apply their own models of progression over the five years of their subject programmes. To focus on formative assessment, and assuming absence of high-stakes summative pressures, it can be seen from our case studies that the models of progression needed for formative purposes are very diverse. For their study of this issue in school science and mathematics (Denvir and Brown, 2004; Wilson and Draney, 2004) detailed models have been developed, based on research studies in the conceptual understanding of many science topics, with guidance to teachers on how to use such models in a formative way.

The study by Anderson and Hounsell (2007) of assessment in higher education presents a very different picture. For biology, the emphasis is on progression in relation to the modes and ground rules for developing and communicating new knowledge, whilst the contrast is sharper still in history, where the aim is for students to learn to experience participation in historical ways of thinking and acting. For such aims, the particular topic is a context for the learning, and whilst assessment is grounded therein, the context as such is not important. This contrast is reflected across schemes of progression, with explicit and analytic models appropriate at one pole, and more holistic models reliant on connoisseurship appropriate at the other. Most subjects attempt a mixture of both approaches.

The other lesson from higher education has been the low profile of regulation, which, given the lack of debate on alignment between assessment and the curriculum, has left teachers with freedom to implement their own models of progression. The same is true, for different reasons, in the case of vocational education, where the priority of encouraging fragile learners to achieve test success has led to coaching to the test, that is, to a shallow model of progression in learning. Workplace learning is different again; here progression is expressed in terms of development from novice to expert. However, there are great variations from one context to another, so that it is hard to codify progression without over-specifying and so undermining professional learning. The compromise tends to be for qualifications based on minimum competence, with progression beyond that level left to individual mentoring and appraisal.

In all of these cases, summative assessment requirements, driven by concerns for uniformity and accountability, constrain the freedom of teachers and trainers to use their own judgement in nurturing progression. This constraint can become far tighter if accountability for progression is required, as in the key stage assessment system in England. When that system was being planned it would have been possible for the curriculum to have been set out without reference to an explicit model of progression. For evidence of attainment at the end of each key stage, the assessment system could have supplied an aggregate mark as the basis for summative grading. However, for evidence of progress in learning, the system would have to be criterion referenced to identify for each student the level of progression for which an acceptable degree of mastery had been attained.

The system of 'levels of attainment' that was eventually put in place attempts to follow the progression model, but the level descriptions that characterize the presumed progression have been under-researched, and the National Curriculum tests, facing the formidable difficulty of criterion referencing, are a vehicle for ranking attainment rather than a source of evidence of progression in learning. Tests, in mathematics as in other National Curriculum 'core' subjects, have become hurdles which provide little useful information for formative purposes.

The combination of high-stakes external assessment with a loose specification of the curriculum elevates the status of the test specification and of the tests based upon it, for it will be to them that teachers look for translation of the vagueness into explicit requirements. Given that test development is constrained by the conditions and resources imposed for high-stakes testing, the result is a summative system which is in tension with formative practices and very weak in its power to reflect or guide progression.

Wilson and Black (2007) draw attention to the paradox that a more tightly prescribed curriculum might be more helpful to learners: if the curriculum were very tightly specified in setting out a detailed sequence of progression, it would follow that the test constructors would have close guidance and would not be faced with deciding how to interpret vague statements of aims in formulating specific and concrete questions. Thus the power of the test constructors, which they may well find an embarrassment, would be reduced, whilst that of the curriculum writers would be enhanced. If the sequence of progression were well founded in relation to models of learning in each subject discipline, then there could be better synergy between assessment and effective pedagogy. Limitations in the criterion referencing for the testing, and in constraints on test validity, would still be obstacles to be tackled, but there might be a clearer basis for tackling them.

Assessment procedures and their impacts

Another major issue to emerge across the case study contexts was the impact of assessment procedures on the alignment between intended or desirable outcomes from learning and those outcomes which actually emerge. From a measurement perspective, alignment is often conceived quite narrowly – in terms of content validity – where misalignment between an assessment instrument and intended learning outcomes represents a threat to the integrity of inferences from assessment results. However, it can be conceived more broadly too, where misalignment represents a threat to the integrity of learning itself. This resonates with the notion of systemic validity, as discussed by Frederiksen and Collins (1989: 27): 'A systemically valid test is one that induces in the education system curricular and instructional changes that foster the development of the cognitive skills that the test is designed to measure'.

The case study contexts highlighted numerous situations in which the nature of an assessment procedure threatened to disrupt the acquisition of desirable learning outcomes by students. This disruption occurred when assessment procedures led either to the failure to acquire desirable outcomes from learning, or to the acquisition of undesirable outcomes from learning. In both cases, potential impacts were attributable either to the design of the assessment instrument or to the nature of the assessment event itself.

The failure to acquire desirable outcomes from learning

Some of the impacts attributable to the design of an assessment instrument occur when only a sub-set of intended learning outcomes are, or can be, routinely assessed. In measurement terms, to design an instrument to this specification would involve intentional construct under-representation. This threat was evident in the school mathematics context, which was characterized by the requirement for short tests to cover a very full curriculum. This tends to rule out 'real-world' problem solving test items requiring extended thinking and analysis. It is also evident in the assessment of English, where speaking and listening are central elements of the national curriculum in England but do not feature in national curriculum tests.

Interestingly, this threat was often avoided in workplace contexts. The very idea of a single curriculum is inappropriate here, given the desirable learning outcomes within workplace learning contexts where each learner will have specific workplace experiences (e.g. nurses in different wards acquiring subtly different sets of learning outcomes). In this situation, a standardized assessment format would seriously risk channelling learners into common learning trajectories, potentially leaving them unfit for the specific requirements of their particular roles.

Another set of impacts occurs when an assessment is designed to assess certain intended learning outcomes, but fails to assess them in practice. In measurement terms, this would reflect unintentional construct under-representation. This threat was perhaps most salient in the higher education context, where an increasing codification of learning outcomes seemed to be associated with a decreasing ability to reward high quality learning. There was a sense of the sum of the parts (the individual learning outcomes which were amenable to description) being unavoidably smaller than the whole (the high quality learning which was far less amenable).

For both of these kinds of impact, the mechanism by which disruption may occur is as follows: students do not need to acquire the desirable learning outcomes to succeed on the assessment; either they, or their teachers, or everyone realizes this; either their teachers decide not to teach these outcomes or the students decide not to acquire them.

Impacts attributable to the nature of the assessment events, rather than to the design of the assessment instruments, occur when the assessment fails to facilitate the acquisition of important learning outcomes, as might otherwise be intended. That is, where the assessment fails as a pedagogical tool in its own right. Again, this was particularly salient in the higher education context, where the increased codification of assessment objectives was reported as hampering effective feedback to students. Subtle feedback relating to higher level outcomes was being replaced by formulaic feedback relating to lower level ones. A similar threat was observed in the workplace context where codified assessment arrangements will tend to inhibit the kind of informal conversations and feedback that are crucial to effective workplace learning.

The acquisition of undesirable outcomes from learning
A different type of impact attributable to the design of an assessment instrument occurs when success on the assessment can be optimized by the acquisition of undesirable, construct-irrelevant learning outcomes. The most obvious of undesirable learning outcomes is cheating behaviour. As above, the mechanism by which disruption occurs is straightforward: students discover that they can succeed on the assessment using construct-irrelevant techniques; so they decide to do so; and these techniques become the primary outcomes from learning. This aspect of the impact of assessment procedures was not prominent in the evidence reviewed by the ASLO project. However, recent changes to coursework requirements for the GCSE examination in England, in maths and in other subjects, have been prompted not only by doubts about the educational value of stereotyped responses to coursework tasks but also by concerns about the prevalence of cheating.

Finally, impacts attributable to the nature of the assessment event also occur when the assessment process actively corrupts the learning process. This threat was observed in the vocational context, as fragmented assessment procedures combined with poorly conceived curricula disposed students towards instrumental approaches to learning.

Reassuringly, there seemed to be no necessary or direct causal relationship between assessment procedures and their impacts. However, we should be acutely aware of consequences arising from the uses to which assessment results are put. The higher the stakes associated with those uses the more sensitive a system may be to disruption.

System-level accountability as a driver of alignment

Accountability takes very different forms, has different purposes and stakeholders and has different effects on the interpretation of learning outcomes within each of the assessment systems we reviewed in the seminar series. Two of the case studies in particular reveal just how influential the political imperatives for system-level accountability can be in determining the role of assessment in shaping relevant constructs but, perhaps more crucially, in shaping how teachers and students then interpret and enact those constructs.

The fierce debates that have surrounded the Mathematics National Curriculum from its inception to recent calls for it to be reshaped in favour of 'functional' mathematics show both the effects of target-driven measures and the shifting emphasis towards aggregate data on pupil attainment as an indicator of the performance of teachers, schools, local authorities and the whole system.

Such problems with alignment in this context become less a matter of how valid a national test in mathematics is as a measure of 'school mathematics' and more a question of how valid the test is as a source of data on system performance. Predictably perhaps, this affects how teachers and students regard both the teaching that leads to the test, and the test itself, with pedagogy geared increasingly towards enhancing pupil performance. In this context, educational questions about the nature, purpose and content of the mathematics curriculum, and how far mathematics should be functional or more broadly based, are distorted by different, often implicit expectations about what counts as valid assessment for different, competing purposes.

Evidence from the EU Learning to Learn Indicators project (Fredriksson and Hoskins, 2007) made clear that this is another case of an assumed learning domain and its associated constructs being shaped by accountability considerations, albeit with a view to attaching due importance to a concept that is widely held to be vital for learning in rapidly changing knowledge economies. As can be seen to occur in other education systems where the main policy driver is system accountability (Herman and Haertel, 2005), it is probable that any adoption by the EU of learning to learn as an indicator of system performance would have substantial 'washback' effects. In this case, the effect could be amplified because the pilot indicator, if adopted, would be used to draw comparisons across national systems.

The case study on vocational education in England showed system-level accountability as being far less driven by debates about what counts as valid vocational education outcomes and measures of those outcomes, within specific vocational subjects. Indeed, the porous and insecure nature of many vocational subjects, and the very diverse purposes of vocational education, mean that accountability is not derived from learning outcomes and measures of those outcomes.

Instead, political targets for retention, student progression and achievement and teachers' concerns that young people who are seen to be educationally and socially disadvantaged should achieve qualifications, pressurize schools and colleges to coach students through assessment criteria in order to maximize achievement. Accountability is also affected by the demands of awarding bodies for standardized achievement rates and grading decisions across subjects and between very diverse providers. This in turn reinforces a compliant, instrumental emphasis on maximizing achievement and showing exactly how grades are arrived at.

It can be argued, then, that system-level accountability in vocational education places much more political emphasis on 'delivering' targets for retention, progression, participation and achievement in general terms, rather than notions of educational or cognitive progression and achievement within clearly defined and debated subject domains. In turn, the dominance of teacher assessment in vocational education leads to strongly regulated moderation and verification procedures to standardize judgements. The combined effect is highly regimented and instrumental approaches to both formative and summative assessment.

Conclusion

The ASLO project's five case studies have mined a rich seam of examples of student learning outcomes being socially constructed in diverse ways. In the two case study contexts where desirable learning outcomes are formally specified through state-led regulatory procedures the constructs involved are strongly and openly contested. In the other three case studies, focusing on sectors of education within the UK rather than on particular domains, the contestation of learning outcomes is also evident.

Each of the case studies exhibits the contested nature of the outcomes in a different way. For school mathematics in England, the state controls the definition of the subject but it is operationalized through the high stakes tests of students at ages 11 and 14 and then mediated through the actions of teachers and students. The search by EU-funded groups for a pragmatic definition of 'learning to learn' and the devising of pilot indicators is an equivalent process on a cross-national basis. The political imperative to identify indicators has brought about a situation that McCormick (2007: 1) has characterized as 'the proverbial assessment tail wagging the curriculum dog'.

On vocational education programmes in England, tightly drawn specifications for qualifications set goals for learners that are then interpreted and mediated in a range of instructional environments. In UK higher education, contestation has been evidenced both at the system level, for example through 'subject benchmarks', and locally as each course is framed by the staff responsible for it and subjected to a process of institutional approval. With workplace learning, whatever the form 'curriculum' may take, it is the way in which a qualification is acquired that defines the domain and the constructs comprising that domain. A recent review of learning outcomes in EU education systems reports an increasing reliance on the identification of learning outcomes, to such an extent that they now have 'a pivotal position in the re-definition of qualifications and the curriculum in VET [vocational education and training], general and higher education' (Leney et al., 2008: 3). It is the drive for comparability of qualifications both within systems and across Europe that is spawning lists of learning outcomes. While the authors of the EU study report that those lists of outcomes currently have only a limited impact on the way learning is being assessed it can be anticipated that, over time, the codified learning outcomes will define and control assessment practices and thereby control the curriculum.

This project's case study evidence has taken the analysis of the relationship between curriculum and assessment beyond the simple notion of explicit outcomes of assessment being in some way aligned to, or congruent with, a pre-specified curriculum. Instead we see a multi-layered process of knowledge being constructed, with numerous influences at work at every level from the national system to the individual learner. Rather than thinking in terms of aligning assessment more closely to curriculum, the construction of learning outcomes is better understood as a complex, non-linear, interacting system with the ultimate goal being a synergy that embraces curriculum, pedagogy and assessment.

Acknowledgements

This article has developed from the ideas discussed in the course of the TLRP seminar series, 'Assessment of Significant Learning Outcomes'. Its authors are grateful for the input from those who presented keynote papers – Jeremy Hodgen, Ulf Fredriksson, Michael Eraut, Dai Hounsell, Kathryn Ecclestone – and for the contributions from all participants in the seminar series. Reports on each of the seminars and the names of participants can be found on the project's website at: http://www.tlrp.org/themes/seminar/daugherty/index.html

The authors also wish to acknowledge the contribution of the other four members of the Assessment Reform Group – John Gardner, Wynne Harlen, Louise Hayward and Gordon Stobart – who have been involved in the ASLO project from the outset and whose ideas have helped shape this article.

Note

1   The evidence reported here relates to the contexts at the time the seminars were held, between January and October 2007.

References

Anderson, C. and Hounsell, D. (2007) 'Knowledge practices: "doing the subject" in undergraduate courses', *The Curriculum Journal*, 18(4): 463–78.
Assessment Reform Group (ARG) (2002) *Assessment for Learning: 10 Principles*. Cambridge: University School of Education.

Crooks, T., Kane, M. and Cohen, A. (1996) 'Threats to the valid use of assessment', *Assessment in Education*, 3(3): 265–85.

Daugherty, R., Black, P., Ecclestone, K., James, M. and Newton, P. (2007) 'Investigating the alignment of assessment to curriculum', paper presented to the annual conference of the British Educational Research Association, September 2007.

Denvir, B. and Brown, M. (2004) 'Understanding number concepts in low attaining 7–9 year olds: Part I, development of descriptive framework and diagnostic instruments; Part II, the teaching studies'. *Educational Studies in Mathematics* 17: 15–36, 143–64.

Eraut, M. (2007) 'How do we represent lifelong professional learning?', expanded version of a paper given in 2006 to a special interest group meeting of the European Association for Research on Learning and Instruction (EARLI).

Frederiksen, J.R. and Collins, A. (1989) 'A systems approach to education testing', *Educational Researcher* 18(9): 27–32.

Fredriksson, U. and Hoskins, B. (2007) 'Indicators of learning to learn', paper presented to ASLO project seminar, London, March 2007. Available at: http://www.tlrp.org/themes/seminar/daugherty/index.html (accessed 30 April 2008).

Gardner, J. (ed.) (2006) *Assessment and Learning*. London: Sage Publications.

Harlen, W. (ed.) (1994) *Enhancing Quality in Assessment*. London: Paul Chapman.

Herman, J. and Haertel, E. (eds.) (2005) *Uses and Misuses of Data for Educational Accountability and Improvement: 104th Yearbook of the National Society for the Study of Education*. Chicago: NSSE.

James, M. and Brown, S. (2005) 'Grasping the nettle: preliminary analysis and some enduring issues surrounding the improvement of learning outcomes', *The Curriculum Journal*, 16(1): 7–30.

Leney, T., Gordon, J. and Adam, S. (2008) *The Shift to Learning Outcomes: Policies and Practices across Europe*. Thessaloniki: European Centre for the Development of Vocational Training (CEDEFOP).

Lissitz, R.W. and Samuelsen, K. (2007) 'A suggested change in terminology and emphasis regarding validity in education', *Educational Researcher*, 36(8): 437–48.

McCormick, R. (2007) 'Learning to learn: reflections on assessment, curriculum and pedagogy', paper presented to ASLO project seminar, London, March. Available at: http://www.tlrp.org/themes/seminar/daugherty/index.html (accessed 30 April 2008).

Messick, S. (1989) 'Validity', in R.L. Linn (ed.), *Educational Measurement*. New York and London: Macmillan and the American Council for Education. pp. 13–103.

Messick, S. (1995) 'Validity in psychological assessments', *American Psychologist*, 50(9): 741–9.

Stobart, G. (2008) *Testing Times: The Uses and Abuses of Assessment*. London: Routledge.

Wilson, M. and Black, P. (2007) 'The idea of a learning progression as a core for both instruction and assessment', paper read at the 2007 annual meeting of the American Educational Research Association, San Francisco.

Wilson M. and Draney, K. (2004) 'Some links between large-scale and classroom assessments: the case of the BEAR Assessment System', in M. Wilson (ed.), *Towards Coherence between Classroom Assessment and Accountability: 103rd Yearbook of the National Society for the Study of Education, Part II*. Chicago: University of Chicago.

Chapter 6

On the Relationship Between Assessment for Formative and Summative Purposes

Wynne Harlen

It is generally agreed that assessment in the context of education involves deciding, collecting and making judgements about evidence relating to the goals of the learning being assessed. This makes no reference to the use of the evidence, who uses it and how. These are matters at the heart of concerns about the appropriate use of assessment in various contexts. The notion of a simple distinction between formative and summative assessment, defined in terms of use either to help learning or to report on learning, has been challenged in the years since the first edition of this book. Both uses are central to effective educational practice, but there are issues relating to whether it is useful to consider them as conceptually or pragmatically distinct, particularly in light of the claim that all assessment should in some way improve teaching and learning.

As a basis for this discussion the first section of the chapter acknowledges a multitude of intended and actual uses and the second section offers a representation of the distinctive features of assessment used mainly for learning or for summarizing learning. The third and fourth sections address questions as to whether evidence gathered at a particular time to summarize learning can be used to help learning, and vice versa. In the last five years research into practice in classroom assessment has been feeding into understanding of the theory, raising questions about the distinctions between formative and summative assessment. Thus the fifth part considers whether the distinction between formative and summative assessment is redundant or whether it is more useful to think in terms of a dimension of purposes and uses rather than a dichotomy. The chapter concludes that it is useful at present to maintain a distinction between formative and summative uses of assessment, whilst recognizing the considerable influences, positive and negative, on students' learning that both can have, particularly when the evidence is collected by teachers.

Purposes, uses and functions of assessment

Newton (2010) has delivered a list of 18 uses of educational assessment, which he also describes as purposes, thus making meaningless the attempt to distinguish between purposes and uses, as for instance, by Harlen (2007) in terms of purposes being the reasons for the assessments and uses being what is actually done with the results. Mansell et al. (2009) note the difference between intended uses and actual uses. Wiliam and Black (1996) avoid the issue by referring to 'functions' of assessment, whilst in Black et al. (2002) formative assessment is defined in terms of the use made of the evidence.

What is clear from recent discussions is that it is not helpful to think in terms of a sharp distinction between formative and summative even in relation to use, since the same assessment results can be used in different ways and there are different ways of serving or reporting learning. Further, Gardner et al. (2010: 31) maintain that 'assessment of any kind should ultimately improve learning'. Whilst self-evident in the case of assessment used for formative purposes, this claim needs some justification in relation to some summative uses, where results are used for reporting achievement after learning has taken place rather than feeding into it. However, the well-known influence of what is assessed on what is taught acknowledges the relationship and makes the point that there is an obligation to ensure that assessment for summative purposes is conducted so that what is assessed and how it is assessed have a positive impact on learning. The existence of the test or examination at a later date inevitably feeds forward into the learning experiences, so it is essential that what is tested reflects the full range of desired learning goals.

Later in this chapter we revisit the value of distinguishing between purposes and uses of evidence provided by assessment. Meanwhile it remains convenient to describe assessment carried out in various ways and used primarily to help students' learning as 'formative', and assessment carried out in various ways to provide information primarily for reporting on students' 'summative'.

A view of how assessment serves formative and summative purposes

Formative purposes

There are many ways in which assessment can serve formative or summative purposes and thus many models of the detailed processes involved. However, in order to explore the relationship it is still useful to identify the general characteristics of assessment that serves mainly formative purposes and how this differs from assessment that serves mainly summative purposes.

Figure 6.1 represents assessment for formative purposes as a cycle of events. Evidence is gathered during activity A and interpreted in terms of progress towards the lesson goals. Some notion of progression in relation to the goal is needed for this interpretation, so that where students have reached can be used to indicate what next step is appropriate. Helping the students to take this next step, leading to activity B, shows how the evidence of current learning is fed back into teaching and learning. This feedback helps to regulate teaching so that the pace of moving towards a learning goal is adjusted to ensure the active participation of the students. As with all regulated processes, feedback into the system is the important mechanism for ensuring effective operation. Just as feedback from the thermostat of a heating or cooling system allows the temperature of a room to be maintained within a particular range, so feedback of information about learning helps ensure that new experiences are not too difficult nor too easy for students.

In the case of teaching, the feedback is both to the teacher and to the students. Feedback to teachers is needed so that they can consider what are the appropriate next steps and the actions that will help the students to take them. Feedback to students is most effective in promoting learning if it involves them in the process of deciding what the next steps should be, so they are not passive recipients of the teacher's judgements of their work. Thus the students are at the centre of the process and the two-headed arrows in Figure 6.1 indicate that they have a role in the collection, interpretation and use of the evidence of their learning.

The actions indicated by the boxes in Figure 6.1 are not 'stages' in a lesson or necessarily conscious decisions made by the teacher. They represent a framework for thinking about what is involved when focusing

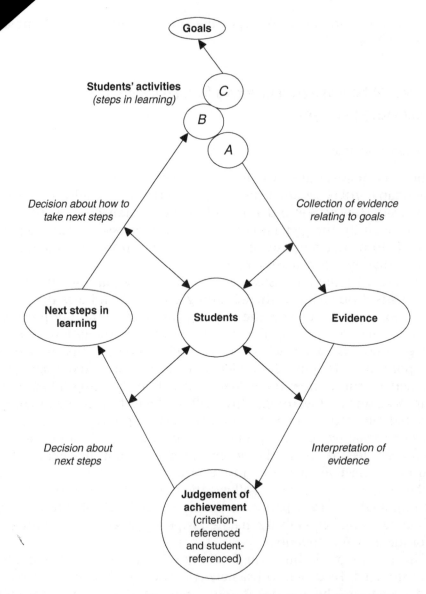

Figure 6.1 Assessment for formative purposes (based on Harlen, 2006)

on what and how students are learning and for using this to help further learning. In some cases it may be possible for teachers and students together to decide on immediate action. For example, if a teacher finds some students' ideas about an event they are investigating in science are not consistent with the scientific explanation, it may be possible for them to help the students to set up a test of their ideas and so see for themselves the need to consider alternative explanations. In other cases, a teacher may take note of what is needed and provide it at a later time. As a further alternative, Carless (2007) has proposed 'pre-emptive' formative assessment. This is action based on the anticipation of students' misconceptions, contrasted with 'reactive' formative assessment which happens 'after incomplete understanding has occurred' (Carless, 2007: 176). However, Carless acknowledges that what is known about misconceptions may not apply to all students, so not everything in a lesson can be planned in advance. If students' current learning is to be taken into account, some decisions will depend on what this learning is. Some ideas can be anticipated from teachers' experience but not all. What a teacher needs is not a prescribed lesson content but a set of strategies to deploy according to what is found to be appropriate on a particular occasion.

Summative purposes

Figure 6.2 proposes a framework for assessment used mainly to report what has been achieved rather than to help teaching and learning. Evidence relating to the goals of learning may be gathered from regular activities or from special assessment tasks or tests. The interpretation of the evidence is in terms of achievement of certain skills, understandings and attitudes as a result of a number of activities. It will be criterion-referenced, using the same criteria for all students because the purposes it serves mean that the basis for reporting achievement ought to be comparable across students. The interpretation and

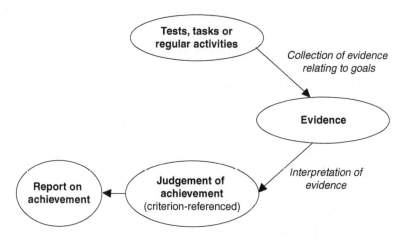

Figure 6.2   Assessment for summative purposes (adapted from Harlen 2006)

judgement may be carried out by teachers, external agencies or partly both. There is no feeding back into teaching – at least not in the same immediate way as in the assessment for learning cycle. In this model the students have no role in the assessment, although some argue that they can and should have a role (see for example, Frederiksen and White, 2004).

Figures 6.1 and 6.2 represent two conceptually different types of use of evidence that enable clear distinctions to be made between assessment used to help learning and to report what has been learned. But are these distinctions quite so sharp in practice? Can evidence collected to summarize learning be used to help learning? Can evidence collected for formative purposes also be used for summative purposes? If so, how is this done and what does it say about any real distinction between formative assessment and summative assessment purposes? These are the questions addressed in the next two sections of this chapter.

Using summative assessment evidence to help learning

The question here is whether evidence gathered so that it efficiently and reliably serves a summative purpose can also serve to help learning. This is evidence that might, for example, be collected by tests or special tasks or a summation of achievement in coursework in order to see to what extent certain skills or understandings have been acquired. Examples of practice provided by Maxwell (2004) and by Black et al. (2003) indicate circumstances in which the process of assessment and evidence obtained for reporting learning can also be used to help further learning.

The approach to assessment used for many years in the Senior Certificate in Queensland, in which a portfolio of evidence, collected over time, provides feedback to students enabling them to improve their performance during the course, as well as showing what they have achieved by the end of the course. Maxwell explains that:

> For this approach to work, it is necessary to express the learning expectations in terms of common dimensions of learning (criteria). Then there can be discussion about whether the student is on-target with respect to the learning expectations and what needs to be done to improve performance on future assessment where the same dimensions appear.

> As the student builds up the portfolio of evidence of their perform-ance, earlier assessment may be superseded by later assessment

covering the same underlying dimensions of learning. The aim is to report 'where the student got to' in their learning journey, not where they started or where they were on the average across the whole course. (Maxwell, 2004: 2–3)

The identification of goals and assessment criteria in terms of a 'common dimension of learning' understood in the same way by all involved, is central to this approach. Descriptions of these dimensions of learning need to be detailed to be capable of giving guidance, yet not so prescriptive as to infringe teachers' ownership of the curriculum. As the research reviewed by Harlen (2004) shows, the dependability of assessment is enhanced when teachers have a thorough understanding of the goals and of the nature of progression towards them. In Queensland, this is facilitated by schools being able to make decisions about their own work plan and by teachers' regular participation in the process of moderation. Time for this participation and respect for the professionalism of teachers are also important (Cumming and Maxwell, 2004). Conditions that promote dependability are clearly essential when teachers' assessment has high stakes for individual students. However, a significant feature of the Queensland system is that the assessment of students in the Senior Certificate is detached from school and teacher accountability procedures.

Black et al. (2003) include the formative use of summative assessment as one of four practices that teachers found were effective ways of implementing formative assessment (the others being questioning, feedback by marking and student peer- and self-assessment). Teachers devised various ways of using classroom tests to enable students to identify their areas of weakness and focus further effort. Whilst most teachers would use the results of classroom tests to inform themselves and the students about what needs to be done, the value in this approach is limited by the frequency and nature of the tests or special tasks. Whilst some external tests and examinations can be used in this way, by obtaining marked scripts and discussing them with students, in practice the approach is one that teachers can use principally in the context of classroom tests over which they have complete control. Black et al. (2003) noted that when external tests are involved, the process can move from developing understanding to 'teaching to the test'. More generally, the pressures exerted by current external testing and assessment requirements are not fully consistent with good formative practices (Black et al., 2003: 56). There would be a strong tendency to gather frequently what is essentially summative evidence as a substitute for evidence that can be used formatively. Whilst the teachers described by Black et al. (2003) used their creativity to graft formative value on to summative procedures, a more fundamental change is needed if assessment is to be designed to serve both purposes from the start.

The 10 principles of assessment for learning (ARG, 2002) provide a means of checking the extent to which evidence from a summative assessment can be truly formative. Before assuming that such evidence is capable of helping learning, a teacher might judge it against these principles by asking, for instance:

- Does it focus on how students learn?
- Is it sensitive and constructive?
- Does it foster motivation?
- Does it promote understanding of goals and criteria?
- Does it help learners to know how to improve?
- Does it develop the capacity for self-assessment?
- Does it recognize all educational achievements?

The Queensland portfolio system could be said to match most of these requirements quite well; indeed, it is designed to serve a formative purpose as well as a summative one. But the same cannot be said of using tests and examinations. These can make a contribution to helping identify further learning, but can never be sufficient to meet the requirement of assessment for learning, because:

- The collection of summative evidence does not occur sufficiently frequently.
- The information is not sufficiently detailed to be diagnostic.
- It is limited in relation to tasks chosen, administered and marked by teachers.
- There is a danger of mistaking frequently collected summative evidence for evidence that can be used formatively with a consequent neglect of genuine formative assessment practices.
- It rarely matches the principles of assessment for learning.

Using evidence gathered for formative assessment for summative purposes

Since evidence gathered during day-to-day work and used to help learning is necessarily collected by teachers, and sometimes also by students, the question of whether evidence from formative assessment can be used for summative purposes becomes a question of whether on-going teachers' assessment can be used for summative reporting.

As part of regular classroom events there are numerous occasions when teachers gather evidence about students' on-going achievements. They do this by observing, questioning, listening to informal discussions among students, reviewing written work and by using students' self-assessment (Harlen and James, 1997). Evidence gathered in this way is often inconclusive and may be contradictory, for what students can do is likely to be influenced by the particular context. This variation, which would be a problem for summative assessment (see Chapter 2), is useful information for formative purposes, suggesting the contexts in which students can be helped to develop their ideas and skills. By definition, since it is gathered in the course of teaching, evidence at this level of detail relates to the goals of specific lessons or activities and can be used in deciding next steps for individual learners or for groups. The question is: can this rich but sometimes inconsistent evidence be used for summative assessment purposes as well as for the formative assessment for which it is so well suited?

A positive answer to this question was given by Harlen and James (1997) who proposed that both formative and summative purposes can be served by evidence collected during teaching provided that a distinction is made between the *evidence* and the *interpretation of the evidence*. For formative assessment, the evidence is interpreted in relation to the progress of a student towards the goals of a particular piece of work, next steps being decided according to where a student has reached. The decision that is informed relates to what needs to be done to help further learning, not what level or grade a student has reached. Moving from this detailed evidence from day-to-day learning tasks to a summary of achievement in terms of grades or levels requires assurance on at least two matters: that the evidence used is valid and adequately reflects the learning goals; and that the judgements are reliable.

The validity of the evidence

If summative assessment is based solely on evidence gathered within the context of regular classroom activities, this evidence will be limited by the range and richness of the educational provision and the efficiency of the teachers in collecting evidence. In some circumstances the evidence required to summarize learning may need to be supplemented by introducing special tasks if, for instance, a teacher has been unable for one reason or another to collect all that is necessary to make judgements about all the students. Also, for formative purposes it is often appropriate to consider the progress of groups rather than of individual students and additional evidence may then be needed when making a report on the achievement of individual students.

However Black et al (2010) found a more basic problem concerning the quality of evidence used for summative assessment. Working with secondary teachers they found it necessary to help teachers improve students' learning tasks if they were to provide evidence validly reflecting the learning goals. Teachers' summative assessment, they reported, was influenced by the nature of external tests rather than a commitment to the goals of the subject. Thus help was needed in identifying the types of task to be included in the portfolios of evidence. In addition, teachers were under pressure from parents and others, who resisted reports that were not based on the result of tests. Black et al. (2010) concluded that any programme aiming to develop teachers' summative assessment 'should start by auditing both existing practices and the various obstacles and constraints that limit the vision and the freedom to manoeuvre of teachers in this area' (2010: 228).

A similar finding was reported by Hume and Coll (2009) from the close study of assessment practice in two schools in New Zealand. They found that the learning experiences – in both cases concerning scientific inquiry – were closely modelled on what was assessed for summative purposes, thus narrowing the learning. Even though they noted that the ability to investigate had been taught, learned and assessed, they expressed concern that 'since there is little evidence of depth and breadth of learning in these limited opportunities to investigate, the question must be asked how transferable this learning might be to novel or hypothetical situations' (Hume and Coll, 2009: 283).

The reliability of summative judgements

The goals of a lesson, which may be shared with the students, will be specific to the subject matter of that lesson. Achieving these specific goals contributes to the development of a more general understanding or improved skill, that is, to goals at a more generic level than the specific lesson goals. For summative reporting teachers are required to make overall judgements about what has been achieved in terms of, for instance, 'knowledge and understanding of life processes and living things' or 'scientific inquiry skills'. This means aggregating data from specific activities to make general judgements about levels reached in terms of the specifications of a curriculum (Harlen, 2004).

One approach to easing the transition from specific learning in context-based activities to the overall curriculum goals is to identify goals at an intermediate level. This is the basis of the Assessing Pupils' Progress (APP) scheme, in which curriculum goals are divided into a number of 'assessment foci' (AFs). For example, in the case of mathematics, the National Curriculum target 'number' is divided into seven AFs for levels 1 to 4 and six AFs for levels 5 and above. Judging levels still means using evidence in different forms and of varying quality. Thus the scheme also provides examples of students' work assessed at different levels. However, trials of the APP and the claim that it supports both formative and summative assessment have encouraged an approach of frequent summative judgements which teachers have found overwhelming (Brodie, 2011).

For summative purposes there needs to be some assurance of dependability. Thus some quality assurance procedures need to be in place, giving confidence that a grade or level has a similar meaning for all students. The more weight that is given to the summative judgement, the more stringent the quality assurance needs to be, possibly including some inter-school as well as intra-school moderation in judgements of evidence. This is difficult in relation to outcomes where the evidence is ephemeral and a consequence of this can be that the end-use of the evidence influences what evidence is gathered and how. This could result in a tick-list approach to gathering evidence or a series of special tasks that give concrete evidence, making formative assessment into a succession of summative assessments.

In summary, limitations on using evidence gathered for formative assessment, if it is to meet the requirements of summative assessment, are:

- It is essential to reinterpret the evidence in relation to the same criteria for each student.
- Since the formative use of evidence depends on teachers' judgements, additional quality assurance procedures will be needed when the information is used for a different purpose.
- Teachers may need to supplement evidence from regular classroom events with special tasks to ensure that the evidence is valid and broad enough adequately to reflect the goals of learning.
- The difficulty of dealing with ephemeral evidence could lead to a tick-list approach or a series of summative tasks.
- The multiple use of evidence may well change the nature of formative assessment, making it more formal.

Is the distinction between formative and summative assessment useful?

The blurred distinction between assessment to help learning and assessment to report learning indicates that the relationship between formative and summative assessment might be better described as a 'dimension' rather than a 'dichotomy'. Some points along the dimension are indicated in Figure 6.3 (derived from Harlen, 1998).

At the extremes are the practices and uses that most typify assessment for learning and assessment of learning. Between these ends it is possible to identify a range of procedures having various roles in teaching and learning. For instance, many teachers would begin a new topic by finding out what the students already know, the purpose being to inform the teaching plans rather than to identify the point of development of each individual. Similarly, at the end of a section of work teachers often give an informal test (or use 'traffic-lighting' – see Chapter 2) to assess whether new ideas have been grasped or need consolidation.

There is some parallel here with intermediate purposes for assessment identified by others. Cowie and Bell (1999) interpreted their observation of the assessment practices of 10 teachers in New Zealand as indicating two forms of formative assessment: planned and interactive. Planned formative assessment concerns the whole class and the teacher's purpose is to find out how far the learning has progressed in relation to what is expected in the standards or curriculum. Information gathering, perhaps by giving a brief class test or special task, is planned and prepared ahead; the findings are fed back

Formative<--->Summative			
	Informal formative	**Formal formative**	**Informal summative**	**Formal summative**
Major focus	What are the next steps in learning?		What has been achieved to date?	
Purpose	To inform next steps in learning	To inform next steps in teaching	To monitor progress against plans	To record achievements of individuals
How evidence collected	As normal part of class work	Introduced into normal class work	Introduced into normal class work	Separate task or test
Basis of judgement	Student- and criterion-referenced	Student- and criterion-referenced	Criterion-referenced	Criterion-referenced
Judged by	Student and teacher	Teacher	Teacher	Teacher or external marker
Action taken	Feedback to students and teacher	Feedback into teaching plans	Feedback into teaching plans	Report to student, parent, other teachers, etc.
Epithet	Assessment for learning	Matching	Dip stick	Assessment of learning

Figure 6.3　A possible dimension of assessment purposes and practices

into teaching. This is similar to 'formal formative'. Interactive formative assessment is not planned ahead in this way; it arises from the learning activity. Its function is to help the learning of individuals and it extends beyond cognitive aspects of learning to social and personal learning; feedback is both to the teacher and the learners and can be immediate. It has the attributes of 'informal formative'. Examples in practice are given by Webb and Jones (2009).

Cowie and Bell's interactive formative assessment is similar to the classroom assessment that Glover and Thomas (1999) describe as 'dynamic'. Like Black and Wiliam (1998), they emphasize the involvement of students in learning and indeed speak of 'devolving power to the learners' and suggest that without this, dynamic assessment is not possible.

There are also different degrees of formality towards the summative end. What is described as 'informal summative' may involve similar practice to 'formal formative'. However, the essential difference is the use made of the evidence. If the cycle is closed, as in Figure 6.1, and the evidence is used in adapting teaching, then it is formal formative. If there is no feeding back into teaching, as in Figure 6.2, then it falls into the category of 'informal summative', even though the evidence may be the same classroom test.

Yet rather than trying to make even more distinctions among assessment procedures, this analysis perhaps ought to be taken as meaning no more than that there are different ways of practising and using formative assessment and summative assessment. If this is so, do we then need the distinction at all?

Recognition of how evidence can be used for both purposes would at first sight seem to add to the case against retaining the distinction between formative and summative assessment. In both cases there are limitations in the dual use of the evidence, but of rather different kinds. The limitation of using evidence which has initially been gathered for a summative purpose to help learning bears on the validity of the evidence; it is just not sufficiently rich and readily available to be adequate for formative use. The limitation of using evidence which has initially been gathered by teachers to help learning to report on learning, bears on the reliability of the evidence.

When procedures are in place to assure quality through moderation and training, then evidence gathered by teachers at a level of detail suitable for helping learning can also be used to meet the requirements for dependable assessment of learning. However, the reverse situation cannot be found; there are no examples of all the needs of assessment for learning being provided from evidence collected for summative purposes. Of course, it is not logical that this could be so.

This asymmetry in dual use seems to be a strong argument for maintaining the distinction in purposes. We need to know for what purpose the evidence was gathered and for what purpose it is used. One can conduct the same assessment and use it for different purposes just as one can travel between two places for different purposes. As the purpose is the basis for evaluating the success of a journey, so the purpose of assessment enables us to evaluate whether the purpose has been achieved. If we fuse or confuse formative and summative purposes, experience strongly suggests that 'good assessment' will mean good assessment *of* learning, not *for* learning.

Conclusion

It is both a weakness and a strength that summative assessment derived by reinterpreting formative evidence means that both are in the hands of the teacher. The weakness arises from the known bias and errors that occur in teachers' judgements. All assessment involves judgement and will therefore be subject to some error and bias. While this aspect has been given attention in the context of teachers' assessment for summative uses, it no doubt exists in teachers' assessment for formative purposes. Although it is not necessary to be over-concerned about the reliability of assessment for this purpose (because it occurs regularly and the teacher will be able to use feedback to correct for a mistaken judgement), the more carefully any assessment is made the more value it will have in helping learning. Procedures for ensuring more dependable summative assessment, which need to be in place in a system using teachers' judgements, will benefit the formative use, the teacher's understanding of the learning goals, the types of learning tasks that are needed and the nature of progression in achieving them. Experience shows that moderation of teachers' judgements, necessary for external uses of summative assessment, can be conducted so that this not only serves a quality control function but also has a quality assurance function, with an impact on the process of assessment by teachers (Harlen, 2007). This will improve the collection and use of evidence for a formative as well as a summative purpose.

This chapter has sought to explore the relationship between formative assessment and summative assessment with a view to using the same evidence for both purposes. We have seen that there are potential dangers for formative assessment in assuming that evidence gathered for summative assessment can serve formative purposes. Similarly, additional measures need to be put in place if summative assessment based on evidence gathered and used for formative assessment is to be adequately reliable. These issues are key to protecting the integrity of assessment and in particular to protecting the integrity of formative assessment so that assessment for both purposes has a positive impact on learning.

References

Assessment Reform Group (ARG) (2002) *Assessment for Learning: 10 Principles.* Cambridge: University of Cambridge Faculty Reform Group. Available from the ARG website: www.assessment-reform-group.org.uk

Black, P. and Wiliam, D. (1998) *Inside the Black Box.* Slough: NFER-Nelson.

Black, P., Harrison, C., Hodgen, J., Marshall, B. and Serret, N. (2010) 'Validity in teachers' summative assessments', *Assessment in Education* 17 (2): 215–32.

Black, P., Harrison, C., Lee, C., Marshall, B. and Wiliam, D. (2002) *Working Inside the Black Box.* Slough: NFER-Nelson

Black, P., Harrison, C., Lee, C., Marshall, B. and Wiliam, D. (2003) *Assessment for Learning: Putting It into Practice.* Maidenhead: Open University Press.

Brodie, D. (2011) 'Assessing pupils' learning', in W. Harlen (ed.), *ASE Guide to Primary Science Education.* Hatfield: Association for Science Education.

Carless, D. (2007) 'Conceptualizing pre-emptive formative assessment', *Assessment in Education,* 14 (2): 171–84.

Cowie, B. and Bell, B. (1999) 'A model of formative assessment in science education', *Assessment in Education,* 6(1): 101–16.

Cumming, J. and Maxwell, G.S. (2004) 'Assessment in Australian schools: current practice and trends', *Assessment in Education,* 11(1): 89–108.

Frederiksen, J.R. and White, B.Y. (2004) 'Designing assessment for instruction and accountability: an application of validity theory to assessing scientific inquiry', in M. Wilson (ed.), *Towards Coherence between Classroom Assessment and Accountability, 103rd Yearbook of the National Society for the Study of Education, Part II.* Chicago: National Society for the Study of Education. pp. 74–104.

Gardner, J., Harlen, W., Stobart, G. with Montgomery, M. (2010) *Developing Teacher Assessment.* Maidenhead: Open University Press.

Glover, P. and Thomas, R. (1999) 'Coming to grips with continuous assessment', *Assessment in Education,* 4(3): 365–80.

Harlen, W. (1998) 'Classroom assessment: a dimension of purposes and procedures', paper presented at the annual conference of the New Zealand Association for Research in Education, Dunedin, December.

Harlen, W. (2004) 'A systematic review of the reliability and validity of assessment by teachers used for summative purposes', in *Research Evidence in Education Library* Issue 1. London: EPPI-Centre, Social Sciences Research Unit, Institute of Education.

Harlen, W. (2005) 'Teachers' summative practices and assessment for learning: tensions and synergies', *Curriculum Journal,* 16(2):207–23.

Harlen, W. (2006) *Teaching, Learning and Assessing Science 5–12* (4th edn). London: Sage Publications.

Harlen, W. (2007) *Assessment of Learning.* London: Sage Publications.

Harlen, W. and James, M.J. (1997) 'Assessment and learning: differences and relationships between formative and summative assessment', *Assessment in Education,* 4(3) 365–80.

Hume, A. and Coll, R.K. (2009) 'Assessment of learning, for learning, and as learning: New Zealand case studies', *Assessment in Education,* 16(3): 269–90.

Mansell, W., James, M. and the Assessment Reform Group on behalf of TLRP (2009) *Assessment in Schools: Fit for Purpose? A Commentary by the Teaching and Learning Research Programme.* London: Economic and Social Research Council Teaching and Learning Research Programme.

Maxwell, G.S. (2004) 'Progressive assessment for learning and certification: some lessons from school-based assessment in Queensland', paper presented at the third Conference of the Association of Commonwealth Examination and Assessment Boards, March, Nadi, Fiji.

Newton, P. (2007) 'Clarifying the purposes of educational assessment', *Assessment in Education,* 14(2): 149–70.

Newton, P. (2010) 'Educational assessment – concepts and issues: the multiple purposes of assessment', in E. Baker, B. McGaw and P. Pearson (eds) *International Encyclopedia of Education.* Oxford: Elsevier.

Webb, M. and Jones, J. (2009) 'Exploring tensions in developing assessment for learning', *Assessment in Education,* 16(2): 165–84.

Wiliam, D. and Black, P. (1996) 'Meanings and consequences: a basis for distinguishing formative and summative functions of assessment?', *British Educational Research Journal,* 23(5): 537–48.

Chapter 7

Quality Assessment Practice

John Gardner

The pursuit of consensus on the quality and purposes of assessment

Assessment is a hot topic in academic circles and across the entire educational spectrum: in schools and classrooms, in local authorities and in the corridors of government. The discourse is often focused on process and outcome matters such as workload issues in schools, results of national and international tests and standards of performance across schools. There are also ongoing debates about the purposes of assessment or, from another perspective, the uses to which assessment information is put. Its relationship to curriculum and pedagogy, in the triangle of key education concepts, waxes and wanes in importance but assessment itself is rarely out of the limelight even when curriculum grabs the lead. For example, in early 2011, the government in England initiated a full review of the National Curriculum (DfE, 2011) and appointed an advisory committee of 15 people, 10 of whom are principals or former principals of schools. In setting out the remit of the review, the government in fact made little reference to assessment but had earlier initiated a parallel review of key stage 2 assessment to be undertaken by Lord Paul Bew (DfE, 2010). This review was designed to:

> consider how to deliver rigorous, valid and reliable assessments which promote attainment and progression and ensure that schools are properly accountable to pupils, parents and the public for the achievement of every child. It will also consider how to ensure that assessments provide parents with good quality information on their child's progress.

The wording of this remit, I would argue, is applicable not only to key stage 2 but to all aspects of any national assessment enterprise. Words and phrases such as 'rigorous', 'valid', 'reliable', 'promote attainment' and 'quality information' are among the most important in the dictionary of quality assessment practice and this chapter looks at them in some detail.

The importance of assessment in a curriculum context cannot be underestimated. Certainly it should not be dismissed as the 'assessment tail wagging the curriculum dog'. If we have learned anything from the last 20 years, whether from the Assessment Reform Group or the many other researchers across the world engaged in the same field, it should be that assessment must be recognized as an integral part of the learning process. As it happens, assessment will likely be well served in the English government's review with the appointment of a four-person 'Expert Panel that will provide an evidence base for the review and will ensure that the construction and content of the new National Curriculum is based upon international best practice' (DfE, 2011). Three of the four experts: Tim Oates, Mary James and Dylan Wiliam, are internationally recognized experts in educational assessment.

The value of experts is widely acknowledged in any enterprise but perhaps more so in the educational contexts of curriculum and assessment. So much confusion exists over such issues as the difference between summative and formative assessment, or the purposes and conduct of assessment, that inevitably the field is littered by a variety of understandings, and indeed misunderstandings. One area of ARG's recent work accentuated this view strongly. The major UK-wide project: *Analysis and Review of Innovations in Assessment* (ARIA, 2009) was funded by the Nuffield Foundation and involved a series of expert seminars. It also reviewed more than a dozen of the largest initiatives involving assessment by teachers since 2000 (see Appendix 7.1 for a list of the initiatives). The analysis considered the documentation relating to these innovative projects (objectives, planning, evaluation reports, etc.) and attempted to answer three broadly framed questions:

1 How can assessment by teachers be improved for formative and summative purposes?

2 What facilitates the dissemination of improved practice in assessment by teachers?

3 What changes are needed in policy relating to assessment by teachers in order to improve students' engagement in learning and raise standards?

The project's seminars were organized across the four countries of the UK and enabled ARG members to collate the views of 200-plus experts on the key issues emerging from the various initiatives. These experts included teachers and head teachers, academics, inspectors of schools, education consultants, school pupils, representatives of the four teaching councils[1] and the professional teacher associations, representatives of the curriculum and assessment bodies, and both local authority officers and government representatives. The engagement of the latter groups of experts proved formative across the board but particularly in the Scottish Government's strategic vision and key principles for assessment in the national initiative: *Curriculum for Excellence* (Scottish Government, 2009).

The main outcomes from the research in relation to all three questions above are set out briefly in the project pamphlet (ARIA, 2009) and are expanded in detail in the book *Developing Teacher Assessment* (Gardner et al., 2010). The project probed every aspect of the task of changing assessment practices in schools and specifically focused on how assessment by teachers could be improved sufficiently for it to be a strong complement to external testing and assessment. However, a major issue emerged very soon after the expert seminars started. Put simply, there was no consistent view of what constitutes quality practice in assessment for any particular purpose. What is 'good' assessment for formative purposes? What is 'good' assessment for summative purposes? Recognizing improved practice in assessment implies knowing what aspects of practice need to be improved and what types of practice are considered to be of a higher quality.

A variety of views on the main purposes of assessment emerged in the seminars: as a classroom process, as a means of evaluating the performance of schools, as a process of awarding qualifications, as a means of promoting learning, and so on. The multiple perspectives around these purposes generated important discussions on the quality of a variety of assessment practices and ultimately led to a shared understanding of the key elements of quality that any type of assessment should have. This in turn led to the identification of a series of quality assessment standards and their underpinning principles (set out in Gardner et al., 2010). At this point, I should draw a distinction between standards of performance (e.g. the score reached in a test), which are arguably the standards we hear most about in assessment discourse, and aspirational standards that set out what is expected of high quality assessment practice. The distinction is important because an assessment activity that does not meet agreed quality standards in its design, administration or the use to which it is put is unlikely to produce dependable outcomes.

As has been argued before (Gardner and Cowan, 2005), and as Paul Black and Dylan Wiliam develop in Chapter 15, the UK does not have a strong record in adhering to internationally recognized standards in assessment practice. For example, in high-stakes tests outside of the UK, most testing bodies comply with the American Educational Research Association's Standards for Educational and Psychological Testing (AERA, APA & NCME, 1999), particularly in publishing reliability data from examinations. The UK bodies seem to be more reluctant to espouse such standards for a variety of reasons, many of which are considered in the chapter mentioned above and Paul Newton's Chapter 16. Three of the AERA Standards, which are not generally found in the UK assessment system, are particularly pertinent to quality assessment practice:

- *Standard 1.1 (on Validity)*: A rationale should be presented for each recommended interpretation and use of test scores, together with a comprehensive summary of the evidence and theory bearing on the intended use or interpretation.
- *Standard 1.2 (on Validity)*: The test developer should set forth clearly how test scores are intended to be interpreted and used. The population(s) for which a test is appropriate should be clearly delimited, and the construct that the test is intending to assess should be clearly described.
- *Standard 2.1 (on Reliability and Errors of Measurement)*: For each total score, sub-score or combination of scores that is to be interpreted, estimates of relevant reliabilities and standard errors of measurement or test information functions should be reported.

While these standards might appear particularly technical they are often voiced in a simpler form as the common concerns or aspirations of a range of educational commentators. One of the major outcomes of the ARIA seminars was the identification of two complementary and less technical sets of aspirational standards. These comprised underpinning principles that should be addressed when quality assuring any proposed assessment (or in assessing its quality after its use); and standards of practice that should be aimed at for consistency across all assessment contexts from classrooms to policy making. The consensus that emerged from the expert seminars therefore included a set of principles underpinning quality assessment and are summarized as:

1 Assessment of any kind should ultimately improve learning.
2 Assessment methods should enable progress in all important learning goals to be facilitated and reported.
3 Assessment procedures should include explicit processes to ensure that information is valid and is as reliable as necessary for its purpose.

4 Assessment should promote public understanding of learning goals relevant to students' current and future lives.

5 Assessment of learning outcomes should be treated as approximations, subject to unavoidable errors.

6 Assessment should be part of a process of teaching that enables students to understand the aims of their learning and how the quality of their achievement will be judged.

7 Assessment methods should promote the active engagement of students in their learning and its assessment.

8 Assessment should enable and motivate students to show what they can do.

9 Assessment should combine information of different kinds, including students' self-assessments, to inform decisions about students' learning and achievements.

10 Assessment methods should meet standards that reflect a broad consensus on quality at all levels from classroom practice to national policy.

These principles are expanded in full in Gardner et al. (2010) and particularly in Wynne Harlen's Chapter 2 of that book, but several of them merit specific attention here. These are outlined below.

Assessment of any kind should ultimately improve learning

The simplicity of this statement belies its profoundness. Regardless of how 'learning' might be conceptualized, for example as the assimilation of new knowledge, the development of new understanding or the acquisition of new skills, and regardless of what theoretical position is taken on learning, be it socio-cultural, constructivist or behaviourist, it is difficult to contest the notion that assessment of the progress or outcome of that learning is beneficial to the learner. If this assessment pinpoints what we know, understand or can do, it affirms our learning. If it pinpoints difficulties or weaknesses, it enables us to focus our efforts, and the efforts of those who support our learning, on identifying how we might improve our learning. Assessment for the sake of assessment makes no sense but assessment for someone else's sake is an industry of epic proportions. In many countries it ranges from commercially provided examinations for qualifications (e.g. for employment and entry to higher education) to international comparative studies between national education systems (e.g. PISA and TIMSS). The former arguably serves the students in terms of 'credentialling' their achievements but generally does not feed into their learning. Indeed the pursuit of qualifications per se often confounds deeper, long-term learning by emphasizing test-taking strategies and privileging knowledge acquisition over understanding. Comparative studies, whether international, national or local, have students participating in tests from which their grades, scores, etc. are aggregated for purposes that can range from having nothing at all to do with facilitating their learning (e.g. monitoring district, local authority and national standards) to only tangentially relating to the improvement of their learning environment (e.g. aiming to 'drive up standards' by comparing school X's school outcomes in ranked 'league' tables of performance).

Very few school students in the UK receive feedback on how their learning has progressed, and in what aspects they might need to improve, from the bewildering array of externally administered summative assessments of their learning. To all intents and purposes, they experience external testing (to different extents, it must be said, depending on the country of the UK in which they live) and their assessments (scores, marks, grades, etc.) are simply taken away without any intention or attempt to support or improve their learning. The cumulative result of this is a growing recognition that: '[Rather,] we can improve educational outcomes through assessment but only when we have better assessment practices. Assessment that is external to an ongoing process of learning and teaching ... will not produce the desired outcomes by itself' (Pellegrino, 1999).

The complementary activity, promoted by the ARG, is Assessment for Learning (AfL), described by David Hargreaves and colleagues (DEMOS, 2005) as one of the few areas of development in education that is based on the convergence of practitioner and scientific evidence. Hargreaves et al. drew on Bransford et al.'s (2000) analysis of how our knowledge of learning at that time suggested that learning environments should be a combination of learner-centred, knowledge-centred, community-centred and assessment-centred. They postulated that in assessment-centred classrooms:

> ... assessment is both formative and summative and becomes a tool to aid learning: students monitor their progress over time and with their teachers identify the next steps needed to improve. Techniques such as open questioning, sharing learning objectives and focused marking have a powerful effect on students' ability to take an active role in their learning. There is always sufficient time left for reflection by students. Whether individually or in pairs, students are given the opportunity to review what they have learnt and how they have learnt it. They evaluate themselves and

one another in a way that contributes to understanding. Students know their levels of achievement and make progress towards their next goal. (DEMOS, 2005: 17)

The central message here is the use of assessment to improve learning – assessment that involves the full gamut of key assessment for learning activities such as (effective) questioning, self- and peer-assessment, sharing learning objectives and identifying next steps in the students' learning. Feedback is not expressly mentioned in this excerpt (it is in other parts of the report) but the term 'focused marking' suggests that the assessment approach should also focus on a summative assessment of the students' achievement of the learning objectives. While most people who espouse assessment for learning will not be unduly troubled by the reference to marking there is considerable debate about whether the giving of marks – the leitmotiv of summative assessment – is beneficial in a formative sense, especially if they constitute the only form of feedback given.

Experience and common sense might suggest that marks alone do not constitute quality assessment feedback but in the absence of much research on the topic, the jury is certainly out. Butler (1987, 1988) is often quoted as having demonstrated that students show greater improvements in their performance when given feedback in the form of comments than when given comments-plus-marks and marks alone. She explained the former as being a result of focusing on the mark and ignoring the comments, and the latter as a result of comparing themselves with others instead of reflecting on what they themselves have done. There is very little research to confirm or reject the notion, and what recent research there has been is often less than conclusive. For example, Smith and Gorard (2005: 36) reported from 'a small study, set in one school, without complete isolation of treatment students and staff from the controls, without representing the full ability range in the Year 7 cohort, and without a standardized "public" test as an outcome' that when some teachers put comments but no marks on students' work these students made less progress than others who were given marks. However, the majority of the teachers' comments illustrated by Smith and Gorard merely commented on how well the students had done and did not provide guidance or suggestions on how to improve the work. After the research was undertaken and reported, a systematically more thorough programme of introducing AfL was undertaken, including support for written feedback, and a year later the Assistant Head of the same school was reporting that the Key Stage 3 results for English, mathematics and science had steadily improved (Burns, 2006).

Smith and Gorard were not seeking to 'test the overall notion that formative feedback is to be preferred in the ways suggested by its advocates' (2005: 36) but their work highlights the need to give any innovative practice enough time to become established. Whether it is through feedback, effective questioning, meaningful participation or self- and peer-assessment, the aspiration embedded in this deceptively simple principle is that quality assessment should ensure that benefit always accrues to learners. If they undertake, participate in or are subjected to any type of assessment of their learning such benefit should comprise them knowing how well they have done and how they might improve.

Assessment methods should enable progress in all important learning goals to be facilitated and reported

Assessment too often tends to be targeted at aspects of learning that are easily 'measured',[2] with sometimes serious consequences for the quality of the assessment process and its outcomes. The assessment of knowledge through tests that require simple recall of facts is the simplest of these types of assessment. More sophisticated tests may require students to apply their understanding of concepts and their relationships. That much is unproblematic. However, unless extensive periods are allocated for the assessment process, the essential weakness of all such time-bounded assessments lies in their inability to assess all learning that is considered important. Time constraints will usually mean that a test can only address a sub-set of the full learning domain for the subject ('There was no question on sulphuric acid manufacture') but more fundamentally the test design may not be capable of assessing the type of learning involved. For example a pen-and-paper test will not be able to examine a student's mastery of a variety of communication techniques.

This is not to say that some types of important learning goals can never be assessed. On the contrary, it should be possible to find a means of assessing even the most complex of learning goals; the limitations are generally related to the extent of resources and time needed to design valid assessment approaches. Some circumstances demand the effort and expense. For example, it is a long time since the competence of medical students was examined solely by pen-and-paper tests and oral examinations. For some 30 years now, Harden and Gleeson's (1979) 'objective structured clinical examinations' (OSCEs) have assessed medical students' diagnostic skills in a

series of simulated clinical situations, complete with 'actors' presenting with ailments and injuries. Reserving a question mark over the
concept of 'objectivity' of the assessments (usually only one judge
monitors the student's appraisal of the patient's condition at each
assessment in a series that may comprise as many as 20 'stations' or
more), it is not unreasonable to conclude that such an approach is
better than writing an essay-type response to a text-based description
of how an imaginary patient may present. Nevertheless, such assessments are expensive in terms of personnel and their time; they
require considerable physical resources and a significant number of
expert judges. Lower down the scale of complexity, for example in
the drama or technology departments of schools, 'authentic' assessments of performance or problem solving will suffer from such
resourcing constraints. Taking them to a national scale will probably
be out of the question.

We continue to learn about and develop new techniques of assessment, especially through the use of digital technologies, to extend
our ability to assess complex types of learning. For example, in creative contexts such as art and technology, portfolios have a long-
established role in the assessment of student work. The ability to
make the work available electronically, with a varied use of media
such as text, video and audio, gives the e-portfolio a boost over traditional paper or artefact-based collections. However, concerns exist
over the time and costs invoved in assessing what can be very complex collections of work. The e-Scape project (e-Scape, 2005–2009)
successfully developed and trialled a portfolio system for assessing
design students' work. Described as a dynamic portfolio process (created over a preset six-hour period by the students) the students
recorded the progress of their work directly to a dedicated web-server
from a variety of input devices including tablet computers, speech
tools, cameras and digital pens. Their portfolios were then electronically distributed to a number of judges and graded on a Thurstone
Pairs basis, that is each portfolio was located on a ranked list according to a minimum number of one-by-one comparisons with other
portfolios. This established a ranked position for each portfolio at
which those below were considered to be less good and the ones
above were considered to be better. The second phase of the project
identified difficulties in scaling the work up but the basic ideas offer
possibilities for tackling the challenges of assessing complex learning
processes and outputs in the future.

Facilitating and reporting progress in all important learning
goals, the focus of the principle that opened this section, is an
exceptionally challenging aspiration but simply ignoring it or not

being able to address it is not considered to be an option in the pursuit of quality assessment.

Assessment procedures should include explicit processes to ensure that information is valid and is as reliable as necessary for its purpose

Validity and quality

It almost goes without saying that assessment that is not valid for its purpose is simply a waste of time. However, it actually does need to be said – not because there are likely to be those who would disagree, but because too many people do not reflect on the validity of the assessments they use in terms of the purposes for which they are needed. Too many do not examine the validity of the interpretations they place on the assessment information their assessments produce. For example, teachers who use multiple-choice quizzes to assess their students' learning in a topic may not be thinking in sufficient depth about the learning that they are trying to facilitate. A student may know something sufficiently to answer a multiple choice (M/C) question correctly but may not understand it or may not be able to apply the knowledge appropriately. There is little point asking a student to identify the principles of 'fair testing' listed in an M/C item if the goal of the original learning is that the student should be able to conduct fair tests; the use of an M/C assessment of this goal is not valid because it is not fit for purpose. It would also be wrong to assume that because a student can identify a set of principles for 'fair testing' in an M/C item, that they are also able to conduct fair tests; the inference is not valid from the assessment information available. However, too often a rather naïve understanding of assessment validity can lead to seriously invalid interpretations of assessment information. Demonstrating a good range of French vocabulary on a sheet of paper gives no indication of how well French is spoken.

Quality practice in any assessment or testing procedure therefore implies that there must be clear information on the limits of valid interpretation of the information from it – and so say AERA Standards 1.1 and 1.2 on p. 106. However, 1.2 also points to the requirement that 'the population(s) for which a test is appropriate should be clearly delimited'. This is arguably not the case in many examination contexts which appear continuously to highlight if not actually consolidate social inequalities (a topic drawn out in more depth in Gardner et al, 2009).[3]

For example, a major UK survey of over 15,000 Year 9 students and their parents (Strand, 2008) has shown that around three points separate the higher levels of White students' performances at Key Stage 3 from those for Pakistani, Black Caribbean and Black African students in the sample. Strand equates this to a whole year of progress in terms of national curriculum levels. The same study showed much more emphatic differences on family background issues with 10 points between students from higher managerial and professional families and those with unemployed parents or guardians, and nine points between students with mothers educated to degree level and those with mothers who had no educational qualifications. The dilemma here is whether the assessment system is merely indicating where social inequality prevails and where educational intervention is needed (for the poorly performing groups) or it is actually contributing to the creation of the differentials in performance. What is more evident, though, is that the existing assessment system is not contributing to the reduction in the differentials by improving outcomes for the under-performing groups.

The double jeopardy of under-performance is that schools and teachers often face the brunt of the criticism for its existence by allegedly not dealing with it. Undoubtedly there are schools and teachers failing to provide an adequate education to their students but the neo-liberal solution that testing and increased accountability will raise the standards of education across the board is a very dubious theory, if not simply a non-sequitur. Much of the research on the effects of testing comes from the US and its conclusions generally point to the impact of educational and social contexts in causing and sustaining the gaps in achievement between groups. Slavin and Madden (2006), for example, provide evidence that

> African Americans, on average, attend schools that are far less well funded than those attended by Whites; their teachers are less highly qualified, and their families are more likely to suffer from the ills of poverty, which have a direct bearing on children's success in schools. (2006: 390)

Perhaps the most researched approach to using assessment as a means to address inequities is the US No Child Left Behind Act (NCLB, 2002). In much of the educational world this policy is largely maligned. For example, Keyes (2007) claims that NCLB is widening the gap between poor and minority students and wealthy White students by restricting the former to answering simple questions in basic skills education while the latter learn to ask complex questions. Nichols et al.'s work (2005) suggests that the problems caused by the high-stakes, standardized tests, which are used to inform actions under NCLB, actually affect minority students disproportionately.

Fusarelli (2004) takes the view that there is much to commend in NCLB but cites the extent to which the withdrawal of Title 1 funding for schools whose students fare badly – most frequently they are '… impoverished schools filled with students of colour' (2004: 87) – is a sanction that defies logic. The states whose schools do best under NCLB are those that are predominantly White, for example: Minnesota (89%), Wyoming (92%) and Connecticut (82%). In a worst case scenario, he argues, the results of the standardized testing approach may include the lowering of state standards, and '… the cure will be worse than the disease' (Fusarelli, 2004: 87). President Obama's administration acknowledged that:

> NCLB highlighted the achievement gap and created a national conversation about student achievement. But it also created incentives for states to lower their standards; emphasized punishing failure over rewarding success; focused on absolute scores, rather than recognizing growth and progress; and prescribed a pass–fail, one-size-fits-all series of interventions for schools that miss their goals. (USDE, 2010)

The administration announced the re-authorization of the NCLB in 2010 but with some refinements, including the intention to reward poorly performing schools that show improvements. The double jeopardy arising from assessments of poor performance has also been shown to exist in England. Levačić and Woods (2002) and Levačić and Marsh (2007) have presented findings that show schools with high proportions of disadvantaged students suffering from reducing budgets over time as the proportion of disadvantaged students tends to increase and their position in the local hierarchy of schools in turn deteriorates. In such circumstances social injustice is likely to be deepened as performance on national assessments continues on a downward trajectory.

Reliability and quality

As later chapters will emphasize, reliability is a sub-element of validity and good practice would also demand that the assessment information must set out the extent to which reliability is important in the context of the assessment, and how reliable the information may be considered to be. Where reliability is important (in high-stakes tests, for example) the information must provide estimates, for example, of the consistency in assessment judgements between judges and in the consistency of the students' scores (including within the test-taking cohort, over time or over a number of assessments). The extent of avoidable errors or unavoidable systemic errors in high-stakes tests is a particularly problematic dimension of reliability that must be reported as these can lead to significant misclassifications of candidates' scores and grades. Later chapters, especially Paul Black and Dylan Wiliam's Chapter 15, will deal with these aspects of reliability in a detailed fashion and this section considers instead reliability issues relating to the bias of assessors.

If every grade was: 'an inadequate report of an inaccurate judgment by a biased and variable judge of the extent to which a student has attained an undefined level of mastery of an unknown proportion of an indefinite material' (Dressel, 1983: 12) then assessments systems would clearly be disastrous. However, Paul Dressel's mischievous description is not completely outlandish as an example shown on BBC Television in 2008 showed. A primary school head teacher presented two pieces of work that had been returned to her as part of the National Curriculum Assessment scripts for her pupils. The issue of unfair and highly dubious marking was revealed as follows:

> Asked to write a story about a fairground inventor called Pip Davenport, one pupil wrote: '*If he wasent doing enthing els heel help his uncle Herry at the funfair during the day. And had stoody at nigh on other thing he did was invent new rides.*' The child was given eight marks out of 12 for composition.

> Another wrote: '*Quickly, it became apparent that Pip was a fantastic rider: a complete natural. But it was his love of horses that led to a tragic accident. An accident that would change his life forever. At the age of 7 he was training for a local competition when his horse, Mandy, swerved sideways unexpectedly, throwing Pip on to the ground, paralysed.*' This pupil was given seven marks out of 12 for composition, while both were awarded five out of eight for sentence structure. (BBC, 2008)

Whether the same person or two different people assessed these students' work, the difference (or sameness) in the judgements is very difficult to explain. Similar problems arise when teachers subconsciously award higher scores to neat work than to work of a comparable quality presented in a relatively untidy style. Unruly or disaffected students, compared to those perceived to be well behaved and committed, might suffer similarly for the same quality of work. Sometimes this can stray consciously or subconsciously into assessment decisions that are influenced by teachers' perceptions of students' backgrounds, their capacity to learn and their capacity to succeed; a form of what George W. Bush once famously described (2004) as the 'soft bigotry of low expectations'.

Assessment of learning outcomes should be treated as approximations, subject to unavoidable errors

Charles Spearman once argued (1904: 272) that all examinations in school subjects and indeed all tests of an individual's attributes 'may be considered so many independently obtained estimates of the one great common intellective function', which he called 'g'. He later argued that every performance depends on two factors one of which is constant (g) while the other varies randomly. Though he eventually referred to IQ as a mere average of a variety of unconnected tests – a 'gallimaufry of tests' (Spearman 1931: 407) – he was convinced that something of considerable importance was being measured and could be used to rank people in terms of ability. Modern understanding of assessment no longer entertains such a simplistic notion and as Chapter 15 on reliability in this edition amply explains, the best description we can allocate to assessments is that they are approximations. Any allusion to precise measurement of a student's learning or any other personal attribute, is merely an illusion.

Random errors therefore conspire to thwart precision in all assessments, though there are well-established steps to ensure some types of assessments are as reliable as possible. However, most people outside of the assessment community (and a fair number within) never have pause to question assessment grades or marks. This incomplete or poorly informed public understanding of assessment contributes to several knock-on problems. For example, widely reported 'errors' such as the problem of the primary school writing assessments above, or human errors such as wrong marks being given or marks being totalled incorrectly, can promote a lack of trust in the system. Even while generally appreciating the concept of human error, the public will often not have a sense of the scale of the problem. For example, few will appreciate the implications of some 65,000 GCSE grades being appealed and over 14,000 (22%) subsequently being revised (BBC, 2007). Although the appeal rate was only around 1% of the total tests sat (around 6.5 million), the need to re-grade as many as 22% of the appeals in any one year is certainly a cause for concern.

A longer-term concern, however, is that the relative complexity of the standard error of measurement (SEM, see Chapter 15), which conspires to cast uncertainty around any score, mark or grade, is a long way from being appreciated by the general public. There is a naïve expectation that somewhere behind the impenetrable scenes of the examinations community, there are processes that ensure that a student's grade B is indisputably a measure of their true ability in the subject; and that this grade B is indisputably better than another student's grade C. On face value 'yes' – perhaps for most practical purposes 'yes', but alas there can be no simple certainty.

Other problems prompted by poor public understanding of assessment include politicians formulating inappropriate assessment policies based on simple notions that, for example, doing tests raises standards of performance. That this is not the case is the expert view of many assessment researchers. Criticism of teacher assessments or lack of attention to reducing bias can also have the effect of steering unwarranted trust towards externally administered testing, that does not involve teachers in the assessment of their own pupils. Just as important as these issues, however, is the potential loss of the learning that effective assessment practice can bring to student performance through feedback and identification of next steps in the learning.

The key dimensions of the perceived lack of public understanding of assessment, validity and reliability, include:

- confusion over the *purposes* of assessment and the designs that achieve these purposes (validity);
- poor grasp of the *dependability* of assessments, usually involving the interpretation and range of content (validity) and accuracy (reliability) of performance indicators such as marks, grades, etc.;
- simplistic notions on the *fairness* of assessments, usually involving the non-sequitur that since everyone takes the same test it is therefore fair;
- no awareness of both systemic and human *error*;
- poor *judgement* in making assessments.

There are signs the situation is beginning to change; prompted, for example, by Newton (2005). In this paper Newton states that: 'The nature and extent of measurement inaccuracy in large-scale tests and examinations should come as news to no one.' (2005: 438). This is not, as it might at first seem, a swipe at examinations; it is part of a careful analysis that argues that greater transparency in assessment practice and public awareness of the limitations will lead to greater trust in both the examination systems and the bodies that organize them. But as O'Neill counsels us, transparency can also undermine trust: 'Transparency can encourage people to be less honest ... those who know that everything they say or write is to be made public may massage the truth ... evasive and uninformative statements may substitute for truth-telling' (2002: 73). If they are not to be deceived, then, the public needs to have a basic understanding of the issues; sufficient to interpret and judge the information they are given.

Concluding remarks

Quality in assessment is a multi-faceted concept. At its simplest level it may be thought of as putting together well-crafted questions to examine a student's knowledge gained from a particular aspect of their learning. These questions will be clearly written and unambiguous, and will invite the students to give the best answers they can. Ideally a quality assessment instrument will strive to cover as much of the learning domain as possible, to give a reasonable picture of the students' accomplishments across the whole of their learning. Realistically, the assessment will not achieve this completely and some students will be disadvantaged because the areas they are most knowledgeable in 'do not come up'. Some will be advantaged by seeing the questions they have been expecting, allowing them to 'put their best foot forward'. To some extent we shrug our shoulders at this situation – you win some, you lose some – but in truth the fault does not lie with the student, it lies with the inadequacy of the assessment.

Domain coverage is one relatively simple feature of ensuring a good quality assessment but the essence of this chapter has been to argue the importance of a selection of simple principles that underpin much more profound dimensions of quality. Quality assessment will contribute to improved learning – and it should do this through feedback and opportunities for the students to reflect on their performance, perhaps in consort with their peers. It should ensure students participate in its processes without compromising its probity, and the students should clearly understand what is being asked of them. Quality assessment will also assess all relevant types and outputs of learning, and not just the easy target of knowledge recall. It should do this by employing realistic attempts to address complex learning outcomes. Its uses will be appropriate; not causing greater disadvantage to struggling students or groups but showing instead the way to improved learning and outcomes. And quality assessment will do these things validly and as reliably as appropriate for its purposes and for the learning it addresses. Finally, quality assessment will be an 'open book' to everyone – its strengths and weaknesses in interpretation and dependability will be clear for all to see and, most importantly, to understand.

Notes

1 The demise of the General Teaching Council for England has since been announced by the English government.
2 The notion of 'measure' is used in its common sense but there is no intention to imply any degree of 'precision'.
3 Some aspects of this chapter draw from the Gardner et al. (2009) report.

References

AERA, APA & NCME (1999) *Standards for Educational and Psychological Testing*. Washington DC: American Educational Research Association (with the American Psychological Association and the National Council on Measurement in Education).

ARIA (2009) Gardner, J., Harlen, W., Hayward, L. and Stobart, G. (2009) *Changing Assessment Practice: Process, Principles and Standards*. London: Assessment Reform Group. Available at www.aria.qub.ac.uk

BBC (2007) 'Thousands given wrong GCSE grades', 16 March. Available at: http://news.bbc.co.uk/1/hi/education/6455977.stm

BBC (2008) 'More questions about Sats results' http://news.bbc.co.uk/l/hi/education/7511922.stm

Bransford, J. D., Brown, A. L. and Cocking, R. R. (2000) *How People Learn: Brain, Mind, Experience and School*. Washington, DC: National Academies Press.

Burns, S. (2006) Developing AfL, monitoring progress and evaluating impact – a case study. Presentation at the conference Assessment for School and Pupil Improvement, London, 27 June.

Bush, G.W (2004) http://archivenewsmax.com/archives/articles/2004/1/9/110923 shtml

Butler, R. (1987) 'Task-involving and ego-involving properties of evaluation: effects of different feedback conditions on motivational perceptions, interest and performance', *Journal of Educational Psychology* 79 (4): 474–82.

Butler, R. (1988). 'Enhancing and undermining intrinsic motivation: the effects of task-involving and ego-involving evaluation on interest and involvement', *British Journal of Educational Pyschology* 58: 1–14.

DEMOS (2005) *About Learning: Report of the Learning Working Group*. London: DEMOS. Available at: http://www.demos.co.uk/publications/aboutlearning

DfE (2010) Review of Key Stage 2 Testing, Department for Education. Available at: http://www.education.gov.uk/b0073043/remit-for-review-of-the-national-curriculum-in-england/remit-for-the-review/links-to-assessment

DfE (2011) 'Review of the National Curriculum in England', Department for Education. Available at: http://www.education.gov.uk/schools/teachingandlearning/curriculum/a0073091/expert-panel-terms-of-reference

Dressel, P. (1983) 'Grades: one more tilt at the windmill', in A. W. Chickering (ed.), Bulletin. Memphis: Memphis State University.

e-Scape (2005–2009) Project e-Scape, Goldsmiths, University of London: http://www.gold.ac.uk/teru/projectinfo/

e-Scape Project (2009) Goldsmith's College, available at http://www.gold.ac.uk/media/e-scape_phase3_report.pdf

Fusarelli, L. D. (2004) 'The potential impact of the No Child Left Behind Act on equity and diversity in American education', *Education Policy* 18 (1) 71–94.

Gardner, J. and Cowan, P. (2005) 'The fallibility of high stakes "11-plus" testing in Northern Ireland', *Assessment in Education: Principles, Policy and Practice*, 12 (2) 145–65.

Gardner, J., Harlen, W., Hayward, L., Stobart, G. with Montgomery, M. (2010) *Developing Teacher Assessment*. London: McGraw-Hill.

Gardner, J., Holmes, B. and Leitch, R. (2009) *Assessment and Social Justice*, Bristol: Futurelab. Available at: http://www2.futurelab.org.uk/resources/publications-reports-articles/literature-reviews/Literature-Review1186

Harden, R. M. and Gleeson, F. A. (1979) 'Assessment of clinical competence using an objective structured clinical examination (OSCE)', *Medical Education*, 13 (1) 41–54.

Keyes, D. (2007) 'Classroom caste system', *Washington Post*, April 9, A13 http://www.washingtonpost.com/wp-dyn/content/artic1e/2007/04/08/AR20070 40800925.html

Levačić, R. and Woods, P. A. (2002) 'Raising school performance in the league tables (Part 1): disentangling the effects of social disadvantage', *British Educational Research Journal*, 28 (2) 207–26.

Levačić, R. and Marsh, A. (2007) 'Secondary modern schools: are their pupils disadvantaged?', *British Educational Research Journal*, 33 (2) 155–78.

NCLB (2002) *No Child Left Behind Act*. The White House. http://www2.ed.gov/ policy/elsec/leg/esea02/107-110.pdf

Newton, P.E. (2005) 'The public understanding of measurement inaccuracy', *British Educational Research Journal*, 31(4): 419–42.

Nichols, S.L., Glass, G.V. and Berliner, D.C. (2005) *High Stakes Testing and Student Achievement: Problems for the No Child Left Behind Act*. Arizona State University: Educational Policy Studies Laboratory http://epicpolicy.org/files/EPSL-0509-105-EPRU.pdf

O'Neill, O. (2002) *A Question of Trust: the BBC Reith Lectures 2002*. Cambridge: Cambridge University Press.

Pellegrino, J. W. (1999) *The Evolution of Educational Assessment: Considering the Past and Imagining the Future*, 6th William H. Angoff Memorial Lecture Series. Princeton, NJ: Educational Testing Service.

Scottish Government (2009) *Assessment for Curriculum for Excellence: Strategic Vision and Key Principles*. Available at: http://www.ltscotland.org.uk/publications/a/ publication_tcm4645133.asp

Slavin, R. E. and Madden, N. A. (2006) 'Reducing the gap: Success for all and the achievement of African American students', *Journal of Negro Education*, 75 (3) 389–400.

Smith, E. and Gorard, S. (2005) 'They don't give us our marks': the role of formative feedback in student progress', *Assessment in Education*, 12(1): 21–38.

Spearman, C. (1904) '"General intelligence", objectively determined and measured', *American Journal of Psychology*, 15 (2) 201–92.

Spearman, C. (1931) 'Our need of some science in place of the word "intelligence"', *Journal of Educational Psychology*, 22 (6) 401–10.

Strand, S. (2008) 'Minority ethnic pupils in the longitudinal study of young people in England', *Cedar Newsletter 20* (Spring) 1 University of Warwick: Centre for Educational Development, Appraisal and Research. Full report at http://www. dcsf.gov.uk/research/data/uploadfiles/dcsf-rr002.pdf

USDE (2010) 'Obama Administration's Education Reform Plan Emphasizes Flexibility, Resources and Accountability for Results', US Department of Education. Available at: http://www2.ed.gov/news/pressreleases/2010/03/03152010.html

Appendix 7.1

[A list of] The main projects reviewed under the auspices of ARIA

- Assessment is for Learning (Learning and Teaching Scotland and the Scottish Government)
- Assessing Pupils' Progress (Key Stage 3) and Monitoring Children's Progress (Key Stage 2) (Qualifications and Curriculum Authority with the Primary and Secondary National Strategies)
- Assessment for Learning in the Northern Ireland Revised Curriculum (Council for Curriculum, Examinations and Assessment (CCEA), Northern Ireland)
- Consulting Pupils on the Assessment of their Learning (Queen's University, Belfast)
- Programme for Developing Thinking and Assessment for Learning (Department for Children, Education, Lifelong Learning and Skills, Welsh Assembly Government)
- Assessment Programme for Wales: Securing Key Stage 2 and Key Stage 3 Teacher Assessment (Department for Children, Education, Lifelong Learning and Skills, Welsh Assembly Government)
- Project e-Scape, Goldsmiths, University of London
- Jersey Actioning Formative Assessment (JAFA) (King's College London and the Education Department of Jersey)
- King's Oxfordshire Medway Formative Assessment Project (KMOFAP) (King's College London, Oxfordshire LA and Medway LA)
- King's Oxfordshire Summative Assessment Project (KOSAP) (King's College London and Oxfordshire LA)
- Learning How to Learn (University of Cambridge)
- Portsmouth Learning Community Assessment for Learning Strand (Portsmouth LA)
- Summative Teacher Assessments at the End of Key Stage 2 (Birmingham LA and Oxfordshire LA)

NB: This list does not include details of the many important local initiatives that participated in ARIA events, for example Gateshead Local Authority, Belfast Education and Library Board and the Highland Council (Scotland).

Part 2

Impact

Chapter 8

Assessment and Learning: The Learner's Perspective

Louise Hayward

This book is about learning and the roles that assessment plays in that process. As Gardner clearly establishes in the Introduction, 'Assessment is our focus but learning is the goal' (p. 2). In this chapter we explore the interaction of learning and assessment from the perspective of learners.

The chapter begins by identifying assessment for learning as a perceived force for good. Bennett (2011) refers to it as a 'promising concept' and reflects on suggestions of what needs to be done if that promise is to be realized. This chapter argues that Bennett's critique of assessment for learning should pay closer attention to the relationship between assessment for learning and children as learners. The chapter suggests that there is a need to understand more deeply the implications of changing relationships between professionals and learners in assessment for learning. It continues by identifying the kinds of roles that learners might expect to play if they were part of a learning experience where the spirit of assessment for learning was in evidence (Marshall and Drummond, 2006). In the context of these expectations, the third section explores evidence from learners of perceptions of their experiences in primary classrooms where teachers were developing assessment for learning. The final section of the chapter reflects on what we might learn from listening to learners and identifies working with learners to explore the world as experienced by them as a research priority for the future development of assessment for learning.

Assessment for learning: a force for good?

The relationship between assessment and learning has been under the spotlight both nationally and internationally. The definition developed at the Third International Conference on Assessment for Learning held in Dunedin, New Zealand, in 2009 was: 'Assessment for Learning is part of everyday practice by students, teachers and peers that seeks, reflects upon and responds to information from dialogue, demonstration and observation in ways that enhance ongoing learning' (Dunedin Conference, 2009).

The allure of improvements in learning linked to ideas of Assessment for Learning has attracted policy makers, practitioners and researchers. Assessment for Learning is now accepted, in some cases rather unreflectively, as a force for good. Describing formative assessment as a 'promising concept', Bennett (2011) argues that formative assessment or assessment for learning is 'work-in-progress' – an idea that would resonate with the writers of this book. Bennett sets an ambitious agenda for formative assessment, suggesting that, 'A meaningful definition requires a theory of action and one or more concrete instantiations' (Bennett, 2011: 19). He suggests that it will require fundamental rethinking of our educational ideas 'from the ground up' (2011: 20). Bennett's analysis touches on many of the issues raised by Black and Wiliam in Chapter 2 of this book.

It seems that, rather than work-in-progress, work-recently-underway might be a more accurate reflection of how much remains to be done to realize the aspirations of formative assessment. Despite its gentle exterior, its focus on subtle changes to existing classroom practices, assessment for learning is radical. In spirit (Marshall and Drummond, 2006), it is a vehicle in education for socio-cultural transformation where learning becomes much more of a community endeavour. This implies different power relationships within classrooms, schools and wider educational and social communities and changes to the ways in which curriculum, pedagogy and assessment play out in schools and classrooms. For example, the traditionally quiet voices of learners and parents would become louder and more influential. The progress made in Assessment is for Learning in Scotland (Hayward, 2009) described by one Scottish Education Minister as 'a quiet revolution in Scottish Education' (Scottish Education Minister, quoted in the *Times Educational Supplement;* Henderson, 2005) would be only the beginning.

One area of assessment for learning that has attracted a great deal of attention has related to changing teachers' practices (Black and Wiliam, 1998a; Black et al., 2002, 2003, 2010; Hallam et al., 2004; Hayward et al., 2004; Condie et al., 2005). There is logic in that position: teachers have significant influence in the culture and climate of the classroom. However, developing a theory of assessment for learning set in a socio-cultural context implies new learning and assessment roles and relationships not only for teachers but also for others, centrally for learners. In this chapter, we turn attention to the learner. In particular we begin to focus on learners' experiences of life in classrooms where teachers are developing assessment for learning principles and practices and to explore the extent to which their experiences represent a 'concrete instantiation' of a theory in action. What is it like to learn in a classroom or school where assessment for learning is being developed? To what extent are pupils aware of and comfortable with the changes in role expected of them and their teachers? What insights can we gain from learners to help point to a future agenda for assessment for learning?

Assessment for learning: what should it be like?

Reflecting on the comprehensive review of evidence on Assessment for Learning (Black and Wiliam, 1998b), Black et al. (2004) argue that 'the central tenet of assessment for formative purposes is the pupil's individual and the pupils' collective awareness of the processes of learning; highlighting the need for learners to have a clear understanding of what they are learning, how they might learn most effectively and how they might judge progress, their own and others'. Pedder and James suggest in Chapter 3 of this book that assessment for learning transforms teaching and learning in classrooms.

> new understandings and perspectives are developed among teachers and students about themselves and each other and, therefore, about the nature of learning and teaching ... new attitudes to and practices of learning and teaching, shaped by explicit and critically reflective modes of participation and relationships are acquired and developed. (p. 38)

In the world of assessment for learning, pupils, they argue, become autonomous, independent and active, qualities which emerge most overtly through sophisticated models of self- and peer-assessment.

> when students: (i) individually or collaboratively, develop the motivation to reflect on their previous learning and identify objectives for new learning; (ii) when they analyze and evaluate problems they or their peers are experiencing and structure a way forward; and (iii) when, through self-regulation, they act to bring about improvement. (Pedder and James, this volume, p. 38)

Sebba, reflecting on her analysis of assessment for learning experiences in selected OECD countries (Chapter 10) includes a further characteristic of what might be expected of assessment for learning in action: the idea that learners themselves would become agents of change in their own schools. However, reporting in 2005, the OECD study found little evidence of well developed examples of this.

Although most of the research on assessment for learning has focused on teachers and systems, there have been notable exceptions. Leitch et al. (2007), in a project undertaken as part of the Teaching and Learning Research Programme, used Article 12 of the UN Convention on the Rights of the Child to examine students' participation in their own assessment. They concluded that children and young people are more than capable of contributing to significant discussions about learning, teaching and assessment and can become actively engaged provided that they are given real opportunities to participate in classrooms. The children are then motivated to focus on their progress and the outcomes of their learning. They are also willing and able to be involved in decision making. The researchers use the framework developed by Lundy (2007) in the context of children's rights to define 'real opportunity'. Lundy concluded that if children are really to engage in consultation they should be given an opportunity to express their views (Space); the expression of their views should be facilitated (Voice); they should be listened to (Audience); and, as appropriate, their view should be acted upon (Influence).

There is then clear evidence from the literature that learners' conscious participation in assessment for learning is at the heart of the business. Learners ultimately control engagement – it is they who decide consciously or subconsciously the extent to which they will become active within the learning community. Ideas of autonomy, independence, engagement and agency matter in changing assessment for learning from a toolbox of assessment techniques into an approach to learning consistent with socio-cultural theories of learning; building communities of learners, democratizing classrooms, deepening learning and raising standards. It is difficult to imagine how such ideas might be developed without recourse to the views of learners. Whether or not to work independently and autonomously is ultimately a choice for each learner.

In conclusion, the insights from Black et al. (2004), Pedder and James (Chapter 3) and Sebba (Chapter 10) offer a basis for reflection that can be used in this chapter to explore the extent to which learners' understandings of their experiences of assessment for learning are consistent with theories of what matters. Findings from Leitch et al.'s TLRP project (2007) suggest that pupils can engage in sophisticated conversations about learning, teaching and assessment if given appropriate opportunities and Lundy offers a model of important characteristics of what constitutes an appropriate opportunity. In the next section of this chapter we will use these ideas to explore how learners understand and interpret their experiences in classrooms where teachers with pupils were attempting to develop principles and practices of assessment for learning.

Assessment for learning: what is it like?

The conversations reported here were held as part of a larger assessment for learning research project funded by The Scottish Government within the Assessment is for Learning programme (Hayward et al, 2008). The children whose views are reported here were all in classes identified by local authority personnel as actively engaged in Assessment for Learning. The groups of primary school children came from four schools in a medium sized Scottish town (each group involved 8–10 children aged 10–11). As the purpose of the conversations was to understand what participants really thought, it was important to employ an approach that encouraged openness and honesty in an authentic conversation (Holstein and Gubrium, 2004). Conversations were recorded, transcribed and analysed using NVivo to identify emerging themes. The quotations used in the section which follows are illustrative of these themes.

The conversations with learners in primary schools focused on two main areas – their understandings of what mattered in learning and how the approaches to learning in their classroom experiences related to these understandings.

The issues raised by the young people suggested that many of them had a fairly sophisticated understanding of what mattered in learning and were able to reflect critically on their own learning environments. What was most interesting, however, were the differences that emerged as children described how ideas about learning were being interpreted in their different classes.

What matters to learners in what they are learning?

Black et al. (2004) suggest that pupils have to have a clear understanding of what they are learning. Pupils in this study (Hayward et al, 2008) realized the importance of knowing what they were intended to learn. However, they wanted more than being given a set of aims or learning goals. They consistently emphasized the importance of their engagement in decisions about the content of the curriculum. They offered examples of the kinds of experience they valued:

> Say if our teacher chooses our topic, like castles that we did last term, we got to choose what we are going to learn about it and where we were going to do it and where we were going to get information from.

and identified the possible impact on motivation of more teacher-dominated models.

> If we do what we want to do, then we'll learn it better but if it is all the teacher's idea, then maybe we'll say, hmmm.....

They also argued for the importance of their involvement in processes of evaluation. It was important that teachers listened to learners' comments on the curriculum:

> So that next year they can make it better, they can make lessons more interesting

> They can improve on what we think is not very good.

Many of them also had confidence in the contribution they would be able to make to improving the quality of the learning experience:

> If they don't listen they won't know how to improve

> They might learn from us what they don't know.

They were also clear that not all teachers involved learners in the ways they would prefer.

> Maybe Teacher x could pay a bit more attention to what we say.

Within the curriculum, choice was important to them although their experiences of what choice meant differed from classroom to classroom. For some the interpretation of choice was very broad. For example, in one school half of each school day over most of the school year was devoted to projects identified by pupils, giving them the opportunity for active engagement in learning in an area of their own choice:

> We get personal projects from the beginning of the year until about past half way and you think of any subject you want ... it

has to be something you don't know anything about, you need to learn about it ...

For others ideas of choice were linked to particular activities:

I liked it when we were doing our glass paintings because we brought in jars and we got to paint them and outline however we wanted and got to paint them all different colours ...

When pupils described situations where they had little choice the tone of their responses became less positive:

We just got put into a pair and she'd had the pictures in a folder and she'd give you the article and you'd have to put the front page or the sports page or whatever you would be doing and you had to get it to look just as same as the front page.

What matters to learners in how they are learning and how do they judge progress?

Black and Wiliam (Chapter 2) and Pedder and James (Chapter 3) agree that through the spirit of assessment for learning learners become autonomous, independent and active, arguing that sophisticated models of self- and peer-assessment lie at the heart of that process. They define sophistication in self- and peer-assessment as involving students in choosing to reflect on their learning and to link that to new learning objectives, to their analyzing and evaluating problems for themselves or for others in their class and then taking action to improve their own learning.

reflect

Learners, in this study, made frequent references to the role of the teacher in supporting learning. At times, the role of the teacher was seen as identifying what was to be learned:

On the board ... it should tell us exactly what we are learning about ... Angles ... and then underneath what we're learning about them.

The teacher was also seen as the arbiter of success, identifying criteria used by pupils to reflect on their own progress. One pupil suggested that he could:

see why we needed success criteria for our work, I thought I did well in that because I did everything that the teacher wanted us to do.

When there was a discrepancy between success criteria and the learners' performance, learners identified a need for them to take action:

> You look at what you need to improve and think ... what am I going to do about that?

However, some learners described self-assessment in ways that might imply that the term was being used to describe fairly traditional classroom practices.

> We correct it from a correcting jotter or if we were using like a book, they've got the answers at the back.

Progress was judged either in terms of the different work provided by their teacher or by the speed at which groups progressed through the curriculum:

> We've got groups for maths, there's group one which is the fast, confident one and with group one, they're on level 7 and group two is on level 6 and group three is on level 5. ... You can get shifted, if you're really fast in group two you can be shifted to group one and if you're slow, you have to move down to group two to get help to get quicker.

Learners emphasized the importance of teacher explanations in supporting their learning but most commonly effective learning was linked to peer explanations. Children liked to learn from one another and peer-assessment and peer-support were often closely linked in children's responses. Peer-explanations were perceived as good learning both for the child offering the explanation

> I like the explaining as well, it helps you learn...

and for the recipient of the explanation

> I would work with Liam because I sit right beside him and usually if I get stuck I just talk to Liam because usually he's near the same questions as me, we're in the same level and I find it a bit easier because he knows what we're trying to do...

When describing engagement in peer-assessment, learners in some classrooms focused on understanding rather than simply looking for the right answer:

We've got peer check partners so once we've done maths we'll go and see if they're done and if they have done it you'll check it together and if we both get a sum a different way, we work it out together.

In some classes learners spoke about enjoying a sense of collective responsibility for learning. For example, taking a 'jigsaw' approach to tasks, with each pupil being responsible for one element of the task was a powerful means of learning:

We all work together and if we're given a problem, if you do different jobs in it and you all come together to solve it.

or supporting one another's learning

If the other person gets it wrong, it isn't just their fault, we both take responsibility because then you were helping them with it so if they get it wrong you're partly to blame as well.

In other classrooms ideas of peer-assessment were interpreted in different ways. In one classroom peer support seemed to be a last resort, if someone really can't do it' and in another, peer-assessment appeared to be more closely related to building and maintaining relationships than making progress in learning.

If you get a good mark, you feel happy but your shoulder partner sometimes gives you different marks because you're their best friend.

Teacher feedback was also identified as an important way for learners to discern progress. Some children welcomed specific comments to guide improvement.

I feel happy ... because it's giving me feedback, even if you got a bad one, try better next time but we never get that. I still feel better because I know what I have to do next time.

Other learners liked teachers to offer strategies they could use to work with problems in different contexts.

At the end of the first section of this chapter, three questions were raised. In this section we considered the first of those questions: What is it like to learn in a classroom or school where assessment for learning is being developed? In common with findings from other studies, whilst some classes appeared to be experiencing the 'spirit' of assessment for learning, others were living the 'letter' (Marshall and Drummond, 2006; Gardner et al., 2010). Pupils' perceptions of their experiences suggested that their experiences were as varied as the classrooms from which they came. Although all the classes had been identified by local authority staff as ones where there had been strong commitment from and support for teachers to develop assessment for learning, it became clear from the children's descriptions of their classroom lives that different theories of learning were leading to very different interpretations of assessment for learning.

Assessment for learning: learning with learners?

In this final section of the chapter we reflect on what we might deduce from the responses of pupils involved in this study to the other two questions: to what extent are pupils aware of and comfortable with the changes in role expected of them and their teachers? What insights can we gain from learners to help point to a future agenda for assessment for learning?

To what extent are pupils aware of and comfortable with the changes in role expected of them and their teachers?

All the children involved seemed enthusiastic about the opportunity to have conversations about their learning both as part of the study and as reported within their schools and classrooms. In Lundy's terms (2007) when offered the space to express their views in a situation where their voice was facilitated, most of the children engaged comfortably in the process. They had a clear sense of audience, emphasizing the importance of being listened to and a strong sense of the importance of influence for the experience to be authentic. As with the TLRP study (Leitch et al., 2007), this study found learners more than capable of contributing to meaningful discussions about learning, teaching and assessment. More than being comfortable with changed roles, most welcomed them and had clear ideas about how their roles and the roles of their teachers might change to improve their learning environment and to motivate them as learners.

The children emphasized the importance of listening and being listened to. These ideas seemed partly to relate to cognitive aspects of learning, knowing what was to be learned and having opportunities to be involved in contributing to that debate. However, pupils mostly argued for the importance of being listened to as a key factor in motivation, almost as a precondition to meaningful engagement in the learning process. Where learners either had no opportunity to contribute to the construction of the curriculum or where views expressed were apparently ignored, there almost seemed to be a conscious intention to disengage

then maybe we'll say, hmmm...

Learners displayed confidence in their ability to help improve the quality of learning and teaching in their classrooms. They argued that inviting feedback from learners would be a key source of evidence for teachers as they reviewed and developed the curriculum. There appeared to be two dimensions to this offer: the first was personal – feedback that would lead to changes in their own educational experiences; the second related to community – a more general willingness to offer advice that would help improve learning for subsequent groups of learners. Learners appeared comfortable with such discussions but some seemed less confident of similar comfort amongst all of their teachers, suggesting that some could 'pay a bit more attention to what we say'.

Choice was also an important motivating theme. It was not clear from the discussion how the open projects so highly rated by the learners developed in class, whether or not learners had complete control over content and process, but there was real enthusiam amongst the learners who described this opportunity. The tone changed (as did the pronouns) when learners described different kinds of experience where their choices were more limited. 'We get personal projects…you think of any subject you want …' and 'I liked it … We … got to paint them all different colours …' became 'we just got put into a pair' and 'she'd had the pictures in a folder and she'd give you the article'.

The importance of motivation in learning is well recognized (e.g. Pollard et al., 2000) as is the potential impact of assessment on motivation (e.g. Harlen and Deakin Crick, 2003). The evidence from the young people in this study suggested that consultation and choice were key features of changed teacher–pupil relationship and that such changes were necessary conditions of motivation and engagement. A strong sense of community permeated the discourse, as did a willingness to negotiate, to work with teachers and learners for the benefit of the wider educational community.

Learners did not challenge the important role of the teacher in learning. They appeared to welcome having clear learning aims made explicit in their classrooms and success criteria against which they could reflect on their own progress. However, it was clear that learners had different experiences of how these ideas were lived in classroom practices and in the values that were being conveyed, for example, from success criteria being negotiated with them to success criteria that were answers in the back of a textbook. Learners recognized the importance of teacher explanations but most of the discussion of what mattered in supporting their learning focused on community activities, group tasks, peer-support and peer-assessment. In some classrooms the learners described experiences demonstrating many of the characteristics of sohisticated self- and peer-assessment as described by Pedder and James (Chapter 3). They appeared to be exceptionally comfortable with learning as part of a community, challenging and supporting one another's learning.

In conclusion, children seemed positively disposed to the range of new roles being asked of them in assessment for learning. Rather than having difficulty with the new roles they were being asked to play, learners in these conversations appeared to have greater difficulty with the more traditional roles that they had been asked to play.

What insights can we gain from learners to help point to a future agenda for assessment for learning?

Theoretically, this chapter argues that the spirit of assessment for learning is situated most comfortably within socio-cultural theory – a theory that recognizes the importance of the inter-relationship between the learner and the social context within which the learning is situated (Lave and Wenger, 1991; Wenger, 1998). Teachers in another part of this study (Hayward et al., 2008) often described self-assessment as a first step in developing assessment for learning. However, learners suggested that it is by working with one another in peer-assessment activities that they develop an understanding of what matters in a task and that it is these understandings that then enable them to reflect on their own learning in a more meaningful way. Peer-assessment provided opportunities for learners to develop their understandings and to support one another's learning. Children recognized the advantages to themselves and to their community of explaining ideas to one another. Concern for the learning of the community lies at the heart of the socio-cultural spirit of assessment for learning. The future agenda of assessment for learning may need to refocus, to play closer attention to the voices of learners – what is important to them that they learn and how they believe that learning might best take place (Hall et al., 2008). Their voices must move from the periphery of practice to become part of its core. The Economic and Social Research Council's major Teaching and Learning

Research Programme identified 10 evidenced-based principles for teaching and learning (TLRP, 2007), one of which was

> **Effective pedagogy fosters both individual and social processes and outcomes.** Learners should be encouraged and helped to build relationships and communication with others for learning purposes, in order to assist the mutual construction of knowledge and enhance the achievements of individuals and groups. Consulting learners about their learning and giving them a voice is both an expectation and a right.

The evidence from this study offers further evidence of the importance of this principle. It also suggests that we are still some way from carrying into practice the right of learners to have their voices heard.

An essential element of building a socio-cultural theory of assessment for learning will require teachers, researchers and policy makers to develop a far deeper understanding of learners' experiences of assessment for learning. If we accept Watkins' (2003) description of socio-cultural theory as building knowledge within a context of working with others, then 'others' must include learners. The word 'with' implies a change in the relationship between teachers and learners. The roles of learners include both contributing to our understanding of the relationship between assessment and learning and being co-developers in moving assessment for learning forward. This new relationship between teachers and learners would seem to be a crucial part of what James (2008) describes as third generation assessment.

The rumblings of the 'quiet revolution' in assessment for learning are beginning to be heard. The teachers involved with the children in this study worked in a local authority with a very sophisticated model of professional learning in assessment for learning. Yet the experiences of the learners suggested different teachers were engaged in very different practices. The most significant difference between teachers living the spirit of assessment for learning as opposed to following the letter appeared to depend on the extent to which teachers saw learners' engagement as core or peripheral to the essence of what they did. If assessment for learning is to become more than a 'promising concept' (Bennett, 2011), the fundamental thinking that needs to be undertaken from the ground up must involve learners more directly. Engaging all teachers in working within the spirit of assessment for learning remains a significant challenge. It may be that learners' voices, their reflections of their experiences in their own classrooms, might open up a space where teachers and learners together can explore the relationship between evidence of what matters in assessment for learning and what might be done in their classrooms to bring theory and practice into closer alignment. There is little doubt that young people do have the potential to become 'agents for change' (OECD, 2005) in schools and classrooms, a role likely to be crucial if the quiet revolution is ever to roar. How such ideas might be realized would seem to be a fruitful area for future research.

References

Bennett, R.E. (2011) 'Formative assessment: a critical review', *Assessment in Education: Principles, Policy and Practice*, 18(1): 5–25.

Black, P. and Wiliam, D. (1998a) *Inside the Black Box: Raising Standards through Classroom Assessment*. London, UK: King's College London School of Education.

Black, P. and Wiliam, D. (1998b) 'Assessment and classroom learning', *Assessment in Education: Principles, Policy and Practice*, 5(7): 13–68.

Black, P., Harrison, C., Hodgen, J., Marshall, M. and Serret, N. (2010) 'Validity in teachers' summative assessments', *Assessment in Education: Principles, Policy and Practice,* 17(2): 215–32.

Black, P., Harrison, C., Lee, C., Marshall, B. and Wiliam, D. (2002) *Working Inside the Black Box: Assessment for Learning in the Classroom*. London, UK: GL Assessment.

Black, P., Harrison, C., Lee, C., Marshall, B. and Wiliam, D. (2003) *Assessment for Learning: Putting it into Practice*. Buckingham, UK: Open University Press.

Black, P. Harrison, C., Lee, C., Marshall., B. and Wiliam, D. (2004) 'Teachers developing assessment for learning: impact on student achievement', *Assessment in Education: Principles, Policy and Practice*, 11(1) 49–65.

Condie, R., Livingston, K. and Seagraves, L. (2005) *The Assessment is for Learning Programme: An Evaluation*. Edinburgh: Scottish Executive Education Department.

Dunedin Conference (2009) 'Position paper on assessment for learning from the Third International Conference on Assessment for Learning', Available at: http://annedavies.com/PDF/11D_PositionPaperAFL-NZ.pdf (accessed 10 February 2011).

Gardner, J., Harlen, W., Stobart, G. with Montgomery, M. (2010) *Developing Teacher Assessment*. Maidenhead: Open University Press.

Hall, K., Murphy, P. and Soler, J. (2008) *Pedagogy and Practice: Culture and Identities*. Buckingham: Open University Press.

Hallam, S., Kirton, A., Peffers, J., Robertson, P. and Stobart, G. (2004) *Evaluation of Project 1 of the Assessment is for Learning Development Programme: Support for Professional Practice in Formative Assessment. Final report*. London, UK: Institute of Education, University of London.

Harlen, W. and Deakin Crick, R. (2003) 'Testing and motivation for learning', *Assessment in Education: Principles, Policy and Practice*, 10(2): 169–208.

Hayward, L. (2009) 'Trust, collaboration and professional learning: Assessment for Learning in Scotland', *Assessment Matters*, 1(1): 64–85.

Hayward, L., Priestly, M. and Young, M. (2004) 'Ruffling the calm of the ocean floor: merging research, policy and practice in Scotland', *Oxford Review of Education*, 30(3): 397–415.

Hayward, L., Boyd, B. and Dow, W. (2008) *Tell Them From me: Pupils' Perspectives of Assessment is for Learning Project. Report to Scottish Government*. Available at: http://wayback.archive-it.org/1961/20100730134201/http://www.ltscotland.org.uk/

resources/t/genericresource_tcm4579651.asp?strReferringChannel=assess (accessed 10 February 2011).

Henderson, D. (2005) 'New tests still to prove their worth', *Times Educational Supplement*, 9 December. Available at: http://www.tes.co.uk/article.aspx?storycode=2170216 (accessed 10 February 2011).

Holstein, J.A. and Gubrium, J.F. (2004) 'The active interview', in D. Silverman (ed.), *Qualitative Research, Theory, Method and Practice*. London: Sage Publications. pp. 140–61.

James, M. (2008) 'Assessment and learning', in S. Swaffield (ed.), *Unlocking Assessment Understanding for Reflection and Application*. Abingdon: Routledge (David Fulton). pp. 20–35.

Lave, J. and Wenger, E. (1991) *Situated Learning: Legitimate Peripheral Participation*. Cambridge: Cambridge University Press.

Leitch, R., Gardner, J., Mitchell, S., Lundy, L., Odena, O., Galanouli, D. and Clough, P. (2007) 'Consulting pupils in "Assessment for Learning" classrooms: the twists and turns of working with students as co-researchers', *Educational Action Research*, 15(3): 459–78.

Lundy, L. (2007) '"Voice is not enough": the implications of Article 12 of the UNCRC for Education', *British Educational Research Journal*, 33(6): 927–42.

Marshall, B. and Drummond, M.J. (2006) 'How teachers engage with Assessment for Learning: lessons from the classroom', *Research Papers in Education*, 21(2): 133–49.

Organisation for Economic Co-operation and Development (2005) 'Formative assessment: improving learning in secondary classrooms', *Policy Brief*, November. Available at: http://www.oecd.org/dataoecd/19/31/35661078.pdf (accessed 10 February 2011).

Pollard, A., Triggs, P., Broadfoot, P., McIness, E. and Osborn, M. (2000) *What Pupils Say: Changing Policy and Practice in Primary Education*. London: Continuum.

Teaching & Learning Research Programme (TLRP) (2007) *TLRP's Evidence-informed Pedagogic Principles*. Available at: http://www.tlrp.org/themes/documents/tenprinciples.pdf

Watkins, C. (2003) *Learning: A Sense-maker's Guide*. London. Association of Teachers and Lecturers.

Wenger, E. (1998) *Communities of Practice*. Cambridge: Cambridge University Press.

Chapter 9

Instrumentalism and Achievement: A Socio-Cultural Understanding of Tensions in Vocational Education

Kathryn Ecclestone

Introduction

> The students ... said to me, 'we want it crystal clear. Pass criteria [sic], number P5, you need to do this, this and this. You've missed this, you haven't done that. Crystal clear, short comment, each criteria, not a holistic comment. Because, they said, 'the holistic comment can be misinterpreted and what I'm thinking might not be what the criteria's asking me to do'. So they want it crystal clear. (David, advanced vocational education lecturer, 2008, quoted in Ecclestone, 2010 p. v)

> Doing their presentations, the students ask 'Is it part of the assessment criteria?' I say, 'Well no, but it is good for you because it's good that you can actually stand up there and it's good for your team work because you actually plan and develop and the more you do it the better you'll get'. 'Oh no, but it's not part of the criteria, so *why* do we have to do it? Does that mean we can be rubbish at it?' (Neil, advanced vocational education lecturer, 2008, quoted in Ecclestone, 2010 p. v, his emphasis)

Over the past 20 years, three trends in assessment throughout the British education system have led to the Holy Grail of 'crystal clarity' (Winter and Maisch, 1996). This phenomenon has become especially strong in vocational education, with far-reaching effects on curriculum content, teaching and assessment methods and teachers' and students' attitudes to learning. The first trend is a shift from using homogenous methods to test and confirm students' knowledge, skills and understanding, to using outcome-based methods that encourage students to accumulate 'evidence of achievement' for an expanding array of educational and social goals. The second is to use assessment diagnostically and formatively, to identify students' starting points, goals, targets, interests and difficulties in learning, and then to provide detailed feedback that helps them recognize their strengths and weaknesses, take an active role in their learning, and motivate and engage them in assessment processes. The third trend is to regard assessment processes as instruments in their own right, as a focus for attention and effort throughout a course.

Combined with target-driven funding regimes in further education (FE) colleges[1], the Holy Grail of transparent assessment has had profound effects on the purposes, practices and outcomes of assessment, and the 'learning cultures' in which these take place. Many of these effects were unanticipated by those promoting the ideal of transparent assessment. Research studies of assessment in vocational education show an almost total merger between summative assignment specifications and criteria, teaching methods, and diagnostic and formative assessment activities. The blurred pedagogy that results is characterized by oral and written feedback that coaches students to improve each grade criterion, and a large proportion of class teaching time devoted to summative assignments (Ecclestone, 2002, 2010). In a study of the impact of different assessment systems on achievements and attitudes to learning in post-compulsory education, carried out in 2003–4, the authors noted that traditional distinctions between summative assessment as 'assessment *of* learning' and formative assessment as 'assessment *for* learning' were pretty much irrelevant: instead, merging summative and formative assessment activities with teaching had led to 'assessment *as* learning' (Torrance et al., 2005).

One outcome of this growing tendency is that participation in, and a positive attitude towards, formative and summative assessment processes have become ends in themselves, 'skills' that teachers and students regard as important for employment. In pre-vocational programmes such as Entry to Employment (e2e), participation is a 'lifeskill' comprising appropriate dispositions and attitudes that can be changed and managed through close personal monitoring and emotional support (see Ecclestone, 2010: Chapter 10).

Yet, while such trends and their outcomes undoubtedly increase participation, retention and achievement, they do so through overwhelmingly instrumental aims and accompanying methods. By 'instrumental', I mean that the instruments and methods become ends in themselves and develop a life of their own. The chapter argues that instrumentalism now dominates many of the 'learning cultures' of vocational education, raising questions about the educational value of assessment for the most unstable, problematic and rarely debated track in the British education system (see Ecclestone, 2002, 2010).

In presenting this argument, the chapter adopts a socio-cultural approach to explore the impact of three features: an expanding array of purposes for vocational education; changing ideas about pedagogy and assessment; and changing images of vocational education students. It draws on the research cited above and an extensive, three-year study of formative assessment in 12 vocational education courses and 18 Skills for Life programmes for adults in literacy, language and numeracy, involving 49 teachers and 58 students and presented more fully in six case studies: Applied Business and Health and Social Care courses for 14–16 year olds, courses in Advanced Vocational Science, Public Services and Entry to Employment for 16–19 year olds, and programmes in literacy, numeracy and English for Speakers of Other Languages for adults (Ecclestone, 2010).

A socio-cultural understanding of assessment

The relationship between historical and political contexts, and participants' identities, dispositions and activities in a particular setting is as much part of pedagogy as specific techniques and strategies. This relationship cannot be isolated from value judgements about the effects of those techniques and strategies. As Hall and Murphy argue:

> Understood from a socio-cultural perspective, pedagogy is also and crucially concerned with what is salient to people as they engage in activity and develop competence in the practice in question. It takes account of two phenomena and their dynamic relationship: a) the social order as reflected in, for example, policy and its associated cultural beliefs and assumptions and b) the experienced world, as reflected in both the enactment and the experience of the policy, including the beliefs underlying the approaches used in its enactment and the beliefs mediating how it is experienced. (Hall et al., 2008: viv)

In a large-scale study of pedagogy in different countries, Robin Alexander argues that teachers' theories, ideas and value judgements about their role in curriculum development and the design of pedagogy and assessment, cannot be divorced from broader questions about the degree of government control over curriculum content, educational purposes, teaching and assessment methods, the quality of teacher education, and social judgements about the purpose and content of education and about what comprises personally and socially useful knowledge (Alexander, 2001; see also Young, 2007).

A socio-cultural approach does not merely explore what knowledge, skills and practices students gain or do not gain, but also what they learn through the assessment practices they experience, how they shape and influence those practices, and what they and other participants consider to be important practices and outcomes. The concept of 'learning culture' is useful as:

> a particular way to understand a learning site as a practice constituted by the actions, dispositions and interpretations of the participants. This is not a one-way process. Cultures are (re)produced by individuals, just as much as individuals are (re)produced by cultures, though individuals are differently positioned with regard to shaping and changing a culture – in other words, differences in power are always at issue too. Cultures, then, are both structured and structuring, and individuals' actions are neither totally determined by the confines of a learning culture, nor are they totally free. (James and Biesta, 2007: 18)

Interactions and practices within and through a course or programme are part of a dynamic, iterative process in which participants and environments shape learning and assessment cultures, and, in turn, those cultures shape the values, beliefs and actions of their participants, including parents, college managers at various levels, policy makers and national awarding bodies, teachers and students. Influential dimensions include:

- the social positions of class, race and gender, age, the 'learning careers' and dispositions and actions of the students and tutors;
- the location and resources of the learning site which are not neutral, but enable some approaches and attitudes, and constrain or prevent others;
- the time tutors and students spend together, their interrelationships, and the range of other learning sites students are engaged with;

- the effects of institutional management, funding and inspection body procedures and regulations, and government policy;
- wider vocational and academic cultures, of which any learning site is part;
- wider social and cultural values and practices around social class, gender and ethnicity, the nature of employment opportunities, social and family life;
- wider social and cultural values and practices in relation to the perceived status of further and adult education, and vocational education, within the education system.

These dimensions interact with 'reified' elements, such as management and government policy texts, syllabuses, learning materials, assessment specifications from awarding bodies, the physical environment, resources and organizational structures. In vocational education, these 'reified elements' are particularly detailed and prescriptive, enforced through strong awarding body procedures that regulate teachers' assessment judgements, and by inspectors. They impose constraints and procedures so that participation in implementing or complying with them also reproduces and enacts certain social and power relations.

A cultural understanding of assessment illuminates the extent to which students and teachers act upon the learning and assessment opportunities and systems they encounter and participate in. The ways in which they do this, and what they choose to highlight, ignore or pay lip service to, are influenced by implicit and explicit values and beliefs about the purposes of a course or qualification, together with certain expectations of students' abilities and motivation, and associated expectations about what they will and will not put up with.

Teachers and students are therefore active agents in shaping expectations and assessment practices around the formal demands of a qualification, thereby influencing what is possible and not possible. Since many expectations exist at the level of dispositions and manifest themselves as cultural ways of doing and being that are considered 'normal' and therefore unproblematic, learning cultures are governed by normative expectations about what comprises 'good' learning, teaching and assessment. Not only are these values and expectations usually implicit but they are also, variously, contradictory, realistic or inaccurate, and vary across and between learning cultures ostensibly with the same purposes and practices (see for a detailed discussion, Colley, 2006; Ecclestone, 2010; James and Biesta, 2007; JVET, 2004).

Influential features of learning cultures in vocational education

Competing goals

With its roots in numerous early initiatives, the vocational education pathway is highly unstable in the UK's education system. It has evolved to enable young people deemed to be unsuitable or unwilling to do general education based on traditional subject disciplines to explore broadly defined areas such as Leisure and Tourism, Health and Social Care, Performing Arts, Hospitality and Catering, and Business Studies. At the ages of 16 and 18, a vocational education qualification offers progression to more focused vocational education and training in further education (FE) colleges and universities as preparation for occupational roles. In recent years, it has widened to encompass 14–16-year-olds in schools, where it is widely seen as a low status alternative to academic qualifications (see Bathmaker et al., 2011: Ecclestone et al., 2011).

Despite repeated attempts to create 'parity of esteem' between vocational and general 'academic' education, choices remain stubbornly segregated (for a detailed discussion see Hodgson and Spours, 2003, 2008). Confusion created by 30 years of changes to the content, teaching and assessment of vocational routes has not created stable qualifications or programmes that are well understood by teachers, students, parents, admissions tutors in universities and employers (see Stanton 1998; Tomlinson Working Group, 2005).

The situation is different in other Western European countries which have a coherent, long-standing vocational education and training pathway that prepares young people for occupational roles at different levels in workplace apprenticeships and/or higher level qualifications in polytechnics. While parity of esteem is an unresolved problem in many if not all countries, good levels of resourcing, including highly qualified teachers, together with stability and continuity in policy, have enabled countries like Finland to have clearly differentiated, well-respected pathways for vocational education and training courses run in partnerships between vocational colleges and local workplaces.

In contrast, British attempts to create a unified system have been dogged by the need to create educationally based methods and activities that young people will find engaging and useful, that will enable them to progress to workplace learning or further and higher education, and to show credible 'standards' of achievement in comparison to academic courses. At the same time, changing employment patterns, the decline of unskilled jobs (or home populations unwilling to do them), growing numbers of young people disaffected from compulsory schooling, and political instability around assessment systems have created an array of competing goals:

- motivating learners who would otherwise not stay on in post-compulsory education or who are disaffected at school, by responding to, and rewarding, their expressed interests and notions of relevance;
- expanding routes into higher education whilst also making sure that expansion does not lead to over-subscription for limited places;
- preparing students for progression into work and job-related training;
- encouraging young people to continue gaining qualifications and acquiring attitudes and dispositions associated with 'lifelong learning';
- convincing young people, parents, teachers, admissions tutors and employers that vocational education has parity of esteem with academic qualifications;
- ameliorating poor levels of achievement in numeracy and literacy through 'key/basic/functional skills';
- satisfying demands from different stakeholders, such as employers, subject and professional associations, etc., to include 'essential' content and skills;
- creating a credible qualification in compulsory schooling where there are lower levels of vocational expertise amongst teachers.

Outcome-based pedagogy and assessment

The slow accretion of these goals is inextricably linked with changing ideas about appropriate assessment methods for certain 'types' of young people deemed to be suited to vocational education. Amidst the many reports and initiatives that have come and gone over the past 30 years, *A Basis for Choice* (ABC), published by the then Further Education Unit in 1979, has had a powerful impact on teaching, curriculum content and assessment methods in FE colleges generally, but especially in vocational education (for discussion of the influence of ABC see, Avis, 2009; Ecclestone and Hayes, 2008; James and Biesta, 2007). Regarded by many teachers, researchers and qualification designers at the time as radical and progressive, ABC challenged 'traditional' teaching and assessment as old-fashioned, elitist, excluding and irrelevant for the vast numbers of young people displaced by mass unemployment into colleges and government-run employment schemes from the late 1970s onwards.

ABC advocated 'student-centred learning', 'ownership of learning', 'experiential' and 'practical' learning, democratic and informal relationships between teachers and students, more 'personalized' ways of working based on collaborative, negotiated projects that generate diverse evidence of outcomes. Now commonplace in FE and vocational education, these ideas have opened up formal, summative assessment to encompass personal, social and work-related dispositions, attitudes and behaviours and characterizes them as 'skills'. In parallel, the erosion of 'general and liberal studies', with topics such as law, politics, sports, film and arts studies, first in favour of 'communication studies' and then 'transferable skills', together with programmes in 'life and social skills' for the unemployed, introduced in 1978, contributed to a widening of 'skill' to encompass young people's perceptions of themselves, as well as their attitudes to learning, work and social, work and personal relationships.

Key to these changes in both the focus and methods of assessment was the introduction of competence-based qualifications in the workplace in 1989, followed by outcome-based assessment (OBA) in vocational education in 1991. This challenged the elitism, selectivity and lack of transparency of norm-referenced assessment and didactic teaching, contrasting these with valid, authentic measures of performance, 'coverage' or 'mastery' of performance specified in the criteria, together with 'ownership' of them through formative assessment, feedback, and setting and reviewing targets. A particular target for attack was the 'elitist', 'irrelevant' and time-consuming place of theory and knowledge (see Jessup, 1991; NcNair, 1995 for discussion and Hyland, 1994; Wolf, 1995; Winter and Maisch, 1996 for critique). With its promise of transparency, outcome-based assessment was seen as inherently democratic, inclusive and motivating. Crucially, it removed the idea that failure is an inevitable adjunct to success and selection; thereby presenting assessment as accessible and relevant, both to the individual's own sense of self and to real-world activities.

Students' learning and assessment 'careers'

In addition to a growing array of goals and skills in vocational education, the promises of OBA and the rise of instrumental forms of 'assessment-as-learning' cannot be understood without some reference to the powerful socializing influences of teaching and especially of assessment (see e.g. Broadfoot and Pollard, 2000; Ecclestone and Pryor, 2003; Filer, 2000; Pollard and Filer, 1999; Reay and Wiliam, 1999; Torrance and Pryor 1998). Research studies in primary and secondary schools and FE colleges show that, by the time they get to Level 3 study at the age of 16, young people have strong expectations about assessment, support, feedback and 'acceptable' teaching methods. These expectations, in turn, are powerful shapers of their teachers' ideas about students' motivation, behaviours, abilities and dispositions.

From a socio-cultural perspective, dispositions are shaped in both the past and present, and are both stable and open to change. They include expectations, values and beliefs about education, learning and assessment practices, and actions, emerging through social structures operating within and through individuals, rather than something outside. According to James and Biesta, dispositions are a product of accumulated lived experience, at home, school and work, in leisure and in local communities, and developed further through teaching and assessment experiences as well as other parts of a student's life that run in parallel with, and sometimes overlap, activities in college. Sometimes existing dispositions are reinforced, modified or changed, or new ones are formed (James and Biesta, 2007).

A significant factor affecting students' and teachers' attitudes to assessment is the nature of 'choice' for a particular track. In vocational education, whether at key transition points of 14 and 16 years of age, students tend to choose progression routes that both reflect and reinforce an image of themselves as a 'type' of learner suited to particular 'types' of assessment. Numerous studies show that young people make educational choices in socio-economic contexts of poor job opportunities and correspondingly uncertain ideas about further or higher education. It is therefore far from evident that students aim to realize vocational aspirations: instead, they frequently have uncertain, erratic goals and little insight about how their vocational qualification will help them 'progress' to the next stage (see Atkins, 2009; Bathmaker, 2002; Davies, 2007; Davies and Biesta, 2006; Ecclestone, 2002).

Other studies confirm that choices are strongly differentiated between social groups because dispositions and attitudes, and the often-stereotyped expectations they both produce and emerge from, create particular ideas about suitable opportunities and institutions. These cannot be isolated from employment prospects, the effects of educational differentiation in a local area, students' social class, gender and cultural background and their image of institutions and courses as appropriate for 'people like them'. Student decision-making and institutional marketing are both predicated on images of what counts as an appropriate learning identity and culture, as well as on narrow and predictable progression routes from vocational qualifications[2].

Comfort zones and second chances

A notable factor in instrumentalism is that fixed expectations about what students like and want from 'learning' have created 'comfort zones' that protect students by minimizing assessment stress (Atkins, 2009;

Bathmaker, 2002; Ecclestone, 2002, 2010; Torrance et al., 2005). Lack of pressure, and a lively, relaxed and informal atmosphere enable students to work in friendship groups, with minimum teacher input, with lesson time used to work on assignments individually or in small groups and extensive individual and group feedback on draft assignments. Many young people want to continue the teaching and assessment activities they have become familiar with. Such expectations are reinforced by the way in which many vocational teachers see themselves as having been 'second chance' students, leading them to regard colleges as a space that offers a secure, tightly knit group for overcoming feelings of failure from school and creating a new identity as a successful learner. These features have come to characterize 'progressive' teaching and assessment.

In some courses, tutors embellish ideas about progressive teaching with strong images of 'vulnerable', 'at risk' students who do not need or want too much pressure and, in parallel, although students believed they worked hard, high levels of collaborative, relaxed work interspersed with socializing led to very little serious work (Atkins, 2009; see also Bathmaker, 2002).

These images, together with certain notions of motivation, engagement, independent learning and student autonomy are therefore integral to progressive teaching and assessment that meets tightly defined targets for retention and achievement. Together with teachers' emphasis on students' personal development rather than vocational knowledge, and students' desire to work in a conducive atmosphere without too much pressure, targets encourage external forms of motivation and much-valued procedural autonomy. Students use the assessment specifications to aim for acceptable levels of achievement, with freedom for what Inge Bates describes as 'hunting and gathering' information to meet the criteria, to escape from 'boring' classrooms and to work without supervision in friendship groups (Bates, 1998a, 1998b).

For many students on vocational education courses, these features of assessment and teaching are crucial to an emerging identity as confident, successful students. Procedural autonomy comes from command of the minutiae of the assessment specifications, in a comfort zone of achievable grades, enabling them to ask questions, first about official requirements and, from there, to develop more subtle insights rooted in a struggle to understand the subject rather than just its procedures or requirements (Ecclestone, 2002; Torrance et al., 2005).

Instrumental use of assessment criteria does appear to enable a minority of students to develop deep forms of motivation and fleeting signs of critical autonomy. Here, prescriptive procedures are a springboard for educationally worthwhile outcomes. In contrast, however, the majority aim for comfortable, safe goals below their potential capacity, based on high levels of instrumental compliance and coaching by tutors to 'fill the gaps' in the criteria. One effect is to pressurize teachers to 'cover' only relevant knowledge to pass the assignment, or to make difficult subjects 'easy' (see Ecclestone, 2002, 2010, chapter 5).

Second chance 'learners', vocational students or vulnerable and 'at risk' young people?

Over the past 30 years, changes to the aims and methods of assessment systems both reflect, and are fuelled by, certain images of 'typical' dispositions, 'needs' and 'barriers to learning'. A view that vocational education is a 'second chance' reflects, in part, a long-standing and very positive ethos in FE. Yet, whilst maintaining this ethos, ABC offered images of young people displaced by mass unemployment in the 1970s as 'reluctant' and 'non-traditional' students. This was a powerful contrast to FE's core population, namely young people following day-release craft qualifications from work, repeating failed examinations at the end of secondary schooling or studying academic Advanced levels in a different environment to school.

Being a 'pre-vocational' student depicted uncertainty about what occupation to follow and a need for functional (literacy, numeracy and ICT) skills as well as personal and social skills. Psychologically or emotionally based images took root, through assertions that these students lacked confidence and self-esteem, were 'failed by the school system', were demotivated and disengaged and therefore unable and unwilling to 'cope with' particular forms of teaching and assessment. Stereotyped expectations of motivation and engagement, and accompanying images of 'vulnerability', being 'at risk' and having 'complex' social, psychological and emotional 'needs', have become very influential (see Atkins, 2009; Ecclestone, 2010, chapter 10; Ecclestone and Hayes, 2008, chapter 4; Turner, 2007; Wiliams, 2009). Political intervention in the transition from school into training, work, education or unemployment has reinforced these images, where school leavers with poor or no qualifications are seen now as acutely 'at risk', with 'complex needs' that make them vulnerable to crime, drug abuse, marital problems, early pregnancy, unemployment and ill health[3].

The growing prevalence of such images adds another dimension to the goals and outcomes of assessment, inside and outside vocational education. In particular, they have elided 'support' and formal 'diagnostic assessment', especially for those leaving school or the care system who are deemed to be at particular risk of unemployment or other problems, and for those expelled from school. Here, assessment combines the welfare case management of social work, counselling and psychological assessments with the sorts of informal support and recreational activities associated with youth work (see Colley 2003; Turner, 2007).

One effect has been a huge growth in one-to-one 'mentoring' and 'support' which demand high levels of emotional and psychological support, and detailed monitoring of activities and targets. This has become commonplace in vocational education (Ecclestone, 2010). The underlying images of young people are significant because those seen as disaffected, alienated and difficult often experience what Helen Colley calls 'engagement mentoring' (see Colley 2003 for detailed discussion). This combines the searching out of individuals' interests and perception of needs with targets that seek to 're-engage' them with institutionalized norms, structures and pathways. The European Commission depicts this as moving them from being alienated and distant from social and economic reality towards social integration and productive activity (Colley, 2003: 92). From this policy perspective, 'alienation', 'distance' and 'exclusion' become additional attributes and dispositions that require psychological or emotional intervention and assessment (see Ecclestone, 2010; Williams, 2009).

New forms of diagnostic and self-assessment, and mentoring, intensify approaches long used in vocational education courses, presenting attitudes, feelings, behaviours and dispositions, together with those of significant others, as 'resources' that young people can draw on for help. They also institutionalize the idea that 'self-efficacy', motivation and engagement are 'resources' which are integral to 'personal capital', and therefore a key focus for assessment (see Ecclestone, 2010, chaps 5 and 10).

The rise of instrumental assessment goals and practices

The ideas about teaching, and beliefs about young people reflected in *A Basis for Choice* and now embedded in outcome-based assessment systems, offer particular images and related assumptions about what those characterized as 'non-traditional' learners will and will not benefit from, the assessment and teaching methods that they should or should not have to experience, and about what they are capable or incapable of achieving. One outcome, introduced by ABC, has been repeated attempts to define personal, functional and social skills and to assess them, first through records of achievement, introduced in 1985, then portfolios of evidence and summative assignments or projects.

Acquisition of a body of vocational knowledge and skills for occupational roles has given way to generic personal 'skills', such as self-awareness, team working and reflecting on one's learning, alongside literacy, numeracy, social and employability skills. A vocational or occupational focus is increasingly an instrument for such skills rather than an end in its own right (see Bathmaker et al., 2011; Ecclestone, 2010; Ecclestone et al., 2011; Young, 2007). Vocational education programmes are therefore characterized by extremely weak subject cultures, and while some are weaker than others, uncertainty about purpose and content is now commonplace amongst teachers, and other stakeholders (see Pring et al., 2009a and 2009b).

Outcome-based assessment systems reinforce the vacuum in subject-content, filling this with 'skills'. Images of young people with particular personal, social and educational 'needs' and 'barriers to learning', together with teachers' low expectations of students' motivation and attitudes to learning, are prevalent. This has led to intensive one-to-one support as new pedagogy in the drive towards transparent criteria. One outcome is high levels of instrumentalism which have changed teaching and assessment methods, eroded subject content, made the relationship between students and teachers increasingly conditional, and changed teachers' educational values and beliefs. In the project that forms the basis for much of the discussion in this chapter, some teachers appeared to have surrendered previous confidence about the purpose of their professional role, to become more compliant, and to have lower expectations of students than they once had. A minority of teachers was highly instrumental and, whilst aware of tensions, largely accepted the target-driven ethos that dominated their practice.

Yet, a socio-cultural approach shows that although images of vulnerability or of 'fragile learning identities' are undoubtedly powerful at the level of policy texts, their influence on expectations, beliefs and assessment practices is far from consistent between the learning cultures of different vocational education courses. This makes it important to evaluate why certain images take hold in some contexts and not others, and why instrumentalism can occasionally be a springboard to deeper, more meaningful learning or resisted in robust and empowered ways. In a minority of learning and assessment cultures, teachers' strong confidence and enthusiasm for their subject, clear beliefs about educational purposes, and positive rather than diminished images of students and their potential, counteracted trends discussed in this chapter (see Ecclestone, 2010, chap. 4).

Conclusions

> There's no point in jumping through hoops for the sake of jumping through hoops and there's no point in getting grades for the sake of getting grades. I know that's not the answer, the answer is ... 'we should be getting them to get grades'. But that's never as I've seen it and it never will be (Derek Armstrong, teacher of Advanced Vocational Science, Moorview Community College, 2008, quoted in Ecclestone, 2010: 154)

Contrasting the themes of instrumentalism and compliance with deeper educational goals illuminates the ways in which political, institutional, social and educational factors can produce very different effects in the same assessment system and methods in different learning cultures. Understanding how these cultures 'work' enables teachers and researchers to evaluate whether assessment leads to educationally worthwhile or narrow and instrumental outcomes.

A socio-cultural understanding also illuminates how the progressive rhetoric of 'empowering' formative assessment can become distorted to little more than coaching to the summative targets in some contexts, whilst in others, the same assessment is embedded in everyday teaching activities with positive educational effects and outcomes. Understanding these differences might go some way to challenge the worst excesses of instrumentalism and enable teachers to identify which factors they can and cannot influence (see Swann and Ecclestone, 1999; Swann et al., in press).

Notwithstanding this optimistic possibility arising from our study, there is a very widespread view that instrumental assessment is realistic given the types of students, teaching resources and targets in vocational education. This view parallels, and is rooted in, an underlying unwillingness to make educational value judgements. Yet, unless teachers treat instrumentalism as a springboard to something educationally worthwhile and genuinely engaging, rather than an end in itself, the goal of acquiring subject knowledge and related practical skills can no longer be taken for granted in vocational education.

This normative view does not overlook the huge pressures that shape assessment practice, some of which teachers and students can influence and some of which they cannot. Many teachers face daunting pressures, including some challenging students, an increase in casual contracts for FE staff, target-led funding, the use of vocational courses in schools for students seen to be low ability or disaffected, cuts in course hours and overloaded, prescriptive assessment systems.

In learning cultures dominated by these pressures, it is not surprising that assessment systems in vocational education have created high levels of instrumentalism. The problem is compounded by an erosion of professional autonomy and confidence to influence curriculum content and to design teaching and assessment activities, rather than using prescriptive and homogenized assessment requirements. This raises the question of how teachers can influence the learning cultures they work in, and help to shape. It also highlights a pressing need to explore educational questions about what sort of person a learning and assessment culture is creating, what it should create, and the forms of knowledge, skills and dispositions that assessment fosters, overlooks or discourages.

Notes

1   Further education colleges in the British education system are similar to vocational or technical colleges in other European countries. FE colleges offer general academic, general vocational, work-related and work-based training, and basic skills for students aged 14 and above, including adults.
2   See Ball et al., (2000), Hodkinson et al. (1996) for discussion of choices on leaving school, Ball et al., (2005) for choices about higher education, and Hoelscher et al. (2008) for progression data from vocational education into university courses.
3   The Social Exclusion Unit, founded in 1997, produced a series of influential reports about the causes and effects of social deprivation and how government agencies should respond (SEU, 1999). For discussion of its claims and assumptions about young people, see Colley and Hodkinson (2001).

References

Alexander, R. (2001) *Culture and Pedagogy: International Comparisons in Primary Education*. Oxford and Boston: Blackwell.

Atkins, E. (2009) *Invisible Students, Impossible Dreams: Experiencing Vocational Education 14–19*. Stoke-on-Trent: Trentham Books.

Avis, J. (2009) *Education, Policy and Social Justice: Learning and Skills (2nd edn)*, Continuum Studies in Lifelong Learning. London: Continuum.

Ball, S.J., David, M. and Reay, D. (2005) *Degrees of Difference*. London: RoutledgeFalmer.

Ball, S.J., Maguire, M. and Macrae, S. (2000) *Choices, Pathways and Transitions Post-16: New Youth, New Economies in the Global City*. London: RoutledgeFalmer.

Bathmaker, A-M. (2002) 'Wanting to be somebody: Post-16 students' and teachers' constructions of full-time GNVQs in a college of further education', PhD, University of Warwick.

Bathmaker, A-M., Ecclestone, K. and Cooke, S. (2011) 'What counts as "proper" knowledge? The role of stakeholders in designing vocational education qualifications', paper presented to *European Association of Educational Research* Conference, University of Berlin, 14 September 2011.

Bates, I. (1998a) 'The empowerment dimension in GNVQs: a critical exploration of discourse, pedagogic apparatus and school implementation', *Evaluation and Research in Education*, 12(1): 7–22.

Bates, I. (1998b) 'Resisting "empowerment" and realising power: an exploration of aspects of the GNVQ', *Journal of Education and Work*, 11(2): 187–205.

Broadfoot, P. and Pollard, A. (2000) 'The changing discourse of assessment policy: the case of English primary education', in Filer, A. (2000) *Assessment: Social Process, Social Product*. London, Falmer Press.

Colley, H. (2003) *Mentoring for Social Inclusion: A Critical Approach to Nurturing Mentoring Relationships*. London: Routledge.

Colley, H. (2006) 'Learning how to labour with feeling: class, gender and emotion in childcare, education and training', *Contemporary Issues in Early Childhood*, 7: 15–29.

Colley, H. and Hodkinson, P. (2001) 'The problem with "Bridging the Gap": the reversal of structure and agency in addressing social exclusion', *Critical Social Policy*, 21(3): 335–59.

Davies, J. (2007) 'Tentative futures: exploring the formation and transformation of young people's vocational aspirations', PhD thesis, University of Exeter.

Davies, J. and Biesta, G. (2006) 'Going to college: aspirations and experiences of vocational education students', *Research Papers in Education*, 22(1): 33–41.

Ecclestone, K. (2002) *Learning Autonomy in Post-compulsory Education: the Politics and Practice of Formative Assessment*. London: RoutledgeFalmer.

Ecclestone, K. (2010) *Transforming Formative Assessment in Lifelong Learning*. Buckingham: Open University Press.

Ecclestone, K. and Hayes, D. (2008) *The Dangerous Rise of Therapeutic Education*. London: Routledge.

Ecclestone, K. and Pryor, J. (2003) '"Learning careers" or "assessment careers"? The impact of assessment systems on learning', *British Educational Research Journal*, 29: 471–88.

Ecclestone, K., Bathmaker A-M. and Cooke, S. (2011) 'Teachers' constructions of knowledge in vocational education: implications for pedagogy and assessment', paper presented to *European Association of Educational Research* Conference, University of Berlin, 15 September 2011.

Filer, A. (2000) *Assessment: Social Process and Social Product*. London: Routledge/ Falmer.

Further Education Unit (1979) *A Basis for Choice*. London: FEU.

Hall, K., Murphy, P. and Soler, J. (2008) *Pedagogy and Practice: Culture and Identities*. Buckingham: Open University Press.

Hodgson, A. and Spours, K. (2003) *Beyond A-levels: Curriculum 2000 and the Reform of 14–19 Qualifications*. London: Kogan Page.

Hodgson, A. and Spours, K. (2008) *Education and Training 14–19: Curriculum, Qualifications and Organization*. London: Sage.

Hodkinson, P., Sparkes, A.C. and Hodkinson, H. (1996) *Triumphs and Tears: Young People, Markets and the Transition from School to Work*. London: David Fulton.

Hoelscher, M., Hayward, G., Ertl, H. and Dunbar-Godet, H. (2008) 'The transition from vocational education and training to higher education: a successful pathway?', *Research Papers in Education*, 23(2): 139–51.

Hyland, T. (1994) *Competence, Education and NVQs*. London: Cassell.

James, D. and Biesta, G. (2007) *Improving Learning Cultures in Further Education*. London: Routledge.

Jessup, G. (1991) *Outcomes: NVQs and the Emerging Model of Education and Training*. London: Falmer.

Journal of Vocational Education and Training (JVET) (2004) Special Edition: Transforming Learning Cultures in Further Education, 55(4): 389–518.

McNair, S. (1995) 'Outcomes and autonomy', in J. Burke (ed.) (1995) *Outcomes, Learning and the Curriculum: Implications for NVQs, GNVQs and Other Qualifications*. London: Falmer Press.

Pollard, A. and Filer, A. (1999) *The Social World of Pupil Career: Strategic Biographies through Primary School*. London: Cassell.

Pring, R., Hayward, G., Hodgson, A., Johnson, J., Keep, E., Oancea, A., Rees, G., Spours, K. and Wilde, S. (2009a) *The Nuffield Review of 14–19 Education and Training in England and Wales*. London: Nuffield Foundation.

Pring, R., Hayward, G., Hodgson, A., Johnson, J., Keep, E., Oancea, A., Rees, G., Spours, K. and Wilde, S. (2009b) *Education for All: The Future of Education and Training for 14–19 Year-Olds*. London: Routledge.

Reay, D. and Wiliam, D. (1999) '"I'll be a nothing": structure, agency and the construction of identity through assessment', *British Educational Research Journal*, 25: 343–54.

Social Exclusion Unit (1999) *Bridging the Gap: New Opportunities for 16–18 Year Olds Not in Education, Employment or Training*. London: Cabinet Office.

Stanton, G. (1998) 'Patterns in development', in S. Tomlinson (ed.), *Education 14–19: Critical Perspectives*. London: Athlone Press.

Swann, J and Ecclestone, K. (1999) 'Empowering lecturers to improve assessment practice in higher education', in J. Swann and J. Pratt (eds), *Improving Education: Realist Approaches to Method and Research*. London: Cassell.

Swann, J., Ecclestone, K. and Andrews, I. (in press) 'Rolling out and scaling up: the effects of a problem-based approach to developing teachers' assessment practice', *Educational Action Research*, 19(4).

Tomlinson Working Group (2005) *Reform of the 14–19 Curriculum*. London: Department for Education and Skills.

Torrance, H. and Pryor, J. (1998) *Investigating Formative Assessment: Teaching, Learning and Assessment in the Classroom*. Buckingham: Open University Press.

Torrance, H., Colley, H., Garratt, D., Jarvis, J., Piper, H., Ecclestone, K. and James, D. (2005) *The Impact of Different Modes of Assessment on Achievement and Progress in the Learning and Skills Sector*. London: Learning and Skills Development Agency.

Turner, P. (2007) 'The transition to work and adulthood', in D. Hayes, T. Marshall and A. Turner (eds), *A Lecturer's Guide to Teaching in Further Education*. Buckingham: Open University Press.

Williams, J. (2009) 'Social inclusion, education and New Labour', PhD thesis, Canterbury, Canterbury Christ Church University.

Winter, R. and Maisch, R. (1996) *Professional Competence in Higher Education*. London: Falmer Press.

Wolf, A. (1995) *Competence-based Assessment*. Buckingham: Open University Press.

Young, M. (2007) *Bringing Knowledge Back In: From Social Constructivism to Social Realism in the Sociology of Education*. London: Routledge.

Chapter 10

Policy and Practice in Assessment for Learning: The Experience of Selected OECD Countries

Judy Sebba

Studies of assessment for learning in countries other than the USA or those in the UK potentially provide a rich and stimulating source of evidence for understanding practices in assessment for learning. This chapter, largely unchanged from the first edition, draws on illustrative case studies of practice from selected countries that participated in an Organisation for Economic Co operation and Development OECD study of formative assessment in 2005. Ball (1990) suggested that policies are pre-eminently statements about practice, intended to bring about solutions to problems identified by individual teachers and schools. Classroom practice can thus be seen as a key measure of policy implementation and it is examples of classroom practice from different countries that are presented and analysed in this chapter. A comprehensive analysis of educational policies and changes since the cases studies were examined in 2005 is beyond the scope of this chapter.

In 2005, the Centre for Educational Research and Innovation (CERI) at OECD published research (OECD, 2005)[1] on 'formative assessment' in lower secondary education, drawing on case studies involving eight countries: Canada, Denmark, England, Finland, Italy, New Zealand, Australia and Scotland. I undertook the case study of Queensland, Australia, which was written up with Graham Maxwell, a senior manager working in the locality. This chapter draws heavily on examples from the OECD study including those case studies in

Canada, Denmark, New Zealand and in particular, Queensland. There were no significant differences between these countries and the others not mentioned – it is simply that these case studies provided illustrations of some emerging themes. It is important to acknowledge that the eight countries did not include a country that by any definition could be described as 'developing'. Furthermore, the analysis cannot be claimed to provide a comprehensive or definitive picture of the countries involved.

The OECD study provides a basis for identifying some common themes in assessment for learning policy and practice that can be compared across countries. These involve, at the most basic level, what is included in assessment for learning ('formative assessment' as it is called in the study), the nature and role of feedback, self- and peer-assessment, the relationship between student grouping strategies and assessment for learning, and teacher development. In addition to these classroom level issues, there are contextual factors in schools and beyond which enhance or inhibit the implementation of assessment for learning strategies. These factors, such as the role of leadership, developing schools as learning organizations and students as agents of change, are not specific to developing assessment for learning and might more appropriately be viewed as strategies for school improvement. They do, however, vary within and across different countries, thus influencing the capacity for assessment for learning strategies to be effective. The links between assessment for learning at the classroom level, teacher development and school improvement are further explored in Chapter 3.

Before considering these themes, four underlying tensions are acknowledged which need to be taken into account when drawing interpretations and inferences from comparisons of assessment for learning across countries. These are: focusing on difference at the expense of similarities; the influence of cultural contexts; problems of transferability of strategies across countries; and the methodological limitations of research involving short visits to a small sector of provision in other countries. These issues have been more extensively debated in the literature on comparative education (e.g. Vulliamy et al., 1990), but need to be mentioned here to urge caution in drawing generalized inferences from the examples presented.

Focusing on difference at the expense of similarities

In undertaking any comparative analysis, there is a danger of focusing exclusively on differences and ignoring or under-acknowledging similarities. Throughout this chapter, an attempt is made to draw parallels between the experiences of assessment for learning across different countries and to seek multiple interpretations of both the similarities and differences observed. It is important to attempt to distinguish between differences in terminology, definitions and meaning and real differences in policy and practice. International comparisons are frequently hampered by a lack of agreed consistent terminology, which acts as a barrier to communication, development of understanding and the drawing of conclusions. For example, much greater emphasis was put in some countries on the use of test data to inform teaching as a component of formative assessment, whereas others saw this as distinctively separate from formative assessment as such.

The influence of cultural contexts

A second underlying tension concerns the need to acknowledge the cultural contexts within which assessment for learning strategies are being implemented. Attempting to understand the cultural differences between countries and indeed, between different areas within countries, is a considerable challenge extensively debated in comparative education (for example Vulliamy et al., 1990). Broadfoot et al. (1993), provided strong evidence of the influence of culture on the educational organization and processes in different countries. The interaction between national cultures and educational policies and structures adds further complexity to this. For example, national policies prescribing curricula, assessment and accountability systems provide structural contexts which may reflect, or indeed create, particular cultural contexts. Vulliamy (2004) argues that the increasing knowledge and information associated with globalization are in danger of strengthening those positivist approaches that threaten the centrality of culture in comparative education.

Problems of transferability

Thirdly, and partly related to issues of cultural context, the transferability of strategies and innovations from one country to another is a further underlying tension. The assumption that educational innovations that have an effect in one context will have the same or any effect in another has been challenged by many writers (e.g. Crossley, 1984). The Black and Wiliam research review (1998), which indicated the substantial impact of assessment for learning strategies on students' learning and generated extensive international interest, drew on a large number of studies from different countries, but was ultimately limited to those written in English. The OECD study included appendices of reviews of the literature in English, French and

German. However, more often the findings of a single study under-taken in one country are taken as evidence for the efficacy of that strategy in another country. Furthermore, as Fielding et al. (2005) have demonstrated, the concept of 'best practice' is contested and its transfer from one individual, institution or group to another is much more complicated than national policies tend to acknowledge.

Methodological limitations of research based on short 'expert' visits

A final underlying tension is the methodological limitations of what Vulliamy et al. (1990) referred to as 'jetting in' experts or researchers to other countries for short periods. The OECD study involved 'experts' from one country visiting another country for a short time (1–2 weeks), and in partnership with 'experts' from the host country, collecting data on assessment for learning. While many comparative studies are probably similarly limited, the methodological weak-nesses in research design and implementation of a study undertaken in a short period with limited understanding of the context, raise serious questions. Drawing inferences from a necessarily partial pic-ture in contexts where others have determined what documents are accessed, who is interviewed and observed, and perhaps the views that are conveyed, is problematic. For example, it is clear that obser-vations undertaken in two schools in Queensland cannot be assumed to be representative of that state, let alone typical of Australia as a whole. Generalizations should therefore be minimized and interpre-tations treated as illustrative rather than indicative.

Despite these limitations, the OECD study provided rich descrip-tions of a variety of forms of practice in assessment for learning, in a range of different contexts, which offered interesting insights and suggested that some classroom practices and challenges may share more similarities than differences.

What is included in assessment for learning/formative assessment?

In the OECD study 'formative assessment' is defined as: 'frequent, interactive assessments of student progress and understanding to iden-tify learning needs and adjust teaching appropriately' (2005: 21). This definition differs significantly from that which is provided in the Introduction to this volume (ARG, 2002). The Assessment Reform Group definition puts considerably greater emphasis on the use to be made by learners of the assessment information. The OECD definition instead stresses the adjusting of teaching in light of the assessment.

Similarities in the strategies encompassed in formative assessment across the eight countries included: establishing learning goals and tracking of individual students' progress towards these goals; ensuring student understanding (rather than just skills or knowledge) is adequately assessed; providing feedback that influences subsequent teaching; and the active involvement of students in the learning process. But the emphasis given to each of these and the additional strategies which were included under the formative assessment umbrella varied considerably. For example, in the Danish case study schools, there was greater emphasis on developing self-confidence and verbal competence. In New Zealand, formative assessment was linked to the Maori Mainstream Programme within which the importance of culture is emphasized through group work, co-construction of knowledge and peer solidarity (Bishop and Glynn, 1999). Several of the case studies included the use of summative assessment data as part of their formative strategies, even where the use has been for whole-school improvement rather than individual learning, which arguably falls outside the ARG definition given in the Introduction to this volume.

The nature and role of feedback

At one of the two schools in Queensland (Sebba and Maxwell, 2005), students were working on their individual assignments in the library using books, articles and the internet to research globalization in the context of a company they had chosen, for example Nike or McDonald's. The teacher individually saw about half of the 25 students in the group to review their progress. She asked challenging open questions to encourage them to extend and deepen their investigations and gave specific feedback on what they needed to target for improvement.

In each of the two schools, I analyzed more than 20 students' files from across year groups and ability ranges (as identified by the teachers) in order to check if and how grades were used. I collected examples of comment marking and looked for evidence that students had acted upon the comments. One of the schools used no grades at all and the comment marking was characterized as very specific and almost always included targets for improvement. What distinguished it in particular from the comment marking I have experienced in England, was that even positive comments were elaborated to ensure that students were left in no doubt about why a piece of work was so good. For example:

> You girls have done a fantastic job!! Not only is your information accurate and well-researched, but you have also successfully completed the extension tasks! Try and keep an eye on the difference between 'endangered' and 'extinct' and watch your spelling. But please keep up this brilliant effort! You have all gone above and beyond in this activity!! Well done!!

The comments, in particular for less high achieving students, were additionally often characterized by empathy and humour:

L, an excellent effort, I would like to join you in your mission to Mars.

At this school, 11-year-old students said that grades or marks were never given. They felt that this helped them work to their own standard and not worry about comparing themselves to other people. They all claimed to read and act upon the comments and suggested that the teacher was always willing to discuss them. In both schools, students claimed to read and act upon comments written on work and there was some evidence of this, though there were no specific consistent strategies to ensure this happened, as observed in a few schools elsewhere, such as keeping a list of comments in the front of a book and expecting students to indicate when and where (indicated by a page reference) these have been acted upon. However, teachers and students identified lessons in which time was allocated to making revisions in response to comments given.

In Denmark (Townshend et al., 2005), one case study school put great emphasis on verbal competencies. Goal-setting and oral feedback were strong features of the formative assessment work. Oral assessment was preferred because it was quick and flexible and allowed an immediate response from the student, enabling misunderstandings to be clarified rapidly. Individual student interviews took place several times a year in order to assess progress and set new goals focusing on subject outcomes, work attitudes and social skills. As in the Queensland schools, the lessons often incorporated periods of reflective feedback from students to teachers which resulted in adjustments to teaching. Students used logbooks to record their reflections and these were used for teacher and student to enter into a dialogue. Forster and Masters (1996–2001) provide further examples of this in their materials developed in Australia on developmental assessment.

Effective feedback seems to be characterized by specific comments that focus on students' understanding, rather than on quality of presentation or behaviour. Oral feedback may allow for greater exploration of understanding and be more immediate, but written comments allow teachers greater flexibility to reflect on students' work and allocate more time to this process, though the dialogue may be delayed and stilted. In contexts with a strong oral tradition such as the Danish case study school, the balance was more in favour of oral than written feedback. Effective oral questioning and feedback seem to require the teacher to be confident and competent in that subject area and to have the flexibility to 'try another way' in their questioning and feedback strategies in order to ensure that the message has been understood. A much fuller account of this issue can be found in Black et al. (2003).

Self- and peer-assessment

In the PROTIC programme in Quebec (Sliwka et al., 2005) teaching is organized around interdisciplinary projects with a strong emphasis on collaborative group exploration. At the start of each project, students identify their individual learning targets and at regular intervals they are given time for writing reflections on their own learning, their team learning and the achievement of their targets. These written reports are the basis for future target setting and choices. Peer assessment is used to give feedback on each other's regular presentations of work and on teamwork skills. Students reported needing to adjust to the level of autonomy expected compared to their previous schools: 'You understand that you are responsible, you are in charge' (Sliwka et al., 2005: 102).

In Saskatchewan (Sliwka et al., 2005), one school uses electronic learning portfolios with younger children to record their own learning. They keep exemplary pieces of work, scan in art work and are taught how to assess their own work. The same researchers noted that in a school in western Newfoundland, portfolios are similarly used by students to record their best work alongside reflective journals. In pairs, they use criteria provided by the teacher to give each other feedback on ways of improving their quality of writing in English. These practices are used formatively to support continuous learning but may also contribute to summative purposes of assessment.

In Queensland, where there is no testing, teachers are trying to ensure that the students are aware of and understand the outcome-based statements and can assess themselves against the standards. The students interviewed described reflection time as a feature of most lessons. This involved the use of their learning journals in which questions to be addressed included 'What do you understand about ... ?' They gave examples of marking each other's work and giving each other feedback on written work. Self- and peer-assessment was a strong feature of the lessons observed in Queensland. Every week there was an allocated time for Year 8 and 9 students to reflect on their learning and write comments about it in their learning journals. Teachers were allowed to read these but not allowed to write in them.

In another lesson at this school, at the end of each activity, the students were invited to assess it on difficulty; student feedback determined whether the teacher moved on to the next activity or gave a further explanation of the previous one. Students and other staff interviewed confirmed that reflections of this type were regularly built into lessons.

In the lessons observed, peer-assessment was less well developed than self-assessment. This may reflect the additional demands on teachers and students of peer-assessment and the skills that we have noted elsewhere needing to be taught (see e.g. Kutnick et al., 2005). Feedback between students tended to be at the level of whether an outcome was correct or not, rather than indicating how to improve it. Students were encouraged to reflect on how effectively they had worked as a group, as well as how well they had completed the task. One student had entered the following comment into her journal:

> Yesterday my group and I made different shapes of a certain size out of newspaper.

> I got frustrated when nobody would listen to me. But we finished a square and two rectangles. Listen. None of our group members listened to each other. We all had ideas but wouldn't explain them. Then it would all end up in a mess.

The relationship between student grouping strategies and assessment for learning

Assessment for learning encourages students to develop greater responsibility for their own learning but also to regard their peers as a potential resource for learning and thus to become less dependent on the teacher. It requires effective group work, in particular in the area of peer-assessment. Well developed peer-assessment is very demanding on students' social and communication skills, in particular listening, turn-taking, clear and concise verbal and written expression, empathy and sensitivity. There is substantial evidence that group work skills need to be taught (e.g. see Kutnick et al., 2005) and that highly effective group work takes a long time to develop. Teaching students to self-reflect was observed in one school in Queensland:

> Sixteen Year 9 pupils in a PSHE [personal and social health education] lesson worked in self-selected groups of four. The school had a 'buddying' system for incoming Year 7 pupils whereby they had an identified 'buddy' from Year 10 help settle

them into school. Most pupils in this Year 9 class had applied to be 'buddies' and were to be interviewed to see if they were suitable for this role. The teacher asked the groups to identify what characteristics 'buddies' need. She gave them 10 minutes to discuss this and draw up a list. She invited the groups to feed back. She then invited them to spend 10 minutes working out what questions the interviewers would ask them to draw out, whether they had these skills and how they would answer these questions. At the end of the third activity and feedback she asked them to assess how they worked in their groups and invited feedback.

Despite the challenges of group work, students and teachers alike in the two Queensland schools reported beneficial outcomes of using these strategies. In interviews in one school, the students claimed that they worked in groups for about half the lessons and that this helped them to develop their understanding through testing out their ideas, examples and explanations on others. They suggested that the disadvantages of working in groups included having 'to work with people you don't like, who hold you back or mess about'. Overall, they felt that the advantages outweighed the disadvantages and favoured the mixed-ability groups that they usually experienced:

> I reckon it's important to have people working together at differ-
> ent levels, then the people at higher levels can teach the people
> at lower levels in their own way. In the real world you work with
> different people, you don't always choose who you work with and
> working with other people you don't know helps you. (Sebba and
> Maxwell, 2005: 202–3)

In a school in Denmark (Townshend et al., 2005), 'core groups' provided opportunities for reflection on goals, effort and outcomes. The students gave each other oral feedback, recorded their views in their logbooks and evaluated one another's academic achievements and presentational skills. This was done for each project that they undertook. School leaders reported that students were more compe-tent at reflecting on their own learning, identifying their targets and engaging in social interaction.

Teacher development

The definition of formative assessment in the OECD study refers to adjusting teaching in response to feedback about learning, and in this sense, formative assessment and teacher development are inextricably linked, as emphasized in Chapter 3. Many of the OECD case studies refer to evaluation of teaching. In Quebec, the university teacher educators acknowledged that in the PROTIC programme (Sliwka et al., 2005) teachers have to adapt to a shift in control and responsibility for learning from teacher to student, as noted in earlier chapters. They are also required to recognize that they are not the only source of knowledge in the classroom. There is evidence that the PROTIC approach has had an impact on the teaching approaches used by other teachers, such as those in Saskatchewan who reported that whereas previously they had worked in complete isolation, they are now much more interested in working together and sharing resources and have developed a clear focus on how students learn since introducing formative assessment. This professional development issue is developed further in Chapter 3.

Teachers at one school in Queensland (Sebba and Maxwell, 2005) shared pieces of work and discussed comments they had made on them as well as the work itself. They reported that this challenged their thinking and developed their practice. Heads of department saw this as professional behaviour for moderation purposes rather than monitoring of marking for accountability purposes. It was seen as relatively easy to do in a small school in which departments are not isolated.

In the case study school in Denmark (Townshend et al., 2005) teacher development is supported through a centre for teaching innovation based in Copenhagen, established specifically to develop innovatory practices and share these with schools across Denmark. They plan and provide in-service courses for teachers, support school improvement in other schools and publish materials in accessible professional journals. Teachers are challenged by self-evaluation in that they are concerned they may be insufficiently 'objective', but there is evidence of a continuing drive for more secure and effective teaching approaches. School leaders in the case study schools acknowledged the cultural change required to implement formative assessment strategies effectively.

School improvement contextual factors

The role of leadership

It was a feature of a number of the schools in the OECD studies that the head teacher or principal had recently changed, and that the school had been restructured and significant new whole-school initiatives introduced. New managers often provided the impetus for change or were appointed to provide this, but frequent changes to senior management teams can be a threat to longer-term sustainability of new initiatives, and assessment for learning strategies is not exempt from this. There was evidence in one of the schools in Queensland that the changes brought about through assessment for learning, including student self-reflection, group work and comment marking, had become embedded in the infrastructure of the school and could thereby 'survive' some degree of senior management change.

Developing schools as learning organizations

The schools where significant progress had been made were characterized by an ongoing commitment to further development. They did not express views, suggesting they thought they had reached their targets and could reduce their energies. Consistent with research on developing schools as learning communities (e.g. McMahon et al., 2004), these schools recognized the importance of engaging with the wider community beyond teachers with many, for example, having well-developed mechanisms for ongoing dialogue with parents about formative assessment. The emphasis on teachers working in teams and helping to develop one another seems to have been another feature of these schools, which is an issue considered in Chapter 3.

Students as agents of change

There was some evidence of students' awareness that their school was different to others and of linking this to aspects of formative assessment. For example, in one school in Queensland students reported that teaching strategies compared very favourably to those used in other schools attended by their friends, suggesting that other schools relied more heavily on worksheets and students in those schools received less full explanations from teachers. Students in one of the Danish schools noted that they enjoyed better relationships with teachers and that instead of just 'getting grades', they were engaged in a process with their teachers which enabled them to get to know them better and to discuss expectations.

There was, however, little evidence from the OECD case studies of well-developed examples of students acting as change agents in their schools in the realm of formative assessment. Fielding (2001) has proposed levels of engagement for students in schools that enable them to become 'true' contributors to, or even leaders of, change.

For example, students might be expected to challenge the school on why peer-assessment opportunities provided in one subject were not created in other subjects. This would seem to be a potential next development for the schools studied.

The impact and relevance of policy

There are important contextual policy factors that seem likely to support the practices observed in the two Queensland schools. Perhaps the national curriculum framework, less prescriptive than that in England at the time of the case studies, is a useful contextual factor enabling a strong focus on formative assessment by reducing the necessity for teachers to determine what to teach. The lack of external tests and examinations passed without comment in the teacher interviews in the Queensland schools, yet, as a systematic review of research on this has shown (Harlen and Deakin Crick, 2003), high-stakes testing and publication of results are associated with teachers adopting a teaching style that favours transmission of knowledge. This not only reduces the use of teaching approaches consistent with assessment for learning but is likely to consume energy that Queensland teachers could instead direct into assessment for learning. Finally, the status ascribed to teacher summative assessment in the Queensland system suggests that formative assessment is better recognized than in some other systems, for both its contribution to learning and to summative assessment. Its role as a key professional skill for teachers, as advocated in the principles in the Introduction to this volume, is recognized in this system.

In Denmark, the 2003 Education Act introduced an outcomes-based curriculum defining competencies for all students. Schools are required to publish annually the results of average grades on their websites, though these seemed not to take account of prior attainment and were therefore regarded by those interviewed as reflecting intake and not effectiveness. There was no evidence that this accountability framework was inhibiting the developments in formative assessment in the schools. At the time the case studies were conducted (2002–3), the Ministry of Education had just changed the definition of the role of headteachers, so in one of the case study schools the head had used formative assessment as part of the change strategy adopted.

Educational policy in Canada is set at province/territory level. At federal level, monitoring across the provinces takes place but curricular guidelines are produced in the provinces and territories and these often emphasize learning to learn skills. In western Newfoundland, the mandate from the Department of Education and school district that required test (attainment) data to be the basis for school improvement has influenced the developing focus on analyzing progress and addressing the needs of 'weaker' students, partly through formative assessment. Initial resistance was followed by a gradual change in culture and analyzing data is now a key focus of staff development activities, closely linked to evaluation by teachers with individual students. This reflects the Assessment Reform Group principle (ARG, 2002) of promoting a commitment to a shared understanding of the criteria by which students are assessed. The tension for teachers remains how to reconcile the demands of summative testing with formative assessment, though this does not seem to be severely limiting developments in assessment for learning.

Conclusion

Despite considerable differences in cultural contexts across the OECD case study schools, what teachers do at the classroom level may be surprisingly similar. For example, the feedback provided to students on their work, the development of self- and peer-assessment and the implications of formative assessment for group work have overlapping practices across countries. Perceptions of these, however, by students, teachers, senior school managers and teacher educators may differ as a result of the considerable differences in national policy contexts. The national assessment and curriculum framework, accountability mechanisms and underlying values reflected in these about the purposes of education, lifelong learning skills and skills for employability, will enhance or inhibit to different degrees the teachers' capacity to adopt, implement and sustain formative assessment practices. Furthermore, as has been the experience of school improvement in general, schools that are effective at implementing a specific strategy, in this case formative assessment, are often those which can redirect the requirements and additional resources made available through national policies to support their established plans.

Note

1   I would like to acknowledge the extensive writing and editing that Janet Looney of the OECD contributed to the report.

References

ARG (2002) *Assessment for Learning: 10 Principles*. University of Cambridge: Assessment Reform Group.

Ball, S. (1990) *Politics and Policy-Making in Education: Explorations in Policy Sociology*. London: Routledge.

Bishop, R. and Glynn, T. (1999) *Culture Counts: Changing Power Relations in Education*. New Zealand: Dunmore Press.

Black, P. and Wiliam, D. (1998), 'Assessment and classroom learning', *Assessment in Education*, 5: 7–71.

Black, P., Harrison, C., Lee, C., Marshall, B. and Wiliam, D. (2003) *Assessment for Learning: Putting it into Practice*. Buckingham: Open University Press.

Broadfoot, P., Osborn, M., Gilly, M. and Bucher, A. (1993) *Perceptions of Teaching: Primary School Teachers in England and France*. London: Cassell.

Crossley, M. (1984) 'Strategies for curriculum change and the question of international transfer', *Journal of Curriculum Studies*, 16: 75–88.

Fielding, M. (2001) 'Students as radical agents of change', *Journal of Educational Change*, 2: 123–41.

Fielding, M., Bragg, S., Craig, J., Cunningham, I., Eraut, M., Gillinson, S., Horne, M., Robinson, C. and Thorp, J. (2005) *Factors Influencing the Transfer of Good Practice*. London: DfES.

Forster, M. and Masters, G. (1996–2001) *Assessment Resource Kit* (complete set). Camberwell: Australian Council for Educational Research.

Harlen, W. and Deakin Crick, R. (2003) 'Testing and motivation for learning', *Assessment in Education*, 10(2): 169–208.

Kutnick, P., Sebba, J., Blatchford, P. and Galton, M. (2005) *The Effects of Pupil Grouping: An Extended Literature Review for DfES*. www.education.gov.uk/publications/OrderingDownload/RR688.pdf

McMahon, A., Thomas, S., Greenwood, A., Stoll, L., Bolam, R., Hawkey, K., Wallace, M. and Ingram, M. (2004) 'Effective professional learning communities'. Paper presented at the ICSEI conference, Rotterdam.

OECD (2005) *Formative Assessment: Improving Learning in Secondary Classrooms*. Paris: OECD.

Sebba, J. and Maxwell, G. (2005) 'Queensland, Australia: an outcomes-based curriculum', in *Formative Assessment: Improving Learning in Secondary Classrooms*. Paris: OECD.

Sliwka, A., Fushell, M., Gauthier, M. and Johnson, R. (2005) 'Canada: encouraging the use of summative data for formative purposes', in *Formative Assessment: Improving Learning in Secondary Classrooms*. Paris: OECD.

Townshend, J., Moos, L. and Skov, P. (2005) 'Denmark: building on a tradition of democracy and dialogue in schools', in *Formative Assessment: Improving Learning in Secondary Classrooms*. Paris: OECD.

Vulliamy, G. (2004) 'The impact of globalisation on qualitative research in comparative and international education', *Compare*, 34: 261–84.

Vulliamy, G., Lewin, K. and Stephens, D. (1990) *Doing Educational Research in Developing Countries: Qualitative Strategies*. London: Falmer.

Chapter 11

The Role of Assessment in Developing Motivation for Learning

Wynne Harlen

This chapter is about motivation for learning and how assessment for different purposes, used in various ways, can affect it, both beneficially and detrimentally. It begins with a brief discussion of some key components of motivation for learning This is followed by reference to research evidence relating to the impact of summative assessment on motivation for learning. Despite the great range and variety in the research studies, their findings converge in providing evidence that some summative assessment practices, particularly high-stakes tests, have a negative impact. At the same time, the evidence points towards ways of avoiding such impact through actions which, not surprisingly, have many of the features of formative assessment. The chapter ends by drawing together implications for assessment policy at the school, local and national levels.

The importance of motivation for learning

Motivation is considered to be one of the most important aspects of human behaviour (Barkoukis et al., 2008), described as 'the conditions and processes that account for the arousal, direction, magnitude, and maintenance of effort' (Katzell and Thompson, 1990: 144). It is a construct of what impels learners to spend the time and effort needed for learning and solving problems (Bransford et al., 2000); the 'engine' that drives teaching and learning (Stiggins, 2001). It is clearly central to learning, but is not only needed as an input into education. It is also an essential outcome of education if students are to be able to adapt to changing conditions and problems in their lives beyond formal schooling. The more rapid the change in these conditions, the more important is strong motivation to learn new skills and to enjoy the challenge. Thus in the twenty-first century it is essential to be aware of what aspects of teaching and learning practice act to promote or inhibit motivation to learn.

Assessment is clearly one of the key factors. Stiggins claims that teachers can enhance or destroy students' desires to learn more quickly and more permanently through their use of assessment than through any other tools at their disposal (2001: 36). In this chapter we look at this association and at ways of using assessment to enhance motivation for learning. However, it is first necessary to consider briefly the nature of motivation, for it is not a single or simple entity. By recognizing some of its complexity we can see how assessment interacts with it.

The concept of motivation for learning

In some sense all actions are motivated, as we always have some reason for doing something, even if it is just to fill an idle hour, or to experience the sense of achievement in meeting a challenge, or to avoid the consequences of taking no action.

People read books, climb mountains or take heroic risks for these reasons. They may undertake unpleasant and apparently unrewarding tasks because by doing so they avoid the even more unpleasant consequences of inaction or, in other circumstances, achieve the satisfaction of helping others. In tasks that are enjoyed the motivation may be in the enjoyment of the process or in the product; a person might take a walk to enjoy the experience, or because of knowledge that the exercise will be good for the health. In such cases the goals are clear and the achievement, or non-achievement, of them is made evident in a relatively short time. In relation to learning, however, the value of making an effort is not always apparent to the student. This underlines the importance of understanding how learning contexts and conditions, and particularly the crucial role of assessment, impact on motivation.

Types of motivation

There is a well-established distinction between intrinsic and extrinsic motivation (Deci and Ryan, 1985). When applied to motivation for learning it refers to the difference between the learning process being a source of satisfaction itself or the potential gains from the result of learning being the driving force. In the latter case, extrinsic motivation, the benefit derived may be a result of achieving a certain level of attainment but is not related to what is learned; learning is a means to an end, not an end in itself. On the other hand, intrinsic motivation describes the situation in which learners find satisfaction in the skills and knowledge that result and find enjoyment in the learning.

Different types of intrinsic and extrinsic motivations have been proposed, forming a continuum from the various intrinsic to the extrinsic motives. However, an alternative way of conceiving this dimension of behaviour is in terms of levels of self-determination. High levels of self-determination indicate strong intrinsic motivation, whilst low self-determination is represented by absence of motivation, or amotivation. Those described as amotivated 'simply do not demonstrate the intent to engage in an activity' (Barkoukis et al., 2008: 40). The different forms of extrinsic motivation represent intermediate levels of self-determination along the dimension from intrinsic motivation to amotivation. Thus self-determination is proposed as a dimension describing different types of motivation (Deci and Ryan, 2000).

Intrinsic motivation for learning is seen as the ideal, since it is more likely to lead to a desire to continue learning than learning motivated extrinsically by rewards such as stars, certificates, prizes or gifts in the absence of such external incentives. Most teachers have come across students who constantly ask 'Is it for the examination?' when asked to undertake a new task. This follows years of being told how important it is to pass the examination rather than realising the usefulness and interest of what is being learned. At the same time there is a large area between the extremes where is it difficult to characterize a reward as providing extrinsic or intrinsic motivation. For example, the desire to gain a certificate which enables a learner to pass on to the next stage of learning could be regarded as extrinsic motivation, but on the other hand the certificate can be seen as symbolic of the learning achieved. Similarly, praise can be a confirmation that one has achieved something worthwhile or the main reason for expending effort.

However, to regard all extrinsic sources of motivation as 'bad' and all intrinsic motivation as 'good' ignores the reality of the variety of learning, of learning contexts and of goals. Hidi (2000) suggests that what may apply to short-term or simple tasks may not apply to long-term and complex activities. She contends that 'a combination of intrinsic rewards inherent in interesting activities and external rewards, particularly those that provide performance feedback, may be required to maintain individuals' engagement across complex and often difficult – perhaps painful – periods of learning' (Hidi and Harackiewicz, 2000: 159).

Nevertheless, there is strong evidence, reviewed by Deci et al. (1999), that external rewards undermine intrinsic motivation across a range of activities, populations and types of reward. The review by Crooks (1988) drew attention to research that indicates the problems associated with extrinsic motivation in tending to lead to 'shallow' rather than 'deep' learning. Kellaghan et al. (1996) reported evidence that intrinsic motivation is associated with levels of engagement in learning that lead to conceptual understanding and higher level thinking skills. Brown and Hirschfeld's (2008) study of students' views of the purpose of assessment found that those who considered assessment as helping them to take more responsibility for learning achieved higher grades than those who sought to attribute responsibility for their results to their teachers and those who did not take assessment seriously.

Key aspects of motivation

A systematic review of research into the impact of summative assessment on motivation for learning (Harlen and Deakin Crick, 2002, 2003) confirmed that motivation is too complex a concept to be studied as a single dependent variable. Rather, research studies have concerned one or more of several components of motivation which influence the effort that is required for learning: interest, goal-orientation, locus of control, self-esteem, self-efficacy and self-regulation (see Box 11.1). These are interconnected components of motivation for learning and there is a good deal of evidence that assessment has a key role in promoting or inhibiting them and hence affects the nature of the learning achieved in particular circumstances.

Box 11.1 Components of motivation for learning

Interest refers to the pleasure in undertaking an activity. The development of interest that leads to learning is connected with goal orientation and with the type of feedback received.

Goal orientation relates to how learners see the goals of engaging in a learning task and determines the direction in which effort will be made and how they will organize and prioritize (or not) time spent for learning. Two main types of goal are described as '*learning* goals' and '*performance* goals' (Ames, 1992). Those motivated by goals identified in terms of *learning* apply effort in acquiring new skills, seeking to understand what is involved rather than just committing information to memory. Those oriented towards goals identified as a level of *performance* seek the easiest way to meet requirements and achieve the goals, compare themselves with others, and consider ability to be more important than effort.

Locus of control refers to whether learners perceive the cause of their success or failure to be under their control (internal locus) or to be controlled by others (external locus). Locus of control is a central concept in attribution theory (Weiner, 1979). A sense of internal control is evident in those who recognize that their success or failure is due to factors within themselves, either their effort or their ability. Those with a sense of external control attribute their success or failure to external factors, such as their teacher or luck.

Self-esteem refers to how people value themselves both as people and as learners. It shows in the confidence that the person feels in being able to learn.

Self-efficacy is closely related to self-esteem and to locus of control, but is more directed at specific tasks for subjects. It refers to how capable the learner feels of succeeding in a particular task or type of task. It is characterized as 'I can' versus 'I can't' by Anderson and Bourke (2000: 35) who state that it is a learned response, the learning taking place over time through the student's various experiences of success and failure.

Self-regulation in learning refers to the capacity to evaluate one's own performance, to take responsibility for learning and make choices about how to improve.

Summative assessment and motivation for learning

This section briefly notes some main points from studies of how summative assessment affects one or more of the components of motivation. Overall, studies of summative assessment provide strong evidence of negative impact on students' motivation for learning. However the research also indicates how to decrease the negative and increase the positive impact.

Impacts of assessment to be avoided

High stakes and goal orientation
When assessment is used for selection or certification, carrying high stakes for the students, it creates a strong reason for effort. But this effort, for the vast majority of students, is directed to passing the

test/examination at the necessary level to achieve the reward. Students who are extrinsically motivated in this way see their goal as performance rather than as learning, and the evidence shows that this is associated with seeking the easiest route to the necessary outcome. Students with such goal orientation use passive rather than active learning strategies and avoid challenges; their learning is described as 'shallow' rather than 'deep' (Ames and Archer, 1988; Benmansour, 1999; Crooks, 1988; Harlen and James, 1997). Students are encouraged, sometimes unwittingly, by their teachers in this approach to their work. The way in which teachers introduce tasks to students can orientate students to goals as performance rather than goals as learning (Brookhart and DeVoge, 1999; Schunk, 1996). Repeated tests, in which are they encouraged to perform well to get high scores, teaches students that performance is what matters. This permeates throughout classroom transactions, affecting students' approach to their work and their self-esteem (Pollard et al., 2000; Reay and Wiliam, 1999).

Tests and examination results also have high stakes for teachers when they are used to evaluate teaching and schools. Pollard et al. (2000) suggest that making teachers accountable for test scores but not for effective teaching, encourages the administration of practice tests. Many teachers also go further and actively coach students in passing tests rather than spending time in helping them to understand what is being tested (Gordon and Reese, 1997; Leonard and Davey, 2001). Thus the scope and depth of learning are seriously undermined. Even when not directly teaching to the tests, teachers change their approach. Johnston and McClune (2000) reported that teachers adjusted their teaching style in ways they perceived as necessary because of the tests. They spent the most time in direct instruction and less in providing opportunities for students to learn through enquiry and problem solving. This impairs learning, and the feeling of being capable of learning, for those students who prefer to do this in a more active way.

Feedback, self-efficacy and interest
The research confirms that feedback to students has a key role in determining their self-efficacy, the feeling of being capable of learning, of tackling their classroom activities and assessment tasks successfully. Feedback can come from several sources: from the reactions of the teachers to their work, from others, including their peers, and from their own previous performance on similar tasks. In relation to teachers' feedback, there is strong evidence that, in an atmosphere dominated by high-stakes tests, teachers' feedback is largely judgemental and rarely formative (Pollard et al., 2000). Butler's (1988)

experimental study of different kinds of feedback indicated that such feedback encourages interest in performance rather than in learning and is particularly detrimental to interest in the work, and the achievement, of lower achieving students.

The feedback that students obtain from their own previous performance in similar work is a significant element in their feeling of being able to learn in a particular situation (Brookhart and DeVoge, 1999). Consequently, if this is generally judgemental in nature it has a cumulative impact on their self-efficacy. The opportunity for past experience to help further learning is lost.

School support, self-esteem and effort

The kind of feedback received adds to the general impression that students have of their teachers' helpfulness and interest in them as learners. Roderick and Engel (2001) reported on how a school providing a high level of support was able to raise the effort and test performance of very low achieving and disaffected students to a far greater degree than a comparable school providing low level support for similar students. High support meant creating an environment of social and educational support, working hard to increase students' sense of self-efficacy, focusing on learning-related goals, making goals explicit, using assessment to help students succeed and creating cognitive maps which made progress evident. They also displayed a strong sense of responsibility for their students. Low teacher support meant teachers not seeing the target grades as attainable, not translating the need to work harder into meaningful activities, not displaying recognition of change and motivation on the part of students, and not making personal connections with students in relation to goals as learning. There are implications here and in Duckworth et al.'s (1986) study for school management. Pollard et al. (2000) and Hall and Harding (2002) also found that the assessment discourse and quality of professional relationships teachers have with their colleagues outside the classroom influence the quality of teaching and learning inside the classroom.

In summary

Assessment can have a negative impact on student motivation for learning by:

- creating a classroom culture which favours transmission teaching and undervalues variety in ways of learning
- allowing conditions in which summative judgements permeate all teachers' assessment transactions

- focusing the content of teaching narrowly on what is tested
- orienting students to adopt goals as performance rather than goals as learning
- providing predominantly judgemental feedback in terms of scores or grades.

Assessment practices that preserve student motivation

Each item in the above list indicates consequences to be avoided and so suggests what not to do. However, the research evidence also provides more positive implications for practice. One of the more difficult changes to make is to convince teachers that levels of achievement can be raised by means other than by teaching to the tests. Certainly students will have to be prepared for the tests they are required to take, but this best takes the form of explaining the purpose and nature of the test and spending time, not on practising past test items, but on developing understanding and skills by using assessment to help learning. The work of Black et al. (2003) in the development of practical approaches to using assessment for learning has added to the the evidence of the positive effect of formative assessment on achievement (see Chapter 2). Since the measures of change in achievement used in this work are the same statutory tests as are used in all schools, the results show that improvement can be brought about by attention to learning without teaching to the test.

Implications for teachers
There are implications here for two kinds of action that can minimize the negative impact for all students. The first is to ensure that the demands of a test are consistent with the capability of the students, that is, that students are not faced with tests that are beyond their reach (Duckworth et al., 1986). The notion of 'testing when ready' is relevant here so that all students can experience success, which preserves their self-esteem and feeling of self-efficacy. The result also helps students to recognize the progress they are making in their learning, noted as important in the research (Duckworth et al., 1986; Roderick and Engel, 2001). The second action is for teachers actively to promote awareness of the progress that each student is making, and to discourage students from comparing themselves with each other in terms of levels or scores they have attained.

Here the type of feedback is again relevant. Butler's (1988) research showed that feedback which included scores (ego-involving feedback) induced motivation to achieve high marks rather than promoting interest in the task. Feedback promoting task involvement by giving task-related comments and no marks promoted the interest and performance of students. However, the quality of comments feedback is central. In a small-scale experimental study, Smith and Gorard (2005) reported findings in conflict with Butler's, that students who did not receive marks, but only comments on their work, felt at a disadvantage compared with those given marks. They also achieved lower marks. However, it was evident that the feedback was in very general terms, such as urging students to 'try harder' rather than the detailed suggestions for improvement that Black et al. (2003) found effective. In support of more rigorous feedback, Pajares and Graham (1998) reported that Grade 8 students wanted honest comments that helped them improve rather than praise that only made them feel good.

Research findings also underline the value of involving students in self-assessment (Schunk, 1996) and in decisions about tests (Leonard and Davey, 2001; Perry, 1998). Both of these necessitate helping students to understand the reasons for the tests and the learning that will be assessed, thus helping to promote goals as learning. These practices are more readily applied to those tests that teachers control rather than to external tests. However, there is abundant evidence that the majority by far of tests that students undergo are imposed by teachers, either as part of regular checking or in practising for external tests. Thus a key action that can be taken is to minimize the explicit preparation for external tests and use feedback from regular classwork to focus students on the skills and knowledge that will be tested.

Implications for schools

If teachers are to take these actions, they need support at the school level in the form of an ethos and policy that promotes the use of assessment to help learning as well as serving summative purposes. There are implications for the management of schools in establishing effective communication about assessment and developing and maintaining collegiality through structures and expectations that enable teachers to avoid the negative impact of assessment on motivation for learning. These school procedures and policies have also to be communicated to parents.

Implications for assessment policy

There are, of course, implications for local and national assessment policies. The force driving teachers to spend so much time on direct preparation for tests derives from the high stakes attached to the results. The regular national or state-wide tests for all students throughout primary and secondary school have greater consequences for teachers and schools than for students. But whether the stakes are high for the student (as when the results are used for certification or selection) or for the teacher and school (as when aggregated student tests or examination results are used as a measure of teacher or school effectiveness), the consequence is that teaching and learning are focused on what is tested with all the consequences for motivation for learning that have been discussed here.

The irony is that, as an outcome of the high stakes use, the tests do not provide the valid information required for their purposes. In particular, tests taken by all students can only cover a narrow sample (and the most reliably marked sample) of student attainment; teaching how to pass tests means that students may be able to pass even when they do not have the skills and understanding which the test is intended to measure (Gordon and Reese, 1997). Further, the value of the tests as useful indicators of students' attainment is undermined by the differential impact of the testing procedures on a significant proportion of students. Girls and lower achieving students are likely to have high levels of test anxiety that influence their measured performance (Benmansour, 1999; Evans and Engelberg, 1988; Reay and Wiliam, 1999). Older lower achieving students are likely to minimize effort and may even answer randomly since they expect to fail anyway (Paris et al., 1991). Thus results may be unreliable and may exaggerate the difference between the higher and lower achieving students.

Ways forward

To avoid these pitfalls, the Assessment Reform Group (ARG), as a result of consultation with policy makers and practitioners on the implications of the research, concluded that designers and users of assessment systems and tests should:

- be more actively aware of the limited validity of the information about pupil attainment that is being obtained from current high-stakes testing programmes;
- reduce the stakes of such summative assessments by using, at national and local levels, the performance indicators derived from them more selectively and more sensitively. They should take due account of the potential for those indicators to impact negatively on learning, on teaching and on the curriculum;
- recognize the true costs of national systems of testing, in terms of teaching time, practice tests and marking. This should lead

policy makers to come to reasoned conclusions about the benefits and costs of each element in those systems;

- consider that for tracking standards of attainment at national
  level it is worth testing a sample of pupils rather than a full age
  cohort. This would reduce both the negative impacts of high-
  stakes tests on pupil motivation and the costs incurred;
- use test development expertise to create forms of tests and
  assessments that will make it possible to assess all valued outcomes of education, including for example creativity and problem
  solving;
- develop a broader range of indicators to evaluate the performance of schools. Indicators that are derived from summative
  assessments should therefore be seen as only one element in
  a more broadly based judgement. This would diminish the
  likely impact of public judgements of school performance
  on those pupils whose motivation is most 'at risk' (ARG,
  2002: 11–12).

Conclusion

It is natural for students and teachers to aim for high performance,
but when this is measured by external tests and when the results are
accompanied by penalties for low performance, the aim becomes to
perform well in the tests, which is often not the same as to learn well.
Moreover, when there are high stakes attached to test results the tests
are inevitably designed to have high reliability and focus on what
can be most reliably tested. The inevitable consequence, as the
research shows, is to narrow the range of what is assessed and inevitably also of students' learning experiences. However, the impact of
high-stakes testing may well have longer-term consequences than
the narrowness of curriculum experience. Further learning and continued learning throughout life depend on how people view themselves as learners, whether they feel they can achieve success through
effort, whether they gain satisfaction from learning; all aspects of
motivation for learning.

The impact that assessment can have on students can be either
positive or negative. What happens depends on how the teacher
mediates the impact of assessment on students. Chapter 12 shows
that teachers' views of learning affect their pedagogy. When teachers
see their role as helping students to pass tests, by whatever means,
their teaching methods and the experiences of the students are distorted. The alignment of assessment, curriculum and pedagogy is

most easily upset by changes in assessment and this has to be taken into account in designing assessment policy.

References

Ames, C. (1992) 'Classrooms: goals, structures and student motivation', *Journal of Educational Psychology*, 84: 261–71.

Ames, C. and Archer, J. (1988) 'Achievement goals in the classroom: students' learning strategies and motivation processes', *Journal of Educational Psychology*, 80: 260–67.

Anderson, L.W. and Bourke, S.F. (2000) *Assessing Affective Characteristics in Schools* (2nd edn). Mahwah, NJ: Erlbaum.

ARG (Assessment Reform Group) (2002) *Testing, Motivation and Learning*. University of Cambridge Faculty of Education: Assessment Reform Group.

Barkoukis, V., Tsorbatzoudis, H., Grouios, G. and Sideridis, G. (2008) 'The assessment of intrinsic and extrinsic motivation and amotivation: validity and reliability of the Greek version of the Academic Motivation Scale', *Assessment in Education*, 15(1): 39–56.

Benmansour, N. (1999) 'Motivational orientations, self-efficacy, anxiety and strategy use in learning high school mathematics in Morocco', *Mediterranean Journal of Educational Studies*, 4: 1–15.

Black, P., Harrison, C., Lee, C., Marshall, B. and Wiliam, D. (2003) *Assessment for Learning: Putting it into Practice*. Maidenhead: Open University Press.

Bransford, J.D., Brown, A.L. and Cocking, R.R. (1999) *How People Learn: Brain, Mind, Experience and School*. Washington, DC: National Academy Press.

Brookhart, S. and DeVoge, J. (1999) 'Testing a theory about the role of classroom assessment in student motivation and achievement', *Applied Measurement in Education*, 12: 409–25.

Brown, G.T.L. and Hirschfeld, G.H.F. (2008) 'Students' conceptions of assessment: links to outcomes', *Assessment in Education*, 15(1): 3–19.

Butler, R. (1988) 'Enhancing and undermining intrinsic motivation: the effects of task-involving and ego-involving evaluation on interest and performance', *British Journal of Educational Psychology*, 58: 1–14.

Crooks, T. (1988) 'The impact of classroom evaluation practices on students', *Review of Educational Research*, 58: 438–81.

Deci, E.L. and Ryan, R.M. (1985) *Intrinsic Motivation and Self-determination in Human Behaviour*. New York: Plenum.

Deci, E.L. and Ryan, R.M. (2000) 'The "what" and "why" of goal pursuits: human needs and the self-determination of behaviour', *Psychological Inquiry*, 11(4): 227–68.

Deci, E.L., Koestner, R. and Ryan, R.M. (1999) 'A meta-analysis review of experiments examining the effects of extrinsic rewards on intrinsic motivation', *Psychological Bulletin*, 125: 627–88.

Duckworth, K., Fielding, G. and Shaughnessy, J. (1986) *The Relationship of High School Teachers' Class Testing Practices to Students' Feelings of Efficacy and Efforts to Study*. Eugene, OR: Oregon University.

Evans, E. and Engelberg, R. (1988) 'Students' perceptions of school grading', *Journal of Research and Development in Education* 21: 44–54.

Gordon, S. and Reese, M. (1997) 'High stakes testing: worth the price?', *Journal of School Leadership*, 7: 345–68.

Hall, C. and Harding, A. (2002) 'Level descriptions and teacher assessment in England: towards a community of assessment practice', *Educational Research*, 44: 1–15.

Harlen, W. and Deakin Crick, R. (2002) 'A systematic review of the impact of summative assessment and tests on students' motivation for learning (EPPI-Centre Review)', in *Research Evidence in Education Library*. Issue 1. London: EPPI-Centre, Social Science Research Unit, Institute of Education. Available at: http://eppi.ioe.ac.uk/EPPIWebContent/reel/review-groups/assessment/ass_rv1/ass_rv1.pdf

Harlen, W. and Deakin Crick, R. (2003) 'Testing and motivation for learning', *Assessment in Education*, 10(2): 169–208.

Harlen, W. and James, M. (1997) 'Assessment and learning: differences and relationships between formative and summative assessment', *Assessment in Education*, 4(3): 365–80.

Hidi, S. (2000) 'An interest researcher's perspective: the effects of extrinsic and intrinsic factors on motivation', in C. Sansone and J.M. Harackiewicz (eds), *Intrinsic and Extrinsic Motivation: The Search for Optimal Motivation and Performance*. New York: Academic Press.

Hidi, S. and Harackiewicz, J.M. (2000) 'Motivating the academically unmotivated: a critical issue for the 21st century', *Review of Educational Research*, 70(2): 151–79.

Johnston, J. and McClune, W. (2000) Selection Project Sel 5.1: *Pupil Motivation and Attitudes – Self-esteem, Locus of Control, Learning Disposition and the Impact of Selection on Teaching and Learning*. Belfast: Queen's University.

Katzell, R.A. and Thompson, D.E. (1990) 'Work motivation: theory and practice', *American Psychologist*, 45: 144–53.

Kellaghan, T., Madaus, G. and Raczek, A. (1996) *The Use of External Examinations to Improve Student Motivation*. Washington, DC: AERA.

Leonard, M. and Davey, C. (2001) *Thoughts on the 11 Plus*. Belfast: Save the Children Fund.

Pajares, M.F. and Graham, L. (1998) 'Formalist thinking and language arts instructions: teachers and students' beliefs about truth and caring in the teaching conversation', *Teaching and Teacher Education*, 14(8): 855–70.

Paris, S., Lawton, T., Turner, J. and Roth, J. (1991) 'A developmental perspective on standardised achievement testing', *Educational Researcher*, 20: 12–20.

Perry, N. (1998) 'Young children's self-regulated learning and contexts that support it', *Journal of Educational Psychology*, 90: 715–29.

Pollard, A., Triggs, P., Broadfoot, P., McNess, E. and Osborn, M. (2000) *What Pupils Say: Changing Policy and Practice in Primary Education* (chapters 7 and 10). London: Continuum.

Reay, D. and Wiliam, D. (1999) '"I'll be a nothing": structure, agency and the construction of identity through assessment', *British Educational Research Journal*, 25: 343–54.

Roderick, M. and Engel, M. (2001) 'The grasshopper and the ant: motivational responses of low achieving pupils to high stakes testing', *Educational Evaluation and Policy Analysis*, 23: 197–228.

Schunk, D. (1996) 'Goal and self-evaluative influences during children's cognitive skill learning', *American Educational Research Journal*, 33: 359–82.

Smith, E. and Gorard, S. (2005) '"They don't give us our marks": the role of formative feedback in student progress', *Assessment in Education*, 12(1): 21–38.

Stiggins, R.J. (2001) *Student-Involved Classroom Assessment* (3rd edn). Upper Saddle River, NJ: Merrill Prentice Hall.

Weiner, B. (1979) 'A theory of motivation for some classroom experiences', *Journal of Educational Psychology*, 71: 3–25.

Part 3

Theory

Chapter 12

Assessment in Harmony with our Understanding of Learning: Problems and Possibilities

Mary James with Jenny Lewis

The discussion of classroom assessment practice and implications for teachers' professional learning, in Part I, draws attention to the close relationship between assessment and pedagogy. Indeed, the central argument is that effective assessment for learning is central and integral to teaching and learning. This raises some theoretical questions about the ways in which assessment, on the one hand, and learning, on the other, are conceptualized and how they articulate. This chapter considers the relationship between assessment practice and the ways in which the processes and outcomes of learning are understood.

Starting from an assumption that there should be a degree of alignment between assessment and our understandings of learning, the equivalent chapter (James, 2006) in the first edition of this book described and analyzed the perspectives on learning that might be extrapolated from a number of different approaches to the practice of classroom assessment. Learning theorists themselves rarely make statements about how learning processes and outcomes within their models should be assessed, which may account for the lack of development of assessments aligned with some of the most interesting new learning theory. The intention of the earlier chapter was therefore to examine more closely the implications for assessment practice of three clusters of learning theories – behaviourist, cognitive constructivist and socio-cultural – and discuss whether eclectic or synthetic models of assessments, matched to learning, are feasible.

The revision of that chapter offered here has a slightly different purpose. Instead of providing a review across the range of historic theories, it focuses on the problems and possibilities of developing assessment practice congruent with socio-cultural learning theory. There are three particular reasons for this decision, all connected with the present author's more recent work. The first is that discussion of models of assessment consonant with socio-cultural perspectives on learning emerged as a common theme (James, 2010) in a significant number of the 53 articles, from across the world, in the 'Educational Assessment' section of the *International Encyclopedia of Education* (Peterson et al., 2010). The second is that most of the researchers involved in the 90 projects and thematic groups of the UK Economic and Social Research Council's Teaching and Learning Research Programme (TLRP) claimed to take a socio-cultural or social contructivist theoretical position (James and Pollard, 2011). The TLRP aimed to 'improve outcomes for learners of all ages in teaching and learning contexts across the UK'. As such, researchers had an obligation to consider what those outcomes might be and how they might be evaluated, although this task often proved challenging (James and Brown, 2005). This issue was followed up in the Assessment of Significant Learning Outcomes project which is described in Chapter 5. The third reason is that when classroom teachers were introduced, at a conference in late 2006, to some of the ideas in the previous version of this chapter, they responded very enthusiastically to what I tentatively named 'Third Generation Assessment' (James, 2008). Without my knowledge at the time, a few went back to their schools to try to develop it. Some of the results are described later in this revised chapter.

Alignment between assessment and learning

The alignment (Biggs, 1996; Biggs and Tang, 1997) of assessment with curriculum and pedagogy is a basis for claims for the validity of assessments (see Chapters 14 and 15), but the relationship is not straightforward. Indeed there are plenty of examples of assessment practices that have only tenuous or partial relationships to current understanding of learning within particular domains. Take, for instance, short answer tests in science that require recall of facts but do not begin to tap into understanding of concepts or the investigative processes that are central to science as a discipline. Nor do assessment practices always take sufficient account of current understanding of the ways in which students learn subject matter, the difficulties they encounter and how these are overcome.

Historically, much assessment practice was founded on the content and methods of psychology, especially the kind that deals with mental traits and their measurement. Thus classical test theory has primarily been concerned with differentiating between individuals who possess certain attributes, or determining the degree to which they do so. The focus tended to be whether some behaviour or quality could be detected rather than the process by which it is acquired. However, during the twentieth century understanding of how learning occurs developed apace. Learning was no longer seen as largely related to an individual's possession of innate and generally stable characteristics such as general intelligence. Interactions between people, and mediating tools such as language, came to be seen as having a crucial role. Thus the assessment of learning needs to take more account of the social as well as individual processes through which learning occurs. This requires expansion of perspectives on learning and assessment that take more account of insights from the disciplines of social-psychology, sociology and anthropology.

In practical terms, while exciting new developments in our understanding of learning unfold, developments in assessment systems and technology have lagged behind. Even some of the most innovative and novel developments, say, in e-assessment, are underpinned by models of learning that are limited or, in some cases, out of date. This is understandable too because the development of reliable assessments – always an important consideration in large-scale testing – is associated with an elaborate technology which takes much time and the skills of measurement experts, many of whom have often acquired their expertise in the very specialist field of psychometrics. This is especially true in the United States, which has a powerful influence on practice in other countries.

In this book we are primarily interested in classroom assessment by teachers, but research tells us that teachers' assessment practice is inevitably influenced by external assessment (Harlen, 2004) and teachers often use these assessments as models for their own, even if they do not use them directly. By using models of assessment borrowed from elsewhere, teachers may find themselves subscribing, uncritically or unwittingly, to the theories of learning on which they are based. This raises a question about whether it really matters what conceptions of learning underpin classroom assessment practices if they are deemed to 'work' well enough, and whether the need for consistency between teaching, learning and assessment might be overrated.

My view is that it does matter because some assessment practices are very much less effective than others in promoting the kinds of learning needed by young people today and in the future (James and Brown, 2005). The learning outcomes of most value to enable human flourishing – as citizens, as workers, as family and community members and as fulfilled individuals – are those that enable them to continue learning, when and where required, in a rapidly changing, information- and technology-rich environment. There is a need, therefore, for teachers to have a view about the kinds of learning that are most valuable for their students and to choose and develop approaches to teaching and assessment accordingly.

Helping teachers to become more effective may therefore mean both change in their assessment practice and change in their beliefs about learning (James et al., 2007). It will entail development of a critical awareness that change in one will, and should, inevitably lead to the need for change in the other. So, for instance, implementing assessment for learning/formative assessment may require a teacher to rethink what effective learning is, and his or her role in bringing it about. Similarly a change in their view of learning is likely to require assessment practice to be modified. While the focus of this book is mainly on formative assessment, a good deal is relevant to classroom-based summative assessment by which teachers summarize what has been achieved at certain times.

Theoretical foundations of learning and implications for assessment

Within the literature on learning theory, three clusters of theories are often delineated. In the US literature (Greeno, et al., 1996; Bredo, 1997; Pellegrino et. al., 2001) the three perspectives are often labelled 'behavorist', 'cognitive' and 'situated' but within the UK, drawing in more of the European literature, the labels 'behaviourist', 'constructivist', and 'socio-cultural' are sometimes preferred. These two sets of labels are roughly equivalent. For the benefit of teachers, Watkins (2003) has translated these different views of learning into descriptions: (1) Learning is being taught; (2) Learning is individual sense-making; and (3) Learning is building knowledge as part of doing things with others. Each of these perspectives is based on a view of what learning is, and how it takes place, but implications for assessment are rarely developed.

Behaviourism (learning is being taught) has fallen out of favour and there are few who would now subscribe to the view that learning is simply the conditioned response to external stimuli, and that rewards and punishments are powerful ways of forming or extinguishing habits. Another unfashionable tenet of behaviourism is that complex wholes are assembled out of parts, so learning can best be accomplished when complex performances are deconstructed and when each element is practised and reinforced and subsequently built upon. From this perspective, achievement in learning is often equated with the accumulation of skills and the memorization of information in a given domain, demonstrated in the formation of habits that allow speedy performance. Thus progress is often measured through unseen, timed tests with items taken from progressive levels in a skill hierarchy. Performance is usually interpreted as either correct or incorrect and poor performance is remedied by more practice on the incorrect items, sometimes by deconstructing them further and going back to even more basic skills.

Although learning theory has moved on, assessment practice stemming from behaviourism persists. For example, the approach is evident in many vocational qualifications post-16 where learning outcomes are broken down into tightly specified components. In the early days of the National Curriculum in England the disaggregation of attainment levels into atomised statements of attainment reflected this approach, as did the more recent assessment guidelines for Assessing Pupils' Progress, associated with the pre-2010 Labour Government's National Strategies. The widespread and frequent use of practice tests to enhance scores on national tests for 11-year-olds in England also rests on behaviourist assumptions about learning.

Cognitive constructivist theories of learning (learning is individual sense-making) have a much larger group of advocates today, recently joined by influential neuroscientists. Their particular focus is on how people construct meaning and make sense of the world by developing mental models. Prior knowledge is regarded as a powerful determinant of a student's capacity to learn new material. There is an emphasis on 'understanding' (and eliminating misunderstanding), and problem solving is seen as the context for knowledge construction. Differences between experts and novices are marked by the way experts organise 'salient' knowledge in structures that make it more retrievable and useful. From this perspective, achievement is framed in terms of understanding concepts and their relationships, and competence in processing strategies. The two components of meta-cognition – self-monitoring and self-regulation – are also important dimensions of learning.

This perspective on learning has received extensive attention for its implications for assessment. The two companion volumes produced by the US National Research Council (Bransford et al., 2000; Pellegrino et al., 2001) are perhaps the best examples. In view of the importance attached to prior learning as an influence on new learning, formative assessment emerges as an important, integral element of pedagogic practice because it is necessary to elicit students' mental models (through classroom dialogue, open-ended assignments, thinking-aloud protocols), in order to scaffold their understanding of knowledge structures and to provide them with opportunities to apply concepts and strategies in novel situations. In this context teaching and assessment are blended towards the goals of learning, particularly closing gaps between current understanding and the new understandings sought. It is not surprising therefore that many formulations of formative assessment are associated with this particular theoretical orientation (see Chapter 13). Some experimental approaches to summative assessment are also founded on these theories of learning, for example the use of computer software applications for problem solving and concept-mapping as a measure of students' learning of knowledge structures. However, these assessment technologies are still in their infancy and much formal testing still relies heavily on behavioural approaches.

For the reasons set out in the previous section, I have chosen to give more space in this revised chapter to the implications for assessment of socio-cultural learning theory. The socio-cultural perspective on learning (learning is building knowledge as part of doing things with others) is often regarded as a new development, but Bredo (1997) traces its intellectual origins back to the conjunction of functional psychology and philosophical pragmatism in the work of William James, John Dewey and George Herbert Mead at the beginning of the twentieth century. The interactionist views of the Chicago School, which viewed human development as a transaction between the individual and the environment (actor and structure), had something in common with the development of cultural psychology in Russia, associated with Vygotsky (1978), which derived from the dialectical materialism of Marx (see Edwards, 2005, for an accessible account). Vygotsky quoted Dewey, and, in turn, Vygotsky's thinking has influenced theorists such as Bruner (1996) in the US and Engeström (1999) in Finland. Other key theorists who regard individual learning as 'situated' in the social environment include Barbara Rogoff (1990), Jean Lave and Etienne Wenger (Lave and Wenger, 1991; Wenger, 1998), who draw on anthropological work to characterize learning as 'cognitive apprenticeship' in 'communities of practice'. Given their intellectual roots – in social theory, sociology and anthropology as well as from psychology – the language and concepts employed in socio-cultural approaches are often quite different. For example, 'agency', 'community', 'rules', 'roles', 'division of labour', 'artefacts', 'contradictions', feature prominently in the discourse.

According to this perspective, learning occurs in interactions between the individual and the social environment. Thinking is conducted through actions that alter the situation and the situation changes the thinking; the two constantly interact. Especially important is the notion that learning is a *mediated activity* in which cultural artefacts have a crucial role. These can be physical artefacts such as books and equipment but they can be symbolic tools such as language.

Since language, which is central to our capacity to think, is developed in relationships between people, social relationships are necessary for, and precede, learning (Vygotsky, 1978). Thus learning is a social and collaborative activity in which people develop their thinking together.

Learning therefore involves participation, and what is learned is not the property of an individual but *distributed* within the social group. For example, an ability to use language skills is not solely an indication of individual intelligence but of the intelligence of the community that developed the language, which the individual then puts to use. Thus the collective knowledge of the group or community is *internalized* by the individual. Similarly, as an individual creates new knowledge, for example, a new way of using a tool, then he or she will *externalize* that knowledge in communicating it to others who will put it to use and then *internalize* it. Thus knowledge is created and shared in *expansive learning cycles.*

Vygotsky's theory of goal-oriented, tool-mediated learning activity can encompass learning outcomes associated with notions of learning as acquisition of knowledge *and* learning as participation in activity (Sfard, 1998). But it also embraces outcomes associated with creativity, because it provides a description of how knowledge and practices can be transformed. In other words, it can encompass a very wide range of outcomes: higher and lower mental processes; attitudinal, cognitive and behavioural outcomes; individual and shared activity; problem-solving processes and products; the acquisition of existing knowledge and the creation of new knowledge.

As I have argued elsewhere (James, 2010), Vygotsky also has something to offer on the issue of progression. The structures of grades, scales and attainment levels have accustomed us to regard progression as step-by-step and linear. According to Vygotsky, the mastery of tools of the mind takes place in the *zone of proximal development* (ZPD). As Grigorenko (1998: 210–11) points out:

> The word *zone* refers to the nonlinearity of children's development. In this zone, the child might move forward or backward, to the left or to the right. ... The main characteristic of the ZPD is its sensitivity to the child's individuality – its responsiveness to the unique profile of each child's skills. The ZPD is of tremendous importance educationally. Generally, when educators evaluate a child's skills, they focus on what the child demonstrates in his or her independent performance. ... Vygotsky stated that the level of independent performance is an important, but not the only, index of development. To account for the dynamic process of development, we should consider the level of the child's assisted performance.

There are two points to be made here. First, there is value in plotting a learner's development as a profile within a zone and encouraging them to expand, deepen and enrich their knowledge, skills and understanding. Secondly, there is value in assessing how learners respond to assistance and the introduction of new tools by others. Grigorenko argues that by doing this we are more likely to determine students' true level, than by administering tests of unassisted performance.

> Very often, teachers wait for children to demonstrate completely formed functions; teachers think that they can lead a child to the next step only after they have seen evidence that the child has successfully acquired the function taught at the previous step. As a result, children are limited in their learning opportunities to those that correspond to their level of independent performance. In other words, teachers who follow this standard practice minimize the student's ZPD by almost closing it. On the contrary, ideally, the ZPD should be wide open, so that it can expand developmentally appropriate practices up to the level of assisted performance. (Grigorenko, 1998: 212)

Vygotsky's view that what learners can do at lower levels should not limit opportunities for their development of higher psychological functions was almost certainly influenced by his experience of working at a boarding school for children who were both deaf and blind. He claimed that education targeted on the formation of higher mental processes could help people overcome, or compensate for, deficits because it equipped them with adaptive strategies that might be unique for each person.

All of these ideas have implications for assessment. Practical applications of Vygotsky's theories have been developed in versions of 'dynamic assessment'. Some forms of dynamic assessment have been described as little more than superior intelligence tests, but there are clinical versions (Elliott et al., 2010) that use 'hint structures' in scaffolded instruction to maximize feelings of competence and efficacy. This affects test reliability, in a psychometric sense, although advocates claim that these concerns are less important than the quality of the insights that result and the likely magnitude of change in a learner's performance (i.e. their validity). Dynamic assessments of this nature are currently used in one-to-one situations, usually with students with learning difficulties, therefore they are often felt to be impractical for wider application. However, the principles could well be adapted for everyday use by teachers if they were to be integrated with instructional strategies. Moreover they could serve both formative and summative assessment purposes although the formative would take priority. In this sense, versions of dynamic assessment could provide tools for formative assessment integrated into pedagogy.

Suggestions for socio-cultural assessment practice

As noted earlier, much current assessment practice derives from behaviourist or differentialist approaches, many of which are now rejected as 'learning theories' except in very limited senses. Pellegrino et al.'s (2001) important work provides both the underpinning theory and practical examples of more valuable forms of assessment based on sound cognitive science. An Open University Reader (Murphy, 1999) covers some of the debates that have led to socio-cultural approaches gaining ground in education but notes 'a mismatch between curriculum and assessment rhetoric and teaching and learning practice' (1999: xiii). In the absence of detailed guidance on what classroom assessment might look like if it were informed by socio-cultural theory, I (James, 2008: 31) have offered the following pointers to what I have styled 'third generation assessment':

- If learning cannot be separated from the actions in which it is embodied, then assessment too must be 'situated'.
- Assessment alongside learning implies that it needs to be done by the community rather than by external assessors.
- Assessment of group learning is as important as the learning of the individual.
- 'In vivo' studies of complex problem solving may be the most appropriate form for assessments to take. (Some ethnographic methods could be used, including methods for assuring quality of inferences from evidence.)
- The focus should be on how well people exercise 'agency' in their use of the resources or tools (intellectual, human, material) to formulate problems, work productively and evaluate their efforts. This would be a proper justification for course-work assignments with students having access to source materials, because it is the way that these are used that is of most significance.
- Learning outcomes can be captured and reported through various forms of recording, including narrative accounts and audio- and visual media. The portfolio has an important role here.
- Evaluation needs to be more holistic and qualitative, not atomized and quantified as in measurement approaches.

Two examples

Given the preceding discussion, it is not surprising that paradigm examples of a socio-cultural approach to assessment are difficult to find. There is still much work to be done to find ways of bringing assessment into better alignment with some of the most powerful ideas in contemporary learning theory. Nevertheless, two initiatives, one in United States high schools and the other in an infants' school in the East of England, illustrate some possibilities at school and local level. System-wide applications are still somewhat distant.

Performances and exhibitions from the US Coalition of Essential Schools

The Coalition of Essential Schools (CES) was founded by Theodore Sizer, who aims to create and sustain schools that are personalized, equitable, and intellectually challenging. Rejecting the behaviourism that had long dominated approaches to assessment in the US, Sizer (1992) promotes a model of alternative authentic assessment based on ongoing performances or 'exit' exhibitions in which learning outcomes across disciplines might be demonstrated and evaluated. The exhibition is intended to bring together a number of important dimensions of learning and meaningful assessment.

- It asks students to work across disciplines in a respectful way by creating 'real' learning activities. The dominant metaphor is 'student-as-worker'.
- Tasks are not necessarily devised by teachers; students can devise them for themselves, providing they understand the principles that underlie their construction. Helping students to acquire this meta-level understanding is a valued pedagogical objective.
- It asks students to practise using accumulated knowledge and apply it to new situations.
- It insists on effective communication in a number of forms of expression: oral, written and graphic.
- It requires that students be reflective, persistent and well organised.
- It creates a focus for learning by describing the destination for their journey, although precise learning objectives are not tightly pre-specified. The teachers hope to be delighted and surprised by the learning that their students demonstrate.

An outline for an exhibition is given in Figure 12.1.

Discuss behavior patterns as reflected in the insect world, in animals, in human beings, and in literature. Be sure to include references to your course work over the term in Inquiry and Expression, Literature and the Arts, Social Studies, and Science. This may include Macbeth, the drug prevention and communication workshop, Stephen Crane's poetry, 'A Modest Proposal' and other essays you have studied, Mark Twain's fiction, and behaviors you have observed in our School-within-a-School. You may also add references to what you have read about in the news recently.

Procedure

Day one of the exam: You will be given four periods in which to brainstorm, make an outline, write a rough draft, and write a final copy in standard composition form. You will be graded not only on how well you assimilate the material but also how well you reflect the 'student as worker' metaphor and how responsibly you act during the testing period.

Day two of the exam: You will assemble in villages of three, evaluate anonymous papers according to a set of criteria, and come to a consensus about a grade. Each paper will be evaluated by at least two groups and two instructors. Again, a part of your overall semester grade will have to do with how responsibly you act and how well you demonstrate the 'student as worker' metaphor.

(Thanks to Melinda Nickle at Springdale High School, Springdale, Arkansas.)

Figure 12.1 A Final Performance Across the Disciplines

Source: http://www.essentialschools.org/resources/123

Grant Wiggins, the former director of research at the CES, described such 'authentic assessments' as having the following intellectual design features:

- They are 'essential'- not needlessly intrusive, arbitrary, or designed to 'shake out' a grade.
- They are 'enabling'- constructed to point the student towards more sophisticated use of the skills or knowledge.
- They are contextualized, complex intellectual challenges, not 'atomized' tasks corresponding to isolated 'outcomes'.
- They involve the student's own research or use of knowledge, for which 'content' is a means.
- They assess student habits and repertoires, not mere recall or plug-in skills.
- They are representative challenges – designed to emphasise depth more than breadth.
- They are engaging and educational.
- They involve somewhat ambiguous tasks or problems.

Given the multi-disciplinary nature of the exhibition, it is evaluated by a panel of assessors made up of the teacher who acted as the main tutor or supervisor of the work, another adult but not necessarily a teacher (a business representative might be appropriate), and a peer of the student's own choice. The student is aware of the broad criteria by which the exhibition will be assessed because these are negotiated at the beginning of preparation for the task. About 50 minutes is allocated to each exhibition, half of which is devoted to the student's presentations and the other half to discussion with the panel. The panel would be expected to ask penetrating questions about what has been learned, the completed research, reflections on the work covered and its relationship to the broader field, tentative hypotheses and ideas about further work, and reflections on the learning process itself (meta-learning). In some ways this process can be compared to the *viva voce* for the award of PhD degrees in the UK. Indeed, Sizer claims: 'It began in the eighteenth century, as the exit demonstration in New England academies and in colleges like Harvard. The student was expected to perform, recite, dispute, and answer challenges in public session'.[1]

Third generation assessment in an infants' school in England

Jenny Lewis, a teacher at Recreation Road Infant School, Norwich, attended a talk on assessment and learning that I gave in 2006. She made a connection between my speculative account of a socio-cultural approach to assessment, which I labelled 'third generation assessment', and an approach to curriculum development and pedagogy that she had been developing with colleagues in her school. She returned to her school and, with the support of Luke Abbott, a senior local authority adviser, set up an action research project to investigate whether it was possible to develop assessment practices that are in harmony with her chosen pedagogy. The following is an edited version of her account of the project.[2] The version here is reproduced with her permission.

> I am a Year 2 teacher in a large Infant School (4 form entry) near the centre of Norwich. I initially conducted my research with my own class, but then extended the project to include other colleagues. The school has a creative, flexible and emergent curriculum and we use thinking skills, philosophy, drama and inquiry based learning to underpin our teaching and learning. My head actively promotes adult learning, innovation and risk taking and has been involved in the action research group as part of a drive to create a model of excellence in our school approach to formative assessment.
>
> Several colleagues involved in the project, including myself, use a pedagogic system called Mantle of the Expert (MoE). MoE is an

approach to learning devised by education and drama practitioner Dorothy Heathcote. Children and teachers work together to create an imaginary community within which they function as if they were experts, for example mountain rescuers or archaeologists. As the work progresses many possibilities begin to emerge which the learning community uses to define and deepen the imaginary world and explore the lives of the people that inhabit it. The community engages in a series of collaborative tasks, often motivated by a client's demands, with teamwork, communication and problem solving central to the process.

There is a group responsibility for the project as it progresses and the children act and make decisions with responsibility and authority, tackling authentic issues that seem purposeful and urgent to them. Over the last three years I have worked with a team of practitioners, guided by Luke Abbott, on developing the use of MoE as a pedagogy in the classroom.[3]

One of the two Year 2 classes that I taught during this project worked as a salvage company responsible for exploring the sunken *Titanic*. Some of the colleagues involved in the action research group were running their own MoE projects and others were working with their classes on a range of other inquiry-based learning experiences. We all employed a range of assessment for learning systems to trial with our classes and collected evidence to report back to the group. The group then discussed and reflected on these practices and worked collectively to relate them to Mary James's 3G model.

My personal aim was to develop a cyclical and meaningful assessment system based on the third generation model that worked both for me, and the children. I needed a system that was achievable, relevant and based firmly on a socio-cultural view of learning.

Some of the assessment practices we used are standard AfL practices used in many schools and they combine 2G (cognitive constructivist) and 3G (socio-cultural) elements. We have sometimes adapted these to make them more aligned with 3G assessment principles. Others are combinations of our own ideas and those of other researchers and practitioners. The following show the range of assessment practices we trialled:

1   Dialogue as an integral part of ongoing work involving the whole class, groups or pairs of children, with or without an adult.

2   A Blog Diary recording the day-to-day life of our shipwreck salvage company (MoE) October 2006 – May 2007. (This can be

viewed at: http://theseacompany.blogspot.com/) This was a diary, recorded on a blog-site, so that it was available for anyone to read as our MoE project work progressed. Although time consuming to construct it was an invaluable way of recording and reflecting upon the learning of the class community. It revealed that assessment could happen alongside learning and not as an 'after learning event', as in a plenary session at the end of the day! An additional advantage of the blog-site was that the work became open to a wider community so that children, parents and other teachers were able to find out about and understand the learning that has taken place. Comments have been posted from across the world.

3   An ongoing portfolio containing notes and reflections plus a range of collected evidence (annotated photos, self-assessments, transcriptions of dialogue from Dictaphone, video evidence, pieces of work, etc.).

4   Individual learning diaries kept by the children.

5   Daily sessions focusing on meta-learning. The children interact with a puppet (Sniffles the Hopeless Hamster) in a dialogue concerning Guy Claxton's '5 Rs': resilience, reflection, resourcefulness, responsibility and relationships. The children know that Sniffles finds learning difficult and doesn't understand how to put the 5Rs into action so the children help him out by giving him lots of advice.

6   Variety of self/peer assessment tools: easy – hard continuum; hot spot assessments; self-evaluation grids; end of year individual/group evaluations.

7   Home/school contact books contributed to by teacher, children and parents.

8   Learning Surgeries. Someone volunteers a problem they have encountered and the rest of the group offer their tips and ideas.

9   Connections. At the end of a day or a week we brainstorm all the areas of learning we have covered and begin to make connections. These could be between one area of learning and another, or between an area of learning and the wider world.

10 Questionnaires involving parents and children.

11 Evidence of children's work. I see children's workbooks as ongoing working documents. A piece of totally independent work next to a piece of adult supported work can be incredibly useful.

12 Personal Social and Health Education (PSHE) linked assessments: The Blob Tree; The Circle of Courage; Feelings Wall.

We believe that wellbeing and recognition of feelings and emotions have a huge impact on the way children learn and therefore on the way in which we can help them to understand and move forward in their learning. These tools help the children develop an emotional vocabulary.

13 Mind Maps®.

14 Peer teaching.

I am aware that many of the assessment practices we have trialled have a mixture of 2G (cognitivist) and 3G (socio-cultural) elements, although the use of situated dialogue, the blog and the portfolio, are very much 3G tools. Also, like any other school, we are required to assess our children in relation to National Curriculum levels, which is a standard 1G (behaviourist) procedure.

Mary James (2008) concludes her article with the question 'Can all three generations of assessment practice be housed under the same roof? Is inter-generational conflict inevitable?'

I believe that it is possible to house the different elements under the same roof and to blend and bond those key elements. If the statutory (1G) elements are kept to providing NC levels in English, maths and science, we can, as teachers who know our NC, provide this information relatively easily, however little validity we feel they have as an effective way of assessing children's learning.

I still feel, however, that teachers and schools who are determined to assess what they value, can find a way to keep deep learning and formative assessment at the heart of what they do. Many of the 2G/3G assessment tools we have trialled are quick and easy to implement. Formative assessment as ongoing, situated dialogue and reflection is part of all good primary practice and, just because it may not always be recorded, does not mean that it should be less valued. Some of the other tools we have used, especially the blog and transcriptions of dialogue from a Dictaphone, are much more time-consuming. No one would be able to manage to implement the whole range of tools we have worked on in one classroom. It would be up to headteachers and individual teachers to decide which are the most effective assessment tools to use for them. I always use the '2 M' rule – assessment should be meaningful and manageable!

Discussion

What are the important features of these examples? First, assessment does not drive the curriculum or pedagogy. It starts from a strong belief

Children

'All our little ideas have made one big, fantastic idea.'

'It's like real life – there's big trouble! We can learn about solving problems.'

'It's exciting because anything can happen.'

'It's fascinating. You get to learn about things much more. You're learning things while you're having big adventures.'

'You can pretend to do things you can't do in real life.'

'I think it's brilliant because there are so many dilemmas and adventures that never end. I learnt about myself that I keep trying until I get it perfect.'

'I like it because it seems so real. I'm learning about other people and how to work as a team.'

Parents

'He will talk about what he has learned without prompting which isn't normal.

He is excited about the way you are teaching him which is brilliant!'

'She's definitely motivated by this type of learning – there's obviously a great deal of enthusiasm for this project, not to mention the excitement factor. She is always pleased to tell us she will be doing company work today. It's almost role reversal and she's become the adult!'

'It extends and challenges her way beyond the classroom.'

'It's very important for her, as an only child, to learn to work in a team situation. It has stimulated her to ask various questions she might not have asked about before.'

'There are lots of exciting things to do – we've heard all about who is doing what in the company, about diving – looking at the real gear – and about the history of the Titanic. We've taped TV documentaries and looked up things in books to feed the interest developed.'

'It encourages imagination and broadens their horizons – most 7 year olds would probably never give any thought to the considerations of running a company.'

'It seems to give school work a purpose.'

Figure 12.2 Some responses from children and parents to the Titanic salvage company work

about worthwhile learning outcomes and learning experiences and how these are best achieved through authentic, collaborative problem-solving tasks. They illustrate how teachers search for assessment models and practices to support their educational goals and the processes of learning they value. Secondly, they possess a broad conception of 'community' and the roles that various actors, within and beyond the school, have to play both in learning and assessment. This shift will be vitally important if there is to be any hope of creating models of assessment more congruent with our current best understanding of the learning process and its outcomes. The dominance of psychometric models must, in large measure, be attributable to the fact that parents, employers, policy makers, the media and the general public do not really understand what goes on in classrooms. Therefore they are wedded to proxy measures of learning and achievement that have doubtful validity. If the community can be more directly involved, then confidence in teachers' assessments and students' self-assessments can be strengthened. The potential to use the blogosphere, to communicate and assess learning by creating dialogue with near and distant communities, is particularly exciting. Of course, there are problems to be overcome but pursuing the possibilities associated with the Web may be more fruitful than much of the current effort put into the (commercial) development of e-assessments based on quite different models of learning.

The list of characteristics of third generation assessment practices, given above, indicates possibilities for forms of assessment in sympathy with valued teaching and learning practices in schools and workplaces. It is especially suited to the assessment of collaborative group work on complex, extended projects that have a level of authenticity not available to tests. This could make it attractive to employers who increasingly claim they are interested in recruits who can demonstrate their capability to work in teams to find creative solutions to complex problems. It is significant, however, that one of the examples given here comes from an infants' school, where National Curriculum Assessment is based on teachers' judgements rather than formal external testing. At other stages of schooling in England, the challenges of developing new approaches, within a system dominated by high-stakes external tests and formal examinations, based on entirely different models, are much greater. The key challenge will be to devise new assessment practices that can command confidence, and meet the range of needs of diverse users of assessment information, when large numbers of students are involved and when those who are interested in the outcomes of such learning cannot participate in the activities that generate them.

Although socio-cultural approaches can make claims for greater validity, they are a long way from providing convincing assurances about the reliability of assessment results. Nevertheless, apprenticeship models, from which many socio-cultural ideas derive, may offer solutions because underpinning such models is the concept of the 'community of practice' – the guild which is the guardian and arbiter of developing standards. In other words, validation of standards by a community of experts, or, at least, 'more expert others', may be a way of assuring quality.[4] Furthermore, the dialogue and interaction, which socio-cultural approaches prioritise, promise profound educational (formative) benefits because, in assessment conversations between students and their teachers and peers, they can deepen their understanding of what counts as appropriate responses to problems or tasks, what counts as quality and how criteria for judgement are interpreted and applied in complex activities (Sadler, 2010). Clearly, more work needs to be done to develop approaches to assessment that are coherent with socio-cultural perspectives on learning, but the potential is there.

Notes

1   The source of this example and the quotations is Cushman (1990).
2   Jenny's complete report can be downloaded from http://www.mantleoftheexpert.com/category/articles/ (accessed 20th February 2011).
3   MOE has a website at http://www.mantleoftheexpert.com (accessed 20th February 2011).
4   Within UK vocational education, systems of internal and external assessors and verifiers have attempted to do this although large-scale systems almost inevitably become bureaucratic, unwieldy and reductive.

References

Biggs, J.B. (1996) 'Enhancing teaching through constructive alignment', *Higher Education*, 32: 347–64.

Biggs, J. and Tang, C. (1997) 'Assessment by portfolio: constructing learning and designing teaching', paper presented at the annual conference of the Higher Education Research and Development Society of Australasia, Adelaide, July.

Bransford, J.D., Brown, A.L. and Cocking, R. (eds) (2000) *How People Learn: Brain, Mind, Experience, and School*. Washington, DC: National Academy Press.

Bredo, E. (1997) 'The Social Construction of Learning', in G.D. Phye (ed.) *Handbook of Academic Learning: Construction of Knowledge*. San Diego, CA: Academic Press.

Bruner, J. (1996) *The Culture of Education*. Cambridge, MA: Harvard University Press.

Cushman, K. (1990) 'Performance and exhibitions: the demonstration of mastery', paper posted at http://www.essentialschools.org.resources/123, accessed 10th September 2011.

Edwards, A. (2005) 'Let's get beyond community and practice: the many meanings of learning by participating', *The Curriculum Journal*, 16(1): 49–65.

Elliott, J., Grigorenko, E. and Resing, W. (2010) 'Dynamic Assessment', in P. Peterson, E. Baker and B. McGaw (eds) *International Encyclopedia of Education*. Vol. 3. Oxford: Elsevier.

Engeström, Y. (1999). 'Activity theory and individual and social transformation', in Y. Engeström, R. Miettinen and R-L. Punamäki (eds) *Perspectives on Activity Theory*. Cambridge: Cambridge University Press.

Greeno, J.G., Pearson, P.D., and Schoenfeld, A.H. (1996) *Implications for NAEP of Research on Learning and Cognition. Report of a Study Commissioned by the National Academy of Education*. Panel on the NAEP Trial State Assessment, conducted by the Institute for Research on Learning. Stanford, CA: National Academy of Education.

Grigorenko, E. (1998) 'Mastering tools of the mind in school (trying out Vygotsky's ideas in classrooms)', in R. Sternberg and W. Williams (eds) *Intelligence, Instruction and Assessment: Theory and Practice*. Mahwah, NJ: Erlbaum. pp. 201–44.

Harlen, W. (2004) *A Systematic Review of the Evidence of Impact on Students, Teachers and the Curriculum of the Process of Using Assessment by Teachers for Summative Purposes*. London Institute of Education: EPPI-Centre.

James, M. (2006) 'Assessment, teaching and theories of learning', in J. Gardner (ed.) *Assessment and Learning*. London: Sage.

James, M. (2008) 'Assessment and learning', in S. Swaffield, *Unlocking Assessment: Understanding for Reflection and Application*. Abingdon: Routledge (David Fulton). pp. 20–35.

James, M. (2010) 'An overview of educational assessment', in P. Peterson, E. Baker and B. McGaw (eds) *International Encyclopedia of Education*. Vol. 3 Oxford: Elsevier. pp. 161–71.

James, M. and Brown, S. (2005) 'Grasping the TLRP nettle: preliminary analysis and some enduring issues surrounding the improvement of learning outcomes', *The Curriculum Journal*, 16(1): 7–30.

James, M. and Pollard, A. (2011) 'TLRP's ten principles for effective pedagogy: rationale, development, evidence, argument and impact', *Research Papers in Education*, (Special Issue), 26(3): 275–328. Also published in James, M. and Pollard, A. (eds) (2011) *Principles for Effective Pedagogy: International responses to evidence from the UK Teaching and Learning Research Programme*. Abingdon: Routledge.

James, M., McCormick, R., Black, P., Carmichael, P., Drummond, M-J., Fox, A., MacBeath, J., Marshall, B., Pedder, D., Procter, R., Swaffield, S., Swann, J. and Wiliam, D. (2007) *Improving Learning How to Learn – Classrooms, Schools and Networks*. London: Routledge.

Lave, J. and Wenger, E. (1991) *Situated Learning: Legitimate Peripheral Participation*. Cambridge: Cambridge University Press.

Murphy, P. (ed.) (1999) *Learners, Learning and Assessment*. London: Paul Chapman Publishing.

Pellegrino, J.W., Chudowsky, N. and Glaser, R. (eds) (2001) *Knowing what Students Know: The Science and Design of Educational Assessment*. Washington, DC: National Academy Press.

Peterson, P., Baker, E. and McGaw, B. (eds) (2010) *International Encyclopedia of Education*. Oxford: Elsevier.

Rogoff, B. (1990) *Apprenticeship in Thinking: Cognitive Development in Social Context*. New York: Oxford University Press.

Sadler, D. R. (2010) 'Beyond feedback: Developing student capability in complex appraisal', *Assessment & Evaluation in Higher Education*, 35(5): 535–50.

Sfard, A. (1998) 'On two metaphors of learning and the dangers of choosing just one', *Educational Researcher*, 27: 4–13.

Sizer, T. (1992) *Horace's School: Redesigning the American High School*. New York: Houghton Mifflin.

Watkins, C. (2003) *Learning: A Sense-Maker's Guide*. London: Association of Teachers and Lecturers.

Wenger, E. (1998) *Communities of Practice*. Cambridge: Cambridge University Press.

Vygotsky, L.S. (1978) *Mind in Society: The Development of Higher Psychological Process*. Cambridge, MA: Harvard University Press.

Chapter 13

Developing a Theory of Formative Assessment

Paul Black and Dylan Wiliam

Introduction

The descriptions in Chapter 2 present a range of learning activities through which the potential benefits of formative assessment might be achieved. The account there is, in the main, pragmatic and practical. This chapter explores the theoretical underpinning of these activities, for three reasons. The first is to provide a clear rationale for the activities, and to connect them with the research evidence that suggests that such activities are likely to be effective in promoting student achievement. The second is that without an understanding of the theoretical basis of the activities, there is a danger that the adaptations that every teacher must necessarily make to implement the activities in their classrooms will render the activities less effective – what Ed Haertel has termed 'lethal mutations' (Brown and Campione, 1996). The third is that a clear theoretical framing of these activities may suggest ways in which they may be evaluated, and further improved.

The next section below presents a first step with a scheme to inter-link the different activities. This illustrates the centrality of the teacher's role in the classroom, and the subsequent section explores what we regard as the fundamental core activity of formative work – the enrichment of interactive dialogue. A crucial and most difficult part of that enterprise is the task of interpreting the learner's responses to any question or task: this is discussed in detail in the next section. The two sections which follow this look at the broader features which set the context and determine the general direction for this interactive dialogue, discussing in turn the general learning aims, and aims which are specific to different school subjects. The penultimate section then considers the other main agents of learning in the classrooms – the learners themselves. A final section summarizes the argument and indicates some of the difficulties and limitations of our present understanding.

Classroom activities

Teachers and learners

There are many lenses through which we might look at classrooms. For the purposes of this chapter, the idea that a classroom can be understood as a 'community of practice' (Lave and Wenger, 1991; Wenger, 1998) or as a 'figured world' (Holland et al., 1998) provides particularly helpful insights. In both these perspectives, the focus is not so much on 'what is' but rather on what the various actors involved take things to be:

> By 'figured world,' then, we mean a socially and culturally constructed realm of interpretation in which particular characters and actors are recognized, significance is attached to certain acts, and particular outcomes are valued over others. Each is a simplified world populated by a set of agents ... who engage in a limited range of meaningful acts or changes of state ... as moved by a specific set of forces. (Holland et al. 1998: 52)

In the classroom, the actors or agents involved are, of course, the teacher and the students, all of whom exercise agency to a greater or lesser extent, within the constraints and affordances they perceive to be present. This means that their actions are to be interpreted in terms of their perceptions of the structure in which they have to operate, in particular the significance they attach to beliefs or actions through which they engage, that is the ways in which they, as agents, interact with the other agents and forces. These ways may inhibit or encourage any changes, notably those required for successful formative assessment, in which case both teachers and students would have to change the roles that they have adopted. To explore that perspective further, it is necessary to consider the roles of teachers and students in a formative classroom.

Formative activities – a rationale

In Chapter 2, we suggested that formative assessment may be implemented through four main types of activity:

- Classroom dialogue (including discussion);
- Comment-only marking;
- Peer- and self-assessment;
- Formative use of summative tests.

However, precisely how these activities are connected to the central idea of formative assessment was not clearly articulated. A theoretical foundation that does this would clarify both the connection of each of these types of activity to the central idea of formative assessment, and might also indicate relationships between these kinds of activities. It could also go some way to addressing whether these four collectively exhaust the domain of formative assessment practice.

In order to provide a better theoretical grounding for formative assessment, Wiliam and Thompson (2007), drawing on Ramaprasad (1983) and Sadler (1989), highlighted three key processes in learning and teaching:

- Establishing where the learners are in their learning;
- Establishing where they are going;
- Establishing what needs to be done to get them there.

Whilst the teacher clearly has some responsibility for each of these three, it is also necessary to consider the role that the learners themselves, and their peers, play in them. Indeed, the peer- and self-assessment activity introduces two distinctive elements. One is that understanding the success criteria – where they are going – through applying them to one's work, is a crucial foundation for self-assessment. The other is that it is helpful to consider separately the roles of the peer-community of learners and of each student as an individual.

The teacher is responsible for designing and implementing an effective learning environment, and the learner is responsible for the learning within that environment. Furthermore, since the responsibility for learning rests with *both* the teacher *and* the learner, it is incumbent on each to do all they can to mitigate the impact of any failures of the other.

Crossing Ramaprasad's three processes with the different agents, that is teacher, peer and learner, suggests the framework of Figure 13.1 (from Wiliam and Thompson, 2007) which indicates that formative assessment can be conceptualized as consisting of five key strategies.

	Where the learner is going	Where the learner is right now	How to get there
Teacher	1 Clarifying learning intentions and criteria for success	2 Engineering effective classroom discussions and other learning tasks that elicit evidence of student understanding	3 Providing feedback that moves learners forward
Peer	Understanding and sharing learning intentions and criteria for success	4 Activating students as instructional resources for one another	
Learner	Understanding learning intentions and criteria for success	5 Activating students as the owners of their own learning	

Figure 13.1 Aspects of formative assessment (from Wiliam and Thompson, 2007; see also Chapter 4)

The next two sections will discuss in turn activities 2 and 3. Activity 1 will then be analyzed more closely in two further sections, after which will be a section devoted to activities 4 and 5.

The teacher's role in interactive dialogue

In a typical classroom interaction, the teacher addresses a task to the learner, perhaps in the form of a question, the learner responds to this, and the teacher then composes a further intervention, in the light of that response. This basic structure has been described as initiation–response–evaluation or I–R–E (Mehan, 1979), but this structure could represent either a genuinely dialogical process, or one in which students are relegated to a supporting role.

In a dialogical interaction, a crucial step is the teacher's interpretation of the students' responses – which will then lead to a decision about the best response. This decision by the teacher is first of all a strategic one, in that it can only be taken in the light of the overall purpose for which the original task was designed. There is then a tactical decision: how to formulate the detail of the response to best serve the overall strategy. This account applies both to one-on-one tutoring and to the classroom where many learners are involved, through hearing the exchange, perhaps by joining in, so that there may be many teacher–learner and learner–learner interactions.

However, there is evidence (Applebee et al., 2003; Hardman et al., 2003; Smith et al., 2004) that in most classrooms the teacher's use of the I–R–E format is not formative. The teacher asks students to supply missing words or phrases in the teacher's exposition of the material – and the teacher's attention is focused on the correctness of the student's response. In this scenario, the teacher's next action will be aimed at getting the student to make a correct response, through such encouraging responses as, 'Almost' or 'Nearly'.

The assessment initiatives of our project, which emphasized that I-R-E could not encourage learning, led many teachers to think about their teaching in new ways. One teacher described the changes as follows:

> I now think more about the content of the lesson. The influence has shifted from 'What am I going to teach and what are the pupils going to do?' towards 'How am I doing to teach this and what are the pupils going to learn?' (Susan, Waterford School)

Another teacher (see also Chapter 2) noted:

> There was a definite transition at some point, from focusing on what I was putting into the process, to what the pupils were contributing. It became obvious that one way to make a significant sustainable change was to get the pupils doing more of the thinking. I then began to search for ways to make the learning process more transparent to the pupils. Indeed I now spend my time looking for ways to get pupils to take responsibility for their learning at the same time making the learning more collaborative. This inevitably leads to more interactive learning activities in the classroom. (Tom, Riverside School)

It is clear from these quotations that the teachers were also engaged in relating to their students in new ways. It is tempting to characterize these changes as representing a transfer of the responsibility for the learning from the teacher to the student, but the danger with such a characterization is that it can be taken as indicating that the teacher no longer has any responsibility. Accordingly, we describe this as a process of sharing with the students the responsibility for their learning, but by this we have in mind a clear division of responsibilities. Only the learner can create learning, but the teacher has a responsibility to design the learning environment so as to achieve the intended learning, including the steps teachers take to make the learning interesting and engaging to the students. Of course, such steps can only go so far, but we feel it is important to acknowledge the distinct roles that teachers and students play in creating effective learning.

This sharing of responsibility led teachers to give enhanced priority to the need to equip students with the cognitive strategies required to achieve the transition to the new understandings and skills potentially accessible through the subject matter. This implied placing more emphasis on cognitive and meta-cognitive skills and strategies than is usually done in schools. Such changes were evident in the shifts in questioning, in the skilful use of comment on homework, and in the new approach to the use of tests as part of the learning process. It is significant that, a few months into the project, the teachers asked the research team to give them a talk on theories of learning, a topic that we would have judged too 'academic' at the start of the project.

Some teachers have seemed quite comfortable with this sharing of responsibility with students, and the implications for the change in the student's role, and in the character of the teacher–student relationships, are clear. However, others found such changes threatening rather than exciting. Detailed exploration of the trajectories of development of different teachers (see e.g. Black et al., 2003; Lee and Wiliam, 2005) show that the changes have been seen as a loss of control of the learning by some who were trying seriously to implement them. Although one can argue that, objectively, the teacher's control was going to be just as strong and just as essential, subjectively it did not feel like that to these teachers, in part because it implied a change in their conception of how learning is mediated by a teacher.

In summary, the nature of the interaction between teacher and student is a central feature in any study of formative assessment. As already pointed out, our starting position was based in part on the seminal paper of Sadler (1989) on formative assessment. One main feature of his model was an argument that the learner's task is to close the gap between the present state of understanding and the learning goal, that self-assessment is essential if the learner is to be able to do this, and that the teacher's role is to communicate appropriate goals and to promote self-assessment as students work towards them. In this process, feedback in the classroom should operate both from teacher to students and from students to the teacher.

Perrenoud (1998) criticized the treatment of feedback in our 1998 review. Whilst we do not accept some of his interpretations of that paper, his plea that the concept of feedback be treated more broadly, as noted earlier, is a valuable comment. The features to which he draws attention are:

- the nature of the feedback and the cognitive and socio-affective mechanisms activated in the students;
- its inclusion in a contract and didactic organization, and globally in classroom management and a teaching relationship;

- its links with a concept of learning and teaching;
- the degree of individualization and its relevance; and, especially
- the means and effects involved in the regulation of the learning processes. (Perrenoud, 1998: 85–6)

Some aspects of these points have already been alluded to above. However, a more detailed discussion is called for, which will be set out in the following sections.

The analyses of both Sadler and Perrenoud can be understood in the light of the following comment on the management of students' learning:

I would like to suggest several ways forward, based on distinguishing two levels of the management of situations which favour the interactive regulation of learning processes:

- the first relates to the setting up of such situations through much larger mechanisms and classroom management.
- the second relates to interactive regulation which takes place through didactic situations. (Perrenoud, 1998: 92)

The teachers' comments quoted above suggested a shift from the regulation of activity ('what are the students going to do?') to the regulation of learning ('what are the students going to learn?'). Moreover, this regulation occurred at two distinct levels. At the first level, the desire to improve formative assessment forces changes in the prior planning of lessons. The teachers planned the questions and tasks they would use in the classroom with a view to creating 'didactic situations' – in other words, they specifically designed these questions and tasks so that they generated 'teachable moments' – occasions when the teacher could usefully intervene to further learning. Thus the fine grain of such intervention has to be examined closely: this issue will be taken up in the next section. A subsequent section will look more closely at learning aims, for these aims determine the strategy for 'management of situations' and for 'clear communication of the learning goals'.

How can teachers interpret the learner's responses?

In a formative mode the teacher's initial prompt is designed to encourage more thought. The learners are more actively involved, but their responses are not predictable; thus formative interaction is a *contingent* activity. In such situations, the teacher's attention must be focused on what she or he can learn about the student's thinking from their response. However, what the learner actually hears and interprets is not necessarily what the teacher intended to convey, and what the teacher hears and interprets is not necessarily what the student intended to convey. In a genuinely dialogic process, the teacher's own thinking may come to be modified through the exchange (see also Davis, 1997).

The need for a model

Perrenoud, in his response to our 1998 review, identified the same problem as follows: 'Without a theoretical model of the mediations through which an interactive situation influences cognition, and in particular the learning process, we can observe thousands of situations without being able to draw any conclusions.' (1998: 95). Yet in so far as the teacher's focus is on intervention to regulate the learning activity, any intervention has to involve: 'an incursion into the representation and thought processes of the pupil to accelerate a breakthrough in understanding a new point of view or the shaping of a notion which can immediately become operative' (Perrenoud, 1998: 97).

Sadler also discusses this complex activity (1998): he describes the resources that a teacher brings to formative interactions, pointing out that:

> Teachers bring evaluative skill or expertise in having made judgments about student efforts on similar tasks in the past. ... In non-convergent learning environments, this automatically exposes teachers to a wide variety of ways in which students approach problem solving, and how they argue, evaluate, create, analyse and synthesise. (1998: 81)

This complexity presents teachers with a formidable problem, since their feedback needs to be constructed in the light of some insight into the mental life that lies behind the student's utterances. Indeed, as we have noted elsewhere (Black et al., 2003), it was surprising to us how many teachers had functioned reasonably effectively in the classroom for many years, and were widely regarded as good teachers without having developed such insights.

The self-regulated learning model

A promising example of an approach which could meet Perrenoud's requirement for 'theoretical models of the mediation', are theories that come under the general description of self-regulated learning (SRL). One aspect of these is analyzed by Boekaerts and Corno (2005).

In framing a response to any task, a student may pursue the purpose of achieving learning goals that increase resources, that is knowledge and both cognitive and social skills. This process is motivated and steered by personal interest, values and expected satisfaction and rewards, and may be characterized as the *growth* option. However, the student may not do this, but rather seek competitive performance goals or prioritize friendship with peers, which may put at risk a focus on learning goals. This may be triggered by some types of classroom feedback and reward, or merely by boredom. When cues from the environment have this effect, this second option is adopted – that of giving priority to *well-being*. In this perspective, students' responses may be interpreted as adopting one or other of the *growth track* and the *well-being track*, with the possibility of switching to and fro between the two *en route*. Such analysis takes further the discussion in Chapter 12 of assessment and motivation for learning.

A different aspect of the SRL approach (Greene and Azevedo, 2007) draws on information processing theory to propose a representation of the internal processes involved in a learner response. The main elements may be represented, in simplified form, as follows:

1 Identifying a task   A Conditions (of learner and context)

2 Planning a response   B Operations to transform input and own data

3 Enacting a strategy   C Standards: criteria for self-appraisal

4 Adapting: reviewing,   D Evaluation
   perhaps re-cycling

The model combines two kinds of influences: the left hand column represents the stages 1 to 4 of the production of a response whilst the right-hand column represents the various resources, A, B, C or D, which might be brought to bear during these stages. Central to the model is the learner's overall control and monitoring function that steers progress through the stages of production.

Whilst the four stages on the left set out an obvious sequence of activity, it is emphasized that in any phase, the overall control and monitoring function may lead to the work being re-cycled, either after the phase itself, or after evaluation of another phase. A learner may revise her/his definition of the task because of a judgement made in the light of difficulty in phase 3, that it may take too much time, or because the challenge of the original definition implied a high risk of failure, and so start afresh with a revised task definition. On the other hand, if (say) the outcome of phases 1 and 2 is incompetent, but is not perceived as such, then the performance outcome of phase 3 will proceed: if the result then seems to be inadequate, the learner may *Adapt*, that is, undertake a more comprehensively re-cycling, changing both the *Task Identification* and the choice of *Operation* to enact a very different strategy. Such examples will suffice to indicate that multiple and varied cycles may ensue before an outcome is produced.

However, each of 1, 2, 3 and 4 could be associated with any or all of A, B, C, D. Feature A, the *Conditions*, is a broad category comprising the resources available to a person and the constraints inherent in a task or environment. The resources will include past experiences recalled, beliefs, dispositions, motivation, and knowledge of the domain, of the current task and of relevant tactics and strategies, together with a more immediate appraisal of conditions, the time, instructional cues and local context, which are all external to the person.

It follows that *Conditions* influence both the *Operations* and the *Standards* that the learner will deploy. The perspectives formulated at the outset will be transformed in each phase by the *Operations*: these include the searching, assembling, rehearsing and translating processes. Both the ease with which the student can perform these, and the memory capacity on which they draw, are limiting factors here. It is a feature of the model that it is assumed that meta-cognition is not involved in these operations. The learner's *Standards* will depend in part on their interpretation of the task, on their perception of the criteria and targets for success, on their personal orientation towards the task, and on their view of the time constraints. Metacognitive faculties are associated with the monitoring and control functions that are exercised through the cognitive *Evaluations*, the latter being formulated in the light of the *Standards*. Such evaluation may lead to a re-cycling of the whole process as stated above, and indeed an overall feature of the representation is that it includes the possibility of multiple re-cycling between any of the stages 1 to 4 and the resources A to D. However, while all of these elements are internal, there is no implication that they will necessarily be undertaken consciously. What the model does underline is that self-assessment is inevitably deployed by learners before any outcome ensues. The issue is therefore not *whether* to initiate self-assessment – self-assessment is inherent in any classroom activity – but to make it more overt as a step to improvement.

An example which illustrates some of the issues involved is described by Fisher (2005). A teacher says to a 6-year-old drawing a picture of a daffodil: 'What is this flower called?' The child answers: 'I think it's called Betty'. The student has identified the task in terms of her understanding of the term 'called'; her standard for a satisfactory answer is that of everyday talk, not that of a learning discourse in which the distinction between proper and generic names is essential.

The example illustrates the teacher's problem: on receipt of a response, he/she has to decide how the student came to make it. Examples of interpretations could be: the student misunderstood a specific feature of the question, as in the case of the meaning underlying the phrase 'is called', so the student may have no idea of the sort of answers that are called for. Given an interpretation, the teacher has to act on it, and there are choices here even within any one interpretation, for example whether to try to point out a perceived flaw in an argument, or to open up an exploratory discussion to develop the reasoning deployed in arguments of this kind, working with the student's resources, for example by inviting exploration of various uses of the phrase 'is called'. If the teacher can analyze the response in these terms, then the response can be seen as an opportunity to open up discussion on various meanings of the phrase 'is called' leading on to discussion of the distinction between proper and generic names. By contrast, if the teacher were merely concerned with getting the 'right answer', the feedback is simple, to tell the whole class that answer, so the opportunity is not exploited: moreover, the student will be discouraged.

In classroom situations, a teacher's best response to the 'Betty' type of answer might be to ask others in the class to suggest their answers, perhaps asking them to suggest if there are different kinds of answers, and then to develop a discussion between the students drawing on the similarities and differences between the different responses (see Black et al. (2003: 37–9) for an example of such a discussion). Here the SRL literature seems to fall short – assuming the context of students working on their own and relying only on assessing themselves. The studies quoted do not consider interactive discourse and do not consider the dynamics of a succession of feedback interventions by the teacher.

The practical question then is whether the model explored above, or any model with similar aims, can give guidance on how formative feedback should be constructed. The SRL model brings out that an imperfect output may be evidence of a number of the different problems. For example, it may be that the student:

- has misunderstood the language used, e.g. is baffled by a 'why' question because of failure to understand the meaning of 'why';
- has misunderstood the whole purpose and context, e.g. assuming that maths is about getting the algorithm right, that all maths problems have one and only one solution, or that history is about telling it 'how it really was';

- has misunderstood the particular task, e.g. overlooking that the point is to explain, not to give an improved account;
- is using an inappropriate or ineffective strategy to tackle the task;
- has not understood the criteria of quality, e.g. assuming that a good piece of autobiography should present the correct facts clearly and in order, and has to have accurate punctuation, spelling and paragraphing – thus yielding a dull account devoid of feelings;
- has given a relevant answer but needs to attempt an explanation at a deeper level.

For any of the analysis presented above, we must add a final note of caution, as expressed by von Glasersfeld:

> Inevitably, that model will be constructed, not out of the child's conceptual elements, but out of the conceptual elements that are the interviewer's own. It is in this context that the epistemological principle of fit, rather than match is of crucial importance. Just as cognitive organisms can never compare their conceptual organisations of experience with the structure of an independent objective reality, so the interviewer, experimenter, or teacher can never compare the model he or she has constructed of a child's conceptualisations with what actually goes on in the child's head. In the one case as in the other, the best that can be achieved is a model that remains viable within the range of available experience. (p. 13)

The learning aims in classroom dialogue

Preceding sections have considered the theoretical models relevant to the immediate management of dialogic interactions between teacher and learners, for example to the fine grain of processes involved in the implementation of the design of the teaching. The purpose of this and the following section is to supplement those analyses by a more specific focus on the decisions that teachers have to take both in designing and reviewing their work and in their overall strategy in steering any classroom discussion.

The formative potential of the tasks that teachers present to students depends in part on the relevance of these to the conceptual structure of the subject matter, and on their efficacy in relation to the learning capacities of the recipients. This calls for analysis of the interplay between, on the one hand, teachers' views of the nature of the subject matter, particularly of appropriate epistemology and ontology, together with the resulting selections and articulation of goals and subject matter, and on the other hand, their models of cognition and of learning.

The focus in this section is on those components of a teacher's aims that are concerned with developing the general learning skills and practices of the students. The formative practices discussed in Chapter 2 reflect very general principles of learning, notably social constructivism and meta-cognition. However, it is possible to give far more – and more explicit – emphasis on learning aims, even to the extent of setting aside the subject or content-specific aims. This approach is illustrated here by discussion of two very distinctive programmes of instruction, namely cognitive acceleration and dynamic assessment, in both of which the improvement of learning capacity using an explicit and detailed theory of learning is given priority over subject-specific aims.

Learning model priority: the cognitive acceleration programmes

The cognitive acceleration (CA) programmes developed by Shayer and Adey (Shayer and Adey, 2002; Adey, 2005) are a distinctive form of instruction in that they offer a comprehensive innovation programme, with an explicit theoretical basis, a closely specified set of classroom activities, and prescribed pedagogic practices for which teachers require specific training. There is strong evidence that they lead to significant long-term improvements in school achievement, and that the improvements they secure extend beyond the particular subject context in which a programme has been implemented.

The theoretical basis derives from both Piaget and Vygotsky. One central aim is to encourage cognitive growth by creating cognitive conflict, following Vygotsky's dictum from *Mind in Society*:

> learning which is oriented toward developmental levels that have already been reached is ineffective from the viewpoint of a child's overall development. It does not aim for a new stage of the developmental process, but rather lags behind this process. The only good learning is that which is in advance of development. (Vygotsky, 1978: 82)

Within the CA framework, meta-cognition is regarded as a higher level psychological process. By challenging learners to reflect on their own thinking, teachers and their peers help them to make unconscious processes overt and explicit, so making these more available for future use.

A key feature of the programmes is that students must learn through dialogue with others, following another of Vygotsky's principles – that ideas appear first in the external 'social' plane, then become internalized by the individual. The emphasis given to creating cognitive conflict rather than giving answers, to the importance of dialogue to serve the social construction of knowledge, and to meta-cognition involving learners' reflection on their own learning, makes it clear that formative assessment practices are an essential feature of these programmes. Thus, whilst the programme of instruction is distinctive, formative assessment principles lie at the core of its implementation. In SRL terms, the purpose is to change one vital element of the conditions, that is the reasoning resources that a learner might bring to any task.

Learning model priority: dynamic assessment

Dynamic assessment (DA) is a system with an approach very similar to that of formative assessment (Poehner and Lantolf, 2005). The main difference is that it is based on an explicit theory for guiding and interpreting teachers' work (the Learning Potential Assessment Device of Feuerstein et al., 2003). As with the CA programmes, the model guides the formulation of tasks that are designed to elicit and develop these two aspects in comprehensive and increasingly sophisticated ways. It also requires that the teacher's responses be guided by the aim of challenging and developing the learner's thinking. Poehner and Lantolf emphazise that the teacher should not be content with immediate interventions that resolve a particular learning obstacle, but should follow up each issue in a sustained and strategic way to build up further the learner's capacity to learn. They dismiss most of the accounts in the formative literature as too vague because they lack this orientation. However, their judgement that work on formative assessment lacks a theoretical basis is not accepted by Leung (2007) who has expressed a more optimistic view of the synergy between the two. In relation to our argument, the DA programme is in the same category as the cognitive acceleration programmes in two respects. It is a comprehensive pedagogy, with a focused purpose not directly related to the conventional curriculum, and it specifies the particular ways in which its prescribed tasks should be implemented. However, formative assessment practices are central to this implementation.

Learning model priority: comparisons and contrasts

What is common to these and other similar approaches is that they all include particularly effective versions of classroom discourse that,

| 220 | Assessment and Learning

through careful choices of the tasks, the cues, and the feedback, exploit the potential fluidity of the learner's strategies to make significant and cumulative changes in them. Thus they are formative assessment exercises that rely upon interactive dialogue, both between teachers and students and between students themselves, distinguished by the very specifically targeted nature of the reasoning tasks that these methods deploy, the articulation of these in a sustained and coherent sequence, and the specification of aims by the light of which any feedback responses may be guided. The classroom activities discussed in our first main section above fit easily within these programmes – indeed, they are essential to their implementation.

The subject aims in the classroom dialogue

The teacher's responsibility

For most teachers and most classrooms, it cannot be assumed that the teacher has a single pre-determined goal for all students: the aims of any instruction are usually a combination of aims specific to the particular content under consideration, others that are related to the general subject discipline, with yet others directed to improving learning skills in general.

In many classrooms, the more specific aims are now commonly made explicit, with the more general aims being left implicit. However, even when these more general aims are left implicit, the learning intentions still exist, for otherwise the situation would be that 'anything goes'. Some authors (e.g. Knight, 2008) disagree on the grounds that to place the responsibility for the creation of learning with the teacher, is somehow to undermine the creation of student autonomy. It is true that in many situations, particularly those in which high-stakes tests play an important role, teachers often behave as if they believed that they could do the learning for the learner, with disastrous consequences. At the opposite extreme are those who claim not to teach, but to merely act as other participants, or to chair the learning discussions. Such an argument misrepresents the respective responsibilities of the teacher and the learner.

As noted earlier, we believe that the teacher's responsibility is to engineer situations in which the opportunities either for the learner to learn, and/or to develop learning autonomy, are maximized. The teacher must be accountable to the students in terms of taking on board, as far as reasonably practicable, the students' needs, preferences, and so on, but they must also be accountable to the discipline into which the students are being enculturated so that they can eventually operate as effective learners in that discipline. The crucial point here is that the teacher is (presumably) already enculturated into the disciplinary 'habits of mind' valued within the discipline, and the students are not. Part of the teacher's role is therefore to bring the students into the disciplinary 'community of practice' of which the teacher is already a member.

This responsibility to achieve the learning aims is exercised both in the design of the teaching and in the steering of the dialogue through which the underlying learning aims will be achieved. At the design stage, the task or problem put to the student(s) can, if well chosen, engage the students and help draw them into a learning discussion. Different students in the same class might be working towards different goals, and this might be perfectly acceptable to the teacher. However, it will also often be the case that some students appear to be working towards an outcome that is too far from the teacher's intention, and in such a case, the teacher's task would be to draw the student towards a trajectory that is more in keeping with the teacher's intention. More generally, as any particular task is implemented, the 'tuning' of that task to the responses can be very challenging for teachers – Dillon (1994) presents detailed guidance to teachers about this issue.

Teachers, learners, and the subject discipline

The types of classroom interaction entailed in the learning contexts of different subject matters will not necessarily have a great deal in common with one another. Comparisons between our experiences of work with teachers of English, science and mathematics reveal the important effects of the subject disciplines: these create differences between both the identities of teachers and the conduct of learning work in their classes (Grossman and Stodolsky, 1994; Marshall, 2001). For example, in mathematics and science there is a body of subject matter that teachers tend to regard as giving the subject unique and objectively defined aims. It is possible to 'deliver' the subject matter rather than to help students to learn it with understanding, and even where help with understanding is given priority, this help may be designed solely to ensure that every student achieves the 'correct' conceptual goal. In such situations, the teacher will be trying to get all students to the same goal, such as, in mathematics, understanding the notion of equivalent fractions. In other situations, the teacher's aims may be better characterized as having a broad 'horizon' of acceptable outcomes: Hodgen and Marshall's (2005) study brings out these differences in their comparison of mathematics with English classrooms. They show that the picture is quite different in English. In the teaching of writing, there is very little to 'deliver', except in the case of those teachers who focus only on the mechanics in grammar, spelling and punctuation. There is no single goal appropriate for all, and most teachers of this subject are naturally more accustomed to giving individual feedback to help all students to improve the quality of their individual efforts at written communication. There is a vast range of types of quality writing – the goal can be any point in a whole horizon rather than one particular point.

These inter-subject differences would be less sharp if the aims of the teaching were to be changed. For example, open-ended investigations in mathematics or science, or critical study of the social and ethical consequences of scientific discoveries, are activities that have more in common with the production of personal writing or critical appreciation in English.

It is also relevant that many teachers of English, at least at high-school level, are themselves writers, and students have more direct interaction with the 'subject', through their own reading and writing, than they do with (say) science. Nevertheless, whilst teachers might naturally engage more with use of feedback than many of their science colleagues, the quality of the feedback that they provide, and the overall strategies in relation to the meta-cognitive quality of that feedback, still need careful, often radical, development.

It is important in analyzing any subject to distinguish between content knowledge and pedagogical content knowledge (Shulman, 1986). A study of elementary school teachers conducted for the UK's Teacher Training Agency in 1995–1996 (Askew et al., 1997) found no relationship between learners' progress in mathematics and their teachers' level of qualification in mathematics, but a strong positive correlation with their pedagogical content knowledge – a finding also replicated by Hill et al. (2005). The teacher's capacity to explore and re-interpret the subject matter is important for effective pedagogy.

What is less clear is the importance of the interaction between students and the subjects they are studying. In the main, most middle- and high-school students seem to identify a school subject with their subject teacher: the teacher generally mediates the student's relationship with the subject, and there cannot be said to be much direct subject–student interaction. However, one aim of the teacher could well be to enhance the learner's capacity to interact directly with the subject's productions, which would involve a gradual withdrawal from the role of mediator. The meaning to be attached to such a change, let alone the timing and tactics to achieve this end, will clearly be different between different subjects. In subjects that are even more clearly performance subjects, notably physical education, visual arts, and musical performance, feedback is less problematic in that its purpose can be evident to both teacher and student, and it is clear that the learning is entirely dependent on it. The students-as-groups aspect may also emerge more clearly in so far as students work together to reproduce, or at least to simulate, the community practices of the subject areas, for example as actors in a stage drama, or as a team in a science investigation.

The student's role in classroom learning

The perceptions of teachers, as reported in Chapter 2, were that their students had changed role, from being passive recipients to being active learners who can take responsibility for, and manage, their own learning. One teacher reported this as follows:

> They feel that the pressure to succeed in tests is being replaced by the need to understand the work that has been covered and the test is just an assessment along the way of what needs more work and what seems to be fine. ... They have commented on the fact that they think I am more interested in the general way to get to an answer than a specific solution and when Clare [a researcher] interviewed them they decided this was so that they could apply their understanding in a wider sense. (Belinda, Cornbury Estate School)

Other, albeit very limited, interviews with students have also produced evidence that students saw a change in that their teacher seemed really interested in what they thought and not merely in whether they could produce the right answer. Indeed, one aspect of the project has been that students responded very positively to the opportunities and the stimulus to take more responsibility for their own learning.

These changes can be interpreted in terms of two aspects mentioned briefly earlier. The first is the development of meta-cognition, involving, as it must, some degree of reflection by the student about his or her own learning (Hacker et al., 1998). Of significance here also is the particular view of the concept of self-regulated learning developed by Schunk (1996) and Zimmerman and Schunk (1989), and the findings of the Melbourne Project for Enhanced Effective Learning (PEEL) summarized in Baird and Northfield (1992).

Analysis of our work may be taken further along these lines, by relating it to the literature on 'meta-learning' (Watkins et al. 2001). Many of the activities described in our first main section above could readily be classified as meta-cognitive, on the part of both teachers and their students. The distinction, emphasized by Watkins et al., between 'learning orientation' and 'performance orientation' (see Dweck, 2000) is also intrinsic to our approach. The achievement of meta-learning is less clear, for what would be required is that students had reflected on the new strategies in which they had been involved, and would seek to deploy them in new contexts. The practice of active revision in preparation for examinations, or the realization that one needs to seek clarity about aims if one is to be able to evaluate the quality of one's own work, may well be examples of meta-learning, but evidence about students' perceptions and responses to new challenges would be needed to support any claims about outcomes of this type.

A second aspect, reflected in changes in the students' perceptions of their teacher's personal interest in them, is the conative and affective aspects. These have already been discussed in Chapter 8. However, a further perspective which links such issues to the issues explored here is one that was emphasized by Cowie's (2004) study, which explored students' reactions to formative assessment. This work illustrates, in the context of formative assessment in classrooms, the framework proposed by Boekaerts and Corno (2005) and referred to above in the context of self-regulated learning. One of Cowie's general findings was that students are, in any activity, balancing three goals simultaneously, namely completion of work tasks, effective learning, and social-relationship goals. When these conflict, they tend to prioritize the social-relationship goals at the expense of learning goals: so, for example, many will limit disclosure of their ideas in the classroom for fear of harm to their feelings and reputation. The way in which the teacher deals with such disclosures is crucial. The respect shown them by their teacher and their trust in that teacher affects their response to any feedback – they need to feel safe if they are to risk exposure. Cowie also found that the students' responses to formative feedback cannot be assumed to be uniform. Some prioritize learning goals and so look for thoughtful suggestions, preferably in one-to-one exchanges, whilst others pursue performance goals and so want help to complete their work without the distraction of questions about their understanding. Sadly, many felt that the main responsibility for their learning rested with the teacher and not with themselves.

Much writing about classroom learning focuses either on the learner as individual or on learning as a social process. Our approach has been to treat the social-individual interaction as a central feature, drawing on the writings of Bredo (1994) and Bruner (1996). Thus, feedback to individuals and self-assessment has been emphasized, but so have peer-assessment, peer support in learning, and class discussions about their learning.

For the work of students in groups, the emphasis by Sadler (1989, 1998) and others that peer assessment is a particularly valuable way of implementing formative assessment has been amply borne out in the work reported here. Theoretically, this perspective ought to be evaluated in the broader context of the application to classrooms and schools of analyses of the social and communal dimensions of learning, as developed, for example, in Wenger's (1998) study of communities of practice.

The quotation below of a student discussing peer marking of his investigation also bears out Bruner's (1996) emphasis on the importance of externalizing one's thoughts by producing objects or *oeuvres* that, being public, are accessible to reflection and dialogue, leading to enrichment through communal interaction. He points out that awareness of one's own thinking, and capacity to understand the thinking of others, provides an essential reasoned base for interpersonal negotiation that can enhance understanding. This point is illustrated by the following extract from an interview with a student in the KMOFAP project (for details of KMOFAP see Black and Wiliam, 2003):

After a pupil marking my investigation, I can now acknowledge my mistakes easier. I hope that it is not just me who learnt from the investigation but the pupil who marked it did also.

Next time I will have to make my explanations clearer, as they said 'It is hard to understand', so I must next time make my equation clearer. I will now explain my equation again so it is clear.

The importance of peer-assessment may be more fundamental than is apparent in accounts by teachers of their work. For self-assessment, each student has to interact mainly with text; interactions with the teacher, in so far as they are personal, must be brief. Discussing the work of Palincsar and Brown (1984) on children's reading, Wood states:

This work, motivated by Vygotsky's theory of development and by his writings on literacy, started from the assumption that some children fail to advance beyond the initial stages of reading because they do not know how to 'interact' with text – i.e. they do not become actively engaged in attempts to *interpret* what they read. Briefly, the intervention techniques involved bringing into the open, making public and *audible*, ways of interacting with text that skilled readers usually undertake automatically and soundlessly. (Wood, 1998: 220–1, emphasis in original)

Thus if a student's interpretation of aims, and of criteria of quality of performance, is to be enriched, such enrichment may well require 'talk about text', and given that it is impracticable to achieve this through teacher–student interactions, the interactions made possible through peer-assessment may meet an essential need.

Overall, it is clear that changes in the student's role as a learner are a significant feature in the reform of classroom learning, that our formative assessment initiative has been effective in its impact on these features, and that changes in the student's own beliefs and implicit models of learning also underlie the developments involved.

Summary and conclusions

The overall message of this chapter is that it can be seen as a response to a point made by Perrenoud in this commentary on our 1998 review:

> This [feedback] no longer seems to me, however, to be the central issue. It would seem more important to concentrate on the theoretical models of learning and its regulation and their implementation. These constitute the real systems of thought and action, in which feedback is only one element. (Perrenoud, 1998: 86)

This makes clear that a perspective broader than that adopted in Chapter 2 is called for. Accounts which this chapter contributes to the broadening needed include analysis of the underlying rationale which inter-relates the tools of formative assessment, and analyzes of how this rationale links to the necessary changes in the relationship between the subjects, that is, in the relationship between the teacher and the students, and how these in turn prompted changes in the subjects themselves, that is changes in the teacher's and students' roles. This has then led us to the need to look more deeply at the place of learning aims in the design for, and in the control of, learning dialogues, and at the balance between these aims and those that are central to the teaching of individual school subjects.

These various components could be mapped into the scheme of activity theory (Engeström, 1987), as attempted in our earlier version of this chapter. A typical activity theory representation (e.g. Black and Wiliam 2006: 96, Figure 5.2) contains six main elements and 15 possible interactions between them, which serves to illustrate the potential complexity and range of the issues that a broader theory would have to investigate. However, not all of the components and interactions which we now see as central fit comfortably into this scheme. We have since attempted a new approach in a more detailed discussion of some of the issues raised in this chapter (Black and Wiliam, 2009).

Perrenoud's expansion of the agenda could be interpreted as a challenge to incorporate ideas about formative assessment into a comprehensive theory of pedagogy. This seems to be the best way to describe the task that this chapter tries to tackle. However, most theoretical writings about pedagogy pay scant attention to assessment, formative or summative, and although some argue that classroom assessment is concerned with instruction rather than with pedagogy, this simply re-defines the problem of incorporation, but does not solve it. Our general conclusion is that, whilst we regard this chapter as a contribution to the task, there is more work to be done before it could be claimed that the task has been completed.

References

Adey, P. (2005) 'Issues arising from the long-term evaluation of cognitive acceleration programmes', *Research in Science Education*, 35: 3–22.

Applebee, A.N., Langer, J.A., Nystrand, M. and Gamoran, A. (2003) 'Discussion based approaches to developing understanding: classroom instruction and student performance in middle and high school English', *American Educational Research Journal*, 40(3): 685–730.

Askew, M., Brown, M.L., Rhodes, V., Johnson, D.C. and Wiliam, D. (1997) *Effective Teachers of Numeracy: Final Report*. London, UK: King's College London School of Education.

Baird, J.R. and Northfield, J.R. (1992) *Learning from the PEEL Experience*. Melbourne: Monash University.

Black, P. and Wiliam, D. (2003) 'In praise of educational research: formative assessment', *British Educational Research Journal*, 29(5): 623–37.

Black, P. and Wiliam, D. (2006) 'Developing a theory of formative assessment', in J. Gardner (ed.), *Assessment and Learning* (1st edn). London: Sage. pp. 81–100.

Black, P. and Wiliam, D. (2009) 'Developing the theory of formative assessment', *Educational Assessment, Evaluation and Accountability*, 21(1): 5–31.

Black, P., Harrison, C., Lee, C., Marshall, B. and Wiliam, D. (2003) *Assessment for Learning: Putting it into Practice*. Buckingham, UK: Open University Press.

Boekaerts, M. and Corno, L. (2005) 'Self-regulation in the classroom: a perspective on assessment and intervention', *Applied Psychology*, 54(2): 199–231.

Bredo, E. (1994) 'Reconstructing educational psychology', *Educational Psychologist*, 29(1): 23–45.

Brown, A.L. and Campione, J.C. (1996) 'Psychological theory and the design of innovative learning environments: on procedures, principles, and systems', in L. Schauble and R. Glaser (eds), *Innovations in Learning: New Environments for Education*. Hillsdale, NJ: Lawrence Erlbaum Associates. pp. 291–2.

Bruner, J. (1996) *The Culture of Education.* Cambridge, MA: Harvard University Press.

Cowie, B. (2004) 'Student commentary on formative assessment', paper given at the annual conference of the National Association for Research in Science Teaching, Vancouver, March.

Davis, B. (1997) 'Listening for differences: an evolving conception of mathematics teaching', *Journal for Research in Mathematics Education,* 28(3): 355–76.

Dillon, J.T. (1994) *Using Discussion in Classrooms.* London: Open University Press.

Dweck, C.S. (1986) 'Motivational processes affecting learning', *American Psychologist* (Special issue: Psychological science and education), 41(10): 1040–8.

Dweck, C.S. (2000) *Self-Theories: Their Role in Motivation, Personality and Development.* Florence, KY: Psychology Press.

Engeström, Y. (1987) *Learning by Expanding: An Activity-Theoretical Approach to Developmental Research.* Helsinki, Finland: Orienta-Konsultit Oy.

Feuerstein, R., Falik, L., Rand, Y. and Feuerstein, R.S. (2003) *Dynamic Assessment of Cognitive Modifiability.* Jerusalem: ICELP Press.

Fisher, R. (2005) *Teaching Children to Learn* (2nd edn). London: Continuum.

Greene, J.A. and Azevedo, R. (2007) 'A theoretical review of Winne and Hadwin's model of self-regulated learning: new perspectives and directions', *Review of Educational Research,* 77(3): 354–72.

Grossman, P.L. and Stodolsky, S.S. (1994) 'Considerations of content and the circumstances of secondary school teaching', *Review of Research in Education,* 4: 179–221.

Hacker, D. J., Dunlosky, J. and Graesser, A.C. (1998) *Metacognition in Educational Theory and Practice.* Mahwah, NJ: Lawrence Erlbaum Associates.

Hardman, F., Smith, F. and Wall, K. (2003) '"Interactive whole class teaching" in the national literacy strategy', *Cambridge Journal of Education,* 33(2): 197–215.

Hill, H.C., Rowan, B. and Ball, D.L. (2005) 'Effects of teachers' mathematical knowledge for teaching on student achievement', *American Educational Research Journal,* 42(2): 371–406.

Hodgen, J. and Marshall, B. (2005) 'Assessment for learning in mathematics and English: contrasts and resemblances', *The Curriculum Journal,* 16(2): 153–76.

Holland, D., Lachicotte Jr, W., Skinner, D. and Cain, C. (1998) *Identity and Agency in Cultural Worlds.* Cambridge, MA: Harvard University Press.

Knight, O. (2008) 'Create something interesting to show that you have learned something', *Teaching History,* 131: 17–24.

Lave, J. and Wenger, E. (1991) *Situated Learning: Legitimate Peripheral Participation.* Cambridge, UK: Cambridge University Press.

Lee, C. and Wiliam, D. (2005) 'Studying changes in the practice of two teachers developing assessment for learning', *Teacher Development,* 9(2): 265–83.

Leung, C. (2007) 'Dynamic assessment: assessment *for* or *as* teaching?', *Language Assessment Quarterly,* 4(3): 257–78.

Marshall, B. (2001) 'Marking the essay: teachers' subject philosophies as related to their assessment', *English in Education,* 35(3): 42–57.

Mehan, H. (1979) *Learning Lessons: Social Organization in the Classroom.* Cambridge, MA: Harvard University Press.

Palincsar, A.S. and Brown, A.L. (1984) *Reciprocal Teaching of Comprehension Fostering and Monitoring Activities: Cognition and Instruction.* Hillsdale, NJ: Lawrence Erlbaum.

Perrenoud, P. (1998) 'From formative evaluation to a controlled regulation of learning processes: towards a wider conceptual field', *Assessment in Education,* 5(1): 85–102.

Poehner, M.E. and Lantolf, J.P. (2005) 'Dynamic assessment in the language classroom', *Language Teaching Research*, 9(3): 233–65.

Ramaprasad, A. (1983) 'On the definition of feedback', *Behavioral Science*, 28: 4–13.

Sadler, D.R. (1989) 'Formative assessment and the design of instructional systems', *Instructional Science*, 18: 119–44.

Sadler, D.R. (1998) 'Formative assessment: revisiting the territory', *Assessment in Education* 5(1): 77–84.

Schunk, D.H. (1996) 'Goal and self-evaluative influences during children's cognitive skill learning', *American Educational Research Journal*, 33(2): 359–82.

Shayer, M. and Adey, P. (eds) (2002) *Learning Intelligence: Cognitive Acceleration Across the Curriculum 5 to 15 Years*. Milton Keynes: Open University Press.

Shulman, L. (1986) 'Those who understand: knowledge growth in teaching', *Educational Researcher*, 15(1): 4–14.

Smith, F., Hardman, F., Wall, K. and Mroz, M. (2004) 'Interactive whole class teaching in the National Literacy and Numeracy Strategies', *British Educational Research Journal*, 30(3): 395–411.

von Glasersfeld, E. (1987) 'Learning as a constructive activity', in C. Janvier (ed.), *Problems of Representation in the Teaching and Learning of Mathematics*. Hillsdale, NJ: Lawrence Erlbaum Associates. pp. 3–17.

Vygotsky, L. (1978) *Mind in Society*. Cambridge, MA: Harvard University Press.

Watkins, C., Carnell, E., Lodge, C., Wagner, P. and Whalley, C. (2001) *N.S.I.N Research Matters No.13: Learning about Learning Enhances Performance*. London: Institute of Education.

Wenger, E. (1998) *Communities of Practice: Learning, Meaning, and Identity*. Cambridge, UK: Cambridge University Press.

Wiliam, D. and Thompson, M. (2007) 'Integrating assessment with instruction: what will it take to make it work?', in C.A. Dwyer (ed.) *The Future of Assessment: Shaping Teaching and Learning*. Mahwah, NJ: Lawrence Erlbaum Associates. pp. 53–82.

Wood, D. (1998) *How Children Think and Learn: The Social Contexts of Cognitive Development* (2nd edn). Oxford: Blackwell.

Zimmerman, B.J. and Schunk, D.H. (eds) (1989) *Self-Regulated Learning and Academic Achievement: Theory, Research, and Practice*. New York: Springer.

Part 4

Validity and Reliability

Chapter **14**

Validity in Formative Assessment

Gordon Stobart

Validity is central to any assessment. It is about the purpose of the assessment, whether the form of the assessment is fit-for-purpose, and whether it achieves its purpose. Validity includes how the results of an assessment are interpreted and used. We cannot say an assessment is valid without knowing what the intention was in using it and how well this intention was met. For example, if I use a well-constructed and reliably marked maths test to decide which maths group students should be in, this may have high validity. If I use the same test as the sole means of selecting students for a fine arts course, we would immediately say it was invalid – it is not fit-for-purpose and so using the results in this way would be misleading.

In this chapter I apply this approach to formative assessment, a term I use interchangeably with assessment for learning. If the purpose of formative assessment is to stimulate further learning, then validity is about whether this is achieved. I am interpreting formative assessment in the broad sense of any assessment in which information is gathered in order to contribute directly to the learning process. This sits well with our working definition of assessment for learning: 'The process of seeking and interpreting evidence for use by learners and their teachers, to identify where the learners are in their learning, where they need to go to and how best to get there' (ARG, 2002a: 2–3).The focus of this is typically on classroom interactions but may include the formative use of summative assessments. For example, it could include using test information to determine what has not been learned well, so that teaching could address this (the American 'test and remediate' approach). It may also take account of current test information in future teaching, Carless's (2007) 'pre-emptive formative assessment' in which it is primarily the teachers who learn from the evidence and adjust their teaching.

So how do we go about judging the validity of these approaches to improving learning? Can we use the same kind of validity framework that may be used for a summative test? My approach is that while we can use some of the key concepts, there will be distinct differences in emphasis.

I take the key elements in current theorizing about test validity (e.g. Kane, 2006; Stobart, 2009) to be:

1 Validity is based on the purpose(s) of an assessment and how effectively the interpretation and use of the results serve each purpose.
2 It is concerned with how effectively the construct/domain being assessed is being sampled.
3 Reliability and fairness are part of validity. Unreliable results undermine confidence in their interpretation, unfairness will also lead to misinterpretation of the results.

Any validity inquiry in formative assessment will place its emphasis on the first of these. The purpose is to improve learning, so effective formative assessment will do this and the 'threats to validity' are those things that get in its way. This is a *consequential* argument, an approach both championed (Shepard, 1997) and disputed (Popham, 1997) in test validity.[1] The second element is implicated in this – there is a need for clarity, by both teachers and learners, about what is being learned. The third, reliability, is less central as a concern in formative assessment because any assessment of what is needed to be done will vary from learner to learner, so two learners with similar performance may receive different feedback. I take reliability in formative assessment to be more about the quality of information that is gathered and provided in feedback.

Intending to improve learning and achieving it

Earlier writing on assessment for learning tended to use a strict, and circular, definition of formative assessment: that it is only formative when further learning can be seen to have taken place (Black et al., 2003; Stobart, 2006). What this does not sufficiently recognize is that while the intention was to aid learning, in practice the strategy did not do this. The task of any validity inquiry is to find out what helped and what hindered the intention being realized.

Kane (2006), in his authoritative update of validity theory, makes the helpful distinction between a *validation argument* and *validity*. Validation is the process 'of evaluating the plausibility of proposed interpretations and uses', while validity is 'the extent to which the evidence supports or refutes the proposed interpretations and uses' (2006: 17). This is relevant to formative assessment: validation relates to the intention to improve learning, a validity inquiry is whether it achieved this. For example, we may give feedback with the intention of 'closing the gap' between desired and actual performance, yet in many cases it may have the opposite effect (Kluger and DiNisi, 1996). While a validation argument may have made the case for feedback, a validity inquiry may have to investigate why it did not work in these circumstances.

The focus of this chapter, therefore, is to examine what we know about what supports, and what threatens, effective formative assessment. Valid formative assessment is when the intention to improve learning leads to actual improvements. The threats to validity are circumstances or processes which undermine formative assessment. I group these as the *learning context,* both outside and inside the classroom, and the effectiveness of *feedback* – a key process in moving learning forward.

The learning context

If validity is based on whether learning takes place as a consequence of an assessment, what can encourage or undermine this learning? Perrenoud (1998) has argued that formative assessment is affected by what goes on 'upstream' of specific teacher–learner interactions and that this context is often neglected, partly because it is so complex. Some of the cultural assumptions on which assessment for learning is based are a product largely of developed Anglophone cultures (particularly Australia, New Zealand, the UK and the USA), with their 'whole child' approaches, individualism and attitude to motivation. It is therefore worth briefly considering how some different social and cultural factors may affect what goes on in the classroom, since these are likely to provide differing threats to effective formative assessment.

Outside the classroom

At the macro level, the role and status of education within a society will impact on students' motivation to learn and the scope for formative assessment. In a society where high value is placed on education, for exarnple in Chinese education, student motivation to learn may be a 'given' (Watkins, 2000) rather than having to be fostered by schools, as is often the assumption in many UK and North American schools (Hidi and Harackiewicz, 2000; ARG, 2002b). Similarly, the emphasis on feedback being task-related rather than self-related may sit more comfortably in cultures which see the role of the teacher as to instruct (e.g. France) rather than as to care for the 'whole child' (e.g. the UK; see Raveaud, 2004). There are also cultural differences around the extent to which education may be seen as a collective activity with group work as a natural expression of this, or as an individualistic activity in which peer assessment may seem alien (Watkins, 2000).

The curriculum and how it is assessed is another key 'outside' contextual factor. The opportunities for formative assessment, in a centralized curriculum with high-stakes national testing, will be different from those of teachers who enjoy more autonomy over what they have to cover and how they assess it.

Inside the classroom

For formative assessment to lead to learning, the classroom context has to be supportive and the feedback to the learner productive. If the conditions militate against learning they become threats to validity. What I provide below are some examples of how formative assessment may be helped or hindered in the classroom. What they illustrate is the complex contextual nature of classroom assessment and why it is difficult to achieve effective formative assessment. The examples I use represent the more affective elements in learning, the challenge of making clear what is being learned, and the pressures that come from high-stakes summative assessments. These lead into a discussion of effective feedback, a key element in moving learning forward.

Trust and motivation

I am using trust and motivation as examples of the 'classroom climate' which may support or undermine effective learning and in doing so may affect the validity of formative assessment. There is a strong cultural element in how these may be expressed. For example, commentaries on Russian schooling suggest a very different attitude to praise and to building self-esteem. Alexander observes that while there were only a handful of praise descriptors in Russian, 'the vocabulary of disapproval is rich and varied' (2000: 375). Yet in this more critical climate, there is evidence of Russian students pursuing mastery goals and being willing to risk mistakes. Hufton and Elliott report from their comparative study that 'it was not unusual for students who did not understand something, to request to work in front of the class on the blackboard, so that teacher and peers could follow and correct their working' (2001: 10). Raveaud's (2004) account of French and English primary school classes offers some similar challenges to anglophone understandings of fostering trust and motivation. It may be that we need a more robust view of trust to make sense of such findings.

An anglophone 'whole child' view that fragile self-esteem ought to be protected by not exposing failure may prevent children from learning from mistakes and misunderstandings. Finding out 'where learners are in their learning' involves finding out what is known and what is misunderstood. This is why 'rich questioning' is an important classroom practice in formative assessment, since the responses to more open-ended questions may reveal learners' current thinking. The developmental psychologist Reuven Feuerstein and his colleagues (1980, 2006) have pointed out that dealing with error should be seen as a mark of respect for the learner:

> Error cannot be viewed solely as failure: rather, its source must be sought. In doing so the teacher demonstrate their respect for the student as a thinking being who has arrived at a response through reasons that may not correspond to the task, but which, nonetheless, exist and must be explored. (Feuerstein et al., 2006: 353)

Making learning explicit – walking a tightrope.
One of the key assumptions of assessment for learning is that, for learning to be effective, learners and teachers need to be clear on 'where they need to go'. In practice this involves making clear both the learning intentions and what a successful performance will look like. The reasoning is that it is easier to learn when we know what we are learning and that to be able to evaluate our performance we need to know what the required standard is (Sadler, 1989, 2010). Failure to achieve this clarity will be a threat to valid formative assessment since it may limit learning.

The tightrope here is the delicate balancing act between making clear what is to be learned without over-specifying to the point that it leads to fragmented and surface level learning. One of the threats to validity is that students do not understand what they are supposed to be learning and what reaching the intended standard will involve. This was captured nicely by the 15-year-old who commented: 'It's not that I haven't learnt much. It's just that I don't really understand what I'm doing' (Harris et.al., 1995). Lack of understanding of the purposes of learning also makes feedback less likely to be successful – if we do not know what we are trying to achieve it is harder to make sense of, and utilize, feedback.

Explicit but unclear.   While curriculum writers seek to make explicit what is expected at a given level, this is unlikely to be self-evident, particularly to the students. The learning objectives have to be decoded by teachers through exemplars and modelling if students are to understand what they are doing. So, for example, the requirements of the level 4 English Writing attainment target in the National Curriculum in England are:

Level 4

Pupils' writing in a range of forms is lively and thoughtful. Ideas are often sustained and developed in interesting ways and organised appropriately for the purpose of the reader. Vocabulary choices are often adventurous and words are used for effect. Pupils are beginning to use grammatically complex sentences, extending meaning. Spelling, including that of polysyllabic words that conform to regular patterns, is generally accurate. Full stops, capital letters and question marks are used correctly, and pupils are beginning to use punctuation within the sentence. Handwriting style is fluent, joined and legible. (QCDA, 2010).

This is intended to describe the expected attainment of most 11-year-olds, but without examples of what these words mean in practice, the best intentions to make the attainment demands specific are likely to fail. This then undermines the validity of the formative assessment practice of making clear 'where learners need to go'.

Over-explicit learning objectives. The opposing pull is to make the objectives so detailed that they encourage impoverished learning. This kind of micro-teaching can be found in some occupational training in which trainees have to 'tick the boxes' to meet dozens of very specific criteria. The same risk is present with the 'test and remediate' approach to formative assessment in the USA (Popham, 2008). A widespread practice is for a multiple choice test to be given (an 'interim assessment') and the teacher then spends a week remediating the items that students failed. The risk here is that this leads to a very superficial learning experience. The same may be true of examination syllabuses which specify in great detail what is required and which may lead to micro-teaching on how to gain the extra mark here and there.

Torrance (2007) has coined the useful term *criteria compliance* to capture the threat of over-narrow learning objectives:

> Transparency, however, encourages instrumentalism. The clearer the task of how to achieve a grade or award becomes, and the more detailed the assistance given by tutors, supervisors and assessors, the more likely are candidates to succeed; but succeed at what? Transparency of objectives, coupled with extensive use of coaching and practice to help learners meet them, is in danger of removing the challenge of learning and reducing the quality and validity of outcomes achieved. We have identified a move from what we characterise as assessment of learning, through the currently popular idea of assessment for learning, to assessment as learning, where assessment procedures and practices may come completely to dominate the learning experience, and 'criteria compliance' come to replace 'learning'. (2007: 2)

Ecclestone (2002: 36) has summed this up vividly as students becoming 'hunters and gatherers of information without deep engagement in either content or process'.

The formative in a summative climate
One of the most persistent threats to formative assessment is that it is conscripted to support the demands of summative assessment or neglected

once 'real' assessment is imminent. In high-stakes testing cultures this can often mean using formative assessment to 'sugar the pill'. This can take the form of claiming that regular test practice and monitoring of scores is formative. This often masks a confusion, since it is described as formative (as it informs about progress and standards reached) when the function is really summative (a snapshot of where I am now). Much of this type of assessment would be more accurately classified as *frequent summative* or *mini-summative*. It is what is done with this information which will determine whether it *becomes* formative – does it lead to further learning? So the difference is about purpose rather than timing.

What adds complexity to this is that formative and summative functions are often part of a loop rather than independent of each other. For example, if the teacher-assessed part of a qualification has detailed outcomes specified for each level, then the preparation process could be formative – how far short of these outcomes is my present work and what do I need to do to get closer? When I meet these outcomes the process becomes summative and I am awarded this level, only to have this information used in relation to the next level, so it reverts to formative. The risk here is criteria compliance – 'here's what you need to do to move up a level ...'.

Feedback[2]

Feedback is a central element in formative assessment. It is how we move from where we are to where we want to get to, the 'how best to get there' of the ARG definition. What we know is that effective feedback, which does close the gap, is hard to achieve. Kluger and DeNisi concluded from their meta-analysis that: 'In over one third of cases Feedback Interventions reduced performance ... we believe that researchers and practitioners alike confuse their feelings that feedback is desirable with the question of whether Feedback Intervention benefits performance' (1996: 275, 277).

We are learning more about the complexity of feedback. Two more recent reviews of research on feedback, one by Shute (2007) in the US, the other Hattie and Timperley (2007) in New Zealand, have highlighted the complexity of the feedback process. Whether feedback has positive learning effects depends on many interacting factors: motivation, the complexity of the task, the expertise of the learner, and the level and quality of the feedback. This makes it highly situational; the same feedback given to two learners could have opposite effects. Simply telling novice learners that they are wrong may set back learning, telling engaged experts the same may be enough to get them to increase their efforts and change their strategy.

My intention here is simply to highlight some of the ways in which feedback may support, or inhibit, learning. For Kluger and DeNisi (1996) a critical feature is that feedback should be focused on the task rather than the self, and that the level of the feedback determines the level of response:

1 *Task level.* This is often corrective feedback about whether work is accurate, whether more information is needed, and about building more surface knowledge. Simple, rather than complex, tasks benefit from this level of feedback. About 90% of teachers' questions are aimed at this level. This type of feedback is more powerful when it is about faulty interpretations, not lack of information – for which further teaching is more effective.

2 *Process level.* This addresses the processes underlying tasks or relating and extending tasks. Feedback at this level may be in terms of improving error detection and cueing strategies on more complex tasks.

3 *Regulation level.* Hattie and Timperley identify six major factors at this level which mediate the effectiveness of feedback. These are:

> the capability to create internal feedback and to self-assess, the willingness to invest effort into seeking and dealing with feedback information, the degree of confidence or certainty in the correctness of the response, the attributions about success or failure, and the level of proficiency at seeking help (2007: 94).

4 *Self level.* This is personal feedback which offers positive (and sometimes negative) judgements about the learner. This is the 'good girl', 'what a star' language found in many classrooms and used instead of the three task focused levels above. The problem is that it is rarely effective in terms of learning.

This analysis has considerable implications for current classroom practice. It questions the roles of *praise* and *rewards* in feedback, since both direct attention to the self rather than to the task and neither provides information which will move learning on. There are similar questions around the use of *marks* and *grades* which may also provide no direct information about what to do next (and the comments which accompany them are often uninformative or ignored). They too will often be taken at the 'self' level and interpreted in comparison to others, a 'reputational lens', rather than as informing self-regulatory processes.

Where this takes us is that, while feedback is 'a good thing', a validation argument would have to show how a particular form of feedback can be justified in current theorizing. The emphases here may be on the helpfulness of the information being provided, on the cultural context and on the quality of classroom interactions.

The learner's use of feedback

Feedback may be informative, directed at the appropriate level, and focused on the task – and still not lead to further learning. If feedback is seen as a 'gift' from the teacher, the learner has options about what to do with it. It may be negotiated, accepted and used to help move learning forward. However, the emotional and effort costs of acting upon it may be too much, particularly if there is low commitment to it. What can happen then is that the learner can either modify or blur the goal, change it, or reject the feedback.

This brings us back again to the importance of the teacher/learner or learner/learner interactions in the classroom. Feedback does not operate in a vacuum, even task-based feedback still involves strong emotional and motivational reactions. These have to be taken into account if feedback is to help move learning forward.

Conclusion

Formative assessment, like any form of assessment, has to demonstrate its validity. The key element in this is how well formative assessment meets it purpose of improving learning. In this respect it is a consequential validity argument. While formative assessment may be well intentioned, it may not actually improve learning. Validity is then about establishing what has contributed to further learning and what has got in the way of this. This will include the cultural and learning context, the quality of classroom interaction, the teacher's and learner's clarity about what is being learned, and the effectiveness of feedback.

Notes

1   My own position on this is that if a test makes claims about consequences (e.g. 'This testing programme will raise standards', then its validity is based on whether it does so – a consequence).
2   This section draws on Chapter 7 of *Testing Times* (Stobart, 2008).

References

Alexander, R.J. (2000) *Culture and Pedagogy: International Comparisons in Primary Education.* Oxford: Blackwell.

ARG (2002a) *Assessment for Learning: 10 Principles.* Cambridge: University of Cambridge, Assessment Reform Group.

ARG (2002b) *Testing, Motivation and Learning.* Cambridge: University of Cambridge, Assessment Reform Group.

Black, P., Harrison, C., Lee, C. Marshall, B. and Wiliam, D. (2003) *Assessment for Learning: Putting it into Practice.* Buckingham: Open University Press.

Carless, D. (2007) 'Conceptualising pre-emptive formative assessment', *Assessment in Education: Principles, Policy and Practice,* 14(2): 171–84.

Ecclestone, K. (2002) *Learning Autonomy in Post-16 Education.* London: Routledge-Falmer.

Feuerstein, R. (1980) *Instrumental Enrichment: an Intervention Program for Cognitive Modifiability*. Baltimore: University Park Press.

Feuerstein, R., Feuerstein, R.S., Falik, L. and Rand, Y. (2006) *Creating and Enhancing Cognitive Modifiability: the Feuerstein Instrumental Enrichment Program*. Jerusalem: ICELP Publications.

Harris, S., Wallace, G. and Rudduck, J. (1995) '"It's not that I haven't learned much. It's just that I don't really understand what I'm doing": Metacognition and Secondary School Students', *Research Papers in Education*, 10: 253–71.

Hattie, J. and Timperley, H. (2007) 'The power of feedback', *Review of Educational Research*, 77: 81–112.

Hidi S. and Harackiewicz, J.M. (2000) 'Motivating the academically unmotivated: a critical issue for the 21st Century', *Review of Educational Research*, 70(2) 151–79.

Hufton, N. and Elliott, J. (2001) 'Achievement motivation: cross-cultural puzzles and paradoxes', paper presented at the British Educational Research Association Conference, Leeds.

Kane, M.T. (2006) 'Validation' in R.L. Brennan (ed.) *Educational Measurement*. (4th edn.) Westport, CT: American Council on Education/Praeger, 17–64.

Kane, M.T. (2008) 'Terminology, emphasis, and utility in validation', *Educational Researcher*, 37(2): 76–82.

Kluger, A.N. and DeNisi, A. (1996) 'The effects of feedback interventions on performance: a historical review, a meta-analysis, and a preliminary feedback intervention theory', *Psychological Bulletin*, 119: 252–84.

Perrenoud, P. (1998) 'From formative evaluation to a controlled regulation of learning processes: towards a wider conceptual field', *Assessment in Education*, 5(1): 85–102.

Popham, W. J. (1997) 'Consequential validity: right concern – wrong concept', *Educational Measurement: Issues and Practice*, 16(2): 9–13.

Popham, W. J. (2008) *Transformative Assessment*. Alexandria: Association for Supervision and Curriculum Development.

QCDA (2010) *National Curriculum, English*. Available at: http://curriculum.qcda. gov.uk/key-stages-1-and-2/subjects/english/attainmenttagests/index.aspx (accessed 16 October 2010).

Raveaud, M. (2004) 'Assessment in French and English infant schools: assessing the work, the child or the culture?', *Assessment in Education*, 11(2): 193–211.

Sadler, D. R. (1989) 'Formative assessment and the design of instructional systems', *Instructional Science*, 18: 119–44.

Sadler, D.R. (2010) 'Beyond feedback: developing student capability in complex appraisal', *Assessment and Evaluation in Higher Education*, 35, 535–50.

Shepard, L.A. (1997) The centrality of test use and consequences for test validity', *Educational Measurement: Issues and Practice*, 16(2): 5–8.

Shute, V. (2007) 'Focus on formative feedback', *ETS Research Reports*, Princeton, NJ: Educational Testing Service. Available at:http//www.ets.org/media/Research/ pdf/RR-07-11.pdf

Stobart, G. (2006) 'The validity of formative assessment' in J. Gardner (ed.), *Assessment and Learning*. London: Sage. pp. 133–46.

Stobart, G. (2008) *Testing Times*. Abingdon: Routledge.

Stobart, G. (2009) 'Determining validity in national curriculum assessments', *Educational Research*, 51(2): 161–79.

Torrance, H. (2007) 'Assessment as learning? How the use of explicit learning objectives, assessment criteria and feedback in post-secondary education and training can come to dominate learning', *Assessment in Education* 14(3): 281–94.

Watkins, D. (2000) 'Learning and teaching: a cross-cultural perspective', *School Leadership and Management*, 20(2): 161–173.

Chapter 15

The Reliability of Assessments

Paul Black and Dylan Wiliam

Introduction

As many of the chapters in this volume have shown, assessment has a fundamental role in the improvement of educational processes. However, it is also important to acknowledge that assessment is also used simply to measure educational achievement. Within schools and colleges, assessments are used to make decisions about the allocation of students to classes, and whether students should progress to the next stage or repeat the current one. The results of assessments are also used in selecting students for employment, for further stages of education, and for the purpose of holding educational institutions to account. The extent to which educational assessments are fit for this task is therefore a crucial issue in assessment policy.

It is obvious, therefore, that any assessment should be designed so that the users of the results, be they the students, their parents, their teachers or the gatekeepers for further stages of education or employment, can have confidence in the results. This is formally a matter of validity, defined by Samuel Messick (1989: 13) as follows: 'Validity is an integrative evaluative judgment of the degree to which empirical evidence and theoretical rationales support the adequacy and appropriateness of inferences and actions based on test scores or other modes of assessment'. In particular, when we know an assessment result, we should know what kinds of inferences can justifiably be drawn on the basis of the result.

Messick highlighted two threats to valid inferences based on assessment outcomes: construct under-representation and construct-irrelevant variance. Assessment outcomes are said to suffer from construct under-representation when the scores or grades fail to reflect differences in the students' capabilities with respect to the construct of interest. For example, if we use a multiple-choice test to assess students' knowledge of history, then the assessment may well adequately capture students' knowledge of key facts and dates. However, a multiple-choice test is unlikely adequately to assess whether the students can construct historical argument. If this is regarded as part of the construct of 'history' then the multiple-choice test would be regarded as suffering from construct under-representation; important aspects of the construct are under-represented in the assessment.

Construct under-representation therefore occurs when an assessment fails to assess things it should. The opposite threat to valid interpretation – when an assessment assesses things it should not – is called construct-irrelevant variance. The key idea here is that differences in scores between students should represent differences in the construct. For example, in a mathematics test, we want differences in scores to represent differences in mathematics achievement. In other words we want the variation in students' scores to be relevant to the construct of interest. If this is not the case – if, for example, in our mathematics test, the reading demands are so great that it is not clear whether low scores signify lack of knowledge of the mathematics, or lack of ability to read the question – then the scores on the assessment suffer from construct-irrelevant variance. Part of the variance (i.e. variation) in achievement is attributable to factors other than the construct the assessment is intended to address.

In discussing the quality of tests, it is common to talk about reliability and validity. However, in the light of the foregoing discussion, it can be seen that the variation in students' scores caused by random factors, which is what is normally discussed under the heading of 'reliability', is actually just a specific form of construct-irrelevant variance. We want variations in students' scores to be caused by differences that are relevant to the construct of interest, rather than to irrelevant factors, such as who did the scoring, the particular selection of items used for the test, and whether the student was having a 'good' or a 'bad' day.

This chapter explores this specific issue of reliability, although this particular aspect of validity interacts in complex ways with other aspects of validity. As we shall see below, we can make a test more reliable by asking more questions on a particular topic, so that the score a student receives depends less on the particular selection of questions. However, asking more questions on each topic, if we hold the total amount of testing time constant, means that we cover fewer topics, so then the assessment may then under-represent the construct of interest.

These interactions are important, because the public in general, and policy makers in particular, appear not to understand or pay attention to the issue of reliability. They appear to have faith in the dependability of the results of short tests, which suggests they are ignorant of the magnitudes of the inescapable errors that accompany all measurements. This is a serious failing. Decisions that have a significant impact on a student's future may be taken by placing more trust in a test score than in other evidence about that student, when such trust is not justified.

In this chapter, the first section discusses in more detail what is meant by the reliability of the score obtained from a test or other form of assessment and the second examines published evidence about test reliabilities. The third section then looks at decision consistency, that is, the effects of limited reliability on the errors that ensue when candidates are assigned to specific grades or levels on the basis of test scores. The leading issues are then highlighted in a closing summary.

Threats to reliability

No test is perfectly reliable. It is highly unlikely that the score that someone gets on one occasion would be exactly the same as on another occasion, even on the same test, and even if they could not remember how they had answered on the previous occasion. However, if students took the same or similar tests on a number of occasions then the average of all those scores would, in general, be a good indicator of their capability on whatever it was that the test was measuring. This average is sometimes called the 'true score'. Thus, the starting point for estimating the reliability of a test is to hypothesize that each student has a 'true score' on a particular test. Accepting the notion of 'true score' does not entail a belief that a student has a true ability in (say) reading, nor that the reading score is in any sense fixed. It is merely the long-run average of scores on repeated equivalent tests, assuming that there is no learning – what might be called 'Groundhog day' testing.

There are three main sources of construct-irrelevance variance that are generally discussed under the general issue of reliability (Black and Wiliam, 2002):

- Different raters may give different scores for the same piece of work.
- The same student may perform better or worse from one day to another.
- A particular student may perform better or worse depending on the actual questions selected for the particular administration of the test.

In the United States, it is common to regard all three of these sources of variability as aspects of reliablity, although in the United Kingdom, it is common to regard only the first as reliability, while the second and the third are just 'the luck of the draw'. It is certainly possible to define reliability in such a way as to focus only on how different individuals score the same piece of student work, but this limits the kinds of inferences that can be made. If we want to draw conclusions about an individual's future potential, then the fact that they might get a different score on the same test on a different day poses a real problem. How do we know which of the different scores an individual might get on a particular test, depending on the occasion, we should use? And if we want to make comparisons between students who took different versions of the same test, we need to take into account the fact that which version of the test a student took may make a difference to him or her, even though all versions of the test are equally difficult on average.

The first source – often termed 'marker error' or 'rater error' – is, of course, far less of a problem with multiple-choice tests (although there are still issues, such as when a decision needs to be made about whether a student did, in fact, erase an answer or not). With constructed-response questions (i.e. those where a candidate has to construct a response, rather than choose among the alternatives presented), careful selection and training of markers, detailed protocols for markers to follow, and monitoring performance of markers through scrutiny by a more experienced marker of a sample of their marking, all reduce the variability. It is also worth noting that it has been known for a hundred years that the consistency of the same marker on different occasions can be as significant an issue as consistency between markers (Starch and Elliott, 1912).

The second source – inconsistency of student performance from one occasion to another – is not something that can be addressed easily, but it is important to acknowledge its existence, well illustrated in a study by Black (1963). In the study, first-year physics undergraduates took two parallel forms of the same test within a few days of one another and marked by the same markers to common criteria. The tests were designed to decide who should proceed to honours study. Out of 100 candidates, 26 failed the first paper and 26 failed the second, but only 13 failed both. Half of those who would be denied further access to the honours course on one of the papers would have passed on the other. Although errors in marking and differences in the two tests were significant factors here, it is likely that the variability of the performance of the students from test to test was the major factor in the results observed, and yet in previous years, decisions about proceeding to different courses had been taken on the results of a single paper.

The third source – differences in students' scores caused by the particular choice of items selected for a test – is, in the UK at least, the least discussed source of unreliability, and yet it may be the most important. On any syllabus, there will be a very large number of questions that could be set. Questions can differ both in their content (e.g. force, light, electricity in physics) and in the type of attainment that they test (e.g. knowledge of definitions, solution of routine short problems, design of an experiment to test a hypothesis). Those who set public examinations in the UK usually work with a two-dimensional grid with (say) content topics as the rows and types of attainment as the columns. The relative weights to be given to the cells of this grid are usually prescribed in the syllabus (but they can vary between one syllabus and another); so across any one examination, the examiners must reflect this in the distribution of the questions (e.g. one on the definition of force, two on applying the concept in simple quantitative problems, and so on). In addition, they may deploy different types of questions, for example using a set of 40 multiple-choice questions to test knowledge and simple applications so as to cover many cells, and then having a small number of longer problems to test application of concepts and synthesis of ideas (e.g. the design of an experiment involving detection of light with devices which give out electrical signals). Since the number of such extended questions will necessarily be limited, the particular choice of questions will suit some candidates, and not others.

What the examples here demonstrate is that the composition of an examination is a delicate balancing act. There is a huge number of possible questions that could be set on any one syllabus: the examiners have to select a tiny proportion and try to make their selection a fair sample of all the items that might be chosen. If the time allowed for the test or tests is very short, the sample will be very small. The smaller the sample, the less confidence one can have that the result for any one candidate would be the same as that which would be given on another sample composed in the same way. Thus, any examination can become more reliable if it can be given a longer time.

The magntitudes of these three different sources of construct-irrelevant variance are more than matters of academic debate, since without a proper understanding of the relative significance of these sources of unreliability in student achievement, it is likely that time, money and effort will be mis-directed. For example, in the UK, there appears to be much more emphasis on eradicating variation between raters than on other sources of variability, which leads to a situation in which the same work is often scored twice by different raters. However, for many kinds of constructed-response items, there are studies that show that a more reliable result is obtained by having twice as much student work marked once (e.g. Linn and Baker, 1996). Before we can quantify and compare the sources of unreliability, however, we first have to define reliability precisely.

Defining reliability

The most common approach to defining reliability is based on the internal consistency of a test's results. If, for a test composed of several items, candidates are divided according to their overall score on the test, then one can look at each component question (or item) to see whether those with a high overall score have high scores on this question, and those with low overall scores have low scores on this question. If this turns out to be the case, then the question is said to have 'high discrimination'. If most of the questions have high discrimination, then they are consistent with one another in putting the candidates in more or less the same order.

We want the score a student receives to be unaffected by the particular sample of items used in a test, and one way to establish whether this is, in fact, the case, is to split the test into two half-tests (e.g. one might consist of the odd-numbered items and the other the even-numbered items), and then see how well the scores on the two tests correlate. Of course, with any particular test, the value of the correlation coefficient will depend on how the test has been split into two halves. This is why the most popular measure for the reliability of a test is Cronbach's alpha, which, under certain assumptions, can be considered the average value of the split-half correlations across all possible ways of splitting the test in two (Cortina, 1993), and thus provides one of the best measures of the *internal consistency* of the test.

It is sometimes claimed that the value of Cronbach's alpha provides a lower bound on the reliability of a test (see Cortina, 1993 for a discussion of the meaning of coefficient alpha) and in a general sense, this is true, but the assumptions made in demonstrating this are not always, or even commonly, met in practice. Furthermore, there are some aspects of unreliability that Cronbach's alpha is by definition unable to capture. The inconsistency of a student from one day to the next, is impossible to estimate if we only test the student on a single day. Similarly, the fact that an examiner is a consistently harsh scorer is impossible to estimate if all the scripts from a particular school are allocated to one scorer.

Nevertheless, if the internal consistency of a test is high, then it is likely that a much longer test, sampling more of the syllabus, will give approximately the same result. However, if checks on internal consistency reveal (say) that the reliability of a test is unacceptably low, then steps must be taken to increase the reliability of the test.

One way to do this is to remove from the test items that do not discriminate well – items that are answered almost as well by candidates who score poorly on the test as by those who score well. This does increase the reliability, but it can distort the test considerably. To see why, consider an item that is answered incorrectly by almost all 11-year-olds, and correctly by almost all 12-year-olds. Because almost all 12-year-olds answer the question correctly, the item does not discriminate well amongst 12-year-olds, and if it is replaced by an item on which high-scoring students are much more successful than low-scoring students, then the reliabilty of the test will be increased, so the test will be more useful in discriminating between 12-year-olds. However, the price we have paid is to remove an item that measures something that teachers of 12-year-olds are good at teaching. Attempts to make a test more reliable can therefore make the test less useful as an indication of how much students are learning. We have, in the language of threats to validity discussed above, reduced a source of construct-irrelevant variance at the price of increasing construct under-representation.

It is important to note, however, that the main limitations on the accuracy of examination results are not the fault of testing agencies. All of the sources could be tackled, but only if increases in costs, examining times and times taken to produce results were to be accepted by the educational system. Such acceptance seems most unlikely; in this, as in many other situations, the public gets what it is prepared to pay for. This is accepted in many other areas of public policy, but not, apparently, in educational assessment.

Quantifying reliability

As we saw in the previous section, Cronbach's alpha can be thought of as a correlation coefficient, and so has a maximum value of 1. In certain unusual circumstance, it can actually have a negative value, but a negative value is meaningless, so the effective minimum value of Cronbach's alpha is 0. A value of 1 indicates that the assessment is pefectly reliable – every time we undertake the assessment, we get the same result. A value of 0 indicates that the test is effectively just generating random numbers; the test is providing no information about the candidates.

Many writers have argued that the value of Cronbach's alpha must be at least 0.7 for the test to be considered reliable enough to be used, but in fact there is no hard-and-fast rule. While a value of

0.7 might be acceptable in some settings, even a value of 0.9 is inadequate for other uses. To see why, it is necessary to understand what the value of the reliability really means. There are several different ways of definining reliability, but they are all, in effect, equivalent. Earlier, reliability was defined as the correlation between different versions of the test. It can also be defined as a kind of signal to noise ratio (or more precisely as the ratio of signal to signal plus noise). The difference between the student's true score on a test (the long-run average) and the score that a student achieves on any particular occasion can be called the 'error' in that particular observed score. When the errors are small, the scores on any one occasion will be close to the true score, so that the observed score is a reasonable estimate of the true score, and we say that the test is reliable. When the errors are large, the scores on any one occasion can be very different from the true score, so that the observed score is not a good indication of the true score, and we say the test is unreliable. Of course, this is in reality a continuum, not a stark dichotomy between reliable and unreliable tests.

Unfortunately we cannot use the average value of the errors as an indication of how large the errors are because the average value of the errors with any test, however unreliable, is zero (this is actually a consequence of the definition of true score). Instead, we use a measure of how spread out the errors are. The most common way of measuring the spread in a set of data is the *standard deviation*. For typical 'bell curve' data, 68% of the data fall within one standard deviation of the mean, and 96% fall within two standard deviations of the mean. The standard deviation of the errors is generally called the standard error of measurement, or SEM. The key formula is:

SEM = Standard deviation of scores $\times \sqrt{(1 - r)}$

where r is the reliability of the test.

As can be seen from the formula, when a test has a reliability of 0, the SEM is exactly the same as the standard deviation of the students' scores. In other words, when we find out someone's score, we know nothing more about their achievement that we did before we found out their test result. When a test has a reliability of 1, the SEM is 0, so the observed score is exactly the same as the true score. To see how the SEM varies between these extremes, consider a typical test on which the average score is 50 and the standard deviation of the scores is 15.

Provided that the scores on the test are normally distributed, then 96% of the students' scores will be between 20 and 80 (within two standard deviations of the mean). From the formula above, we can see that with a test with a reliability of 0.85, the SEM will be around 6 (r is 0.85, so 1–r is 0.15, so $\sqrt{(1-r)}$ is around 0.4, so the SEM is 0.4×16). What this means is that when a student takes this test, there is a 68% chance that the score obtained on that occasion will be within 6 percentage points of the true score, and a 96% chance it will be with 12 percentage points of the true score.

In other words in a class of 30 students there is likely to be at least one student whose actual score on the test differs from their true score by more than 12%. Unfortunately, we don't know which student it is, nor whether their observed score was higher or lower than their true score.

A reputable standardized test will provide details of the reliability and how it was calculated (see next section), although Camara and Lane (2006) point out that many publishers fail to do this. The reliability of commercially produced educational tests is in the region from 0.8 to 0.9, and can be over 0.9 for tests focusing on a very narrow range of outcomes, although tests produced by teachers can have reliability much lower than this (Frisbie, 1988). The standard error of measurement of a typical test, and how far from the true score the observed score is likely to be, for a test with mean score of 50 and standard deviation of 15, is shown in Table 15.1.

Because the effects of unreliability operate randomly, the average score for a whole class of students on a given test is likely to be quite close to the true score average for the class (for each student who gets an observed score higher than their true score, there is likely to be one that got an observed score lower than their true score). But just as the person with one foot in boiling water and one foot in ice might be quite comfortable 'on average' we must be aware that the results of even the best tests can be wildly inaccurate for a few individual students. As can be seen from Table 15.1, even if the reliability of the test was 0.95 (a value rarely achieved in practice), one student in a class would receive an observed score that differed from their

Table 15.1 Reliability, standard error of measurement, and observed score range for a typical test

Reliability	SEM	68% margin	96% margin
0.70	8.2	±8.2	±16.4
0.75	7.5	±7.5	±15.0
0.80	6.7	±6.7	±13.4
0.85	5.8	±5.8	±11.6
0.90	4.7	±4.7	±9.5
0.95	3.4	±3.4	±6.7

true score by as much as 7 percentage points. This is why testing experts generally say that high-stakes decisions should never be based solely on the results of a single test.

Evidence about reliability

In 1954, the American Psychological Association published its *Technical Recommendations for Psychological Tests and Diagnostic Techniques*. A revised edition, entitled *Standards for Educational and Psychological Testing*, was developed in 1966 by a joint committee of the American Educational Research Association, the American Psychological Association, and the National Council on Measurement in Education, and updated versions have appeared in 1974, 1985 and 1999.

As a result of this evolution, the *Standards* are now pretty comprehensive, with sections on test construction, evaluation, and documentation, on fairness in testing, and on testing applications. One requirement that has been present since the very first version, over half a century ago, is that tests should be adequately documented, the procedures by which the tests were developed should be documented, and evidence regarding the validity of the tests, and specifically the reliability, must be produced.

It is rather sobering to realize, therefore, than until recently, none of the public tests and examinations in use in the United Kingdom would satisfy these widely accepted criteria. Very little in the way of public information about the reliability of public examinations, such as those taken by students at the age of 16 (General Certificate of Secondary Education) and 18 (the Advanced Level of the General Certificate of Education) exists. On the other hand, evidence about the reliability of national curriculum tests has been made available in recent years, and the new regulatory authority for examinations, qualifications and national assessments for England, the Office of Qualifications and Examinations Regulation (Ofqual), has taken much more seriously the need for greater public understanding of the limitations of educational assessment. Since 2008 it has conducted a research programme 'looking at the consistency of assessments, and factors which may affect the reliability of results' (Office of Qualifications and Examinations Regulation, 2010).

The difficulty with any such programme is, of course, that many of the issues are complex, not completely understood, and in a number of cases, highly contentious. Even an apparently simple question like 'How reliable are the national tests for 11-year-olds?' turns out to be surprisingly complex to answer.

Newton (2009) provides a summary of the evidence on the reliability of the national curriculum assessments from 1996 to 2007 and shows that the reliability of national curriculum assessments has increased sightly over this period.

In English at key stage 2 (age 11), there are tests of reading, writing, spelling and handwriting, but the values of Cronbach were calculated only for the reading and spelling tests, for which the values have been around 0.88 to 0.90 over the last 10 years. At key stage 3 (age 14) the assessment consists of assessments of reading, writing, and a specific paper on Shakespeare, but reliability coefficients were calculated only for the reading paper, for which the value has varied quite significantly over the last 15 years, from a value of 0.71 (in 1996) to 0.94 (in 1998) and has averaged around 0.85 in recent years. Values of Cronbach's alpha have not been calculated for the tests of writing and handwriting at key stage 2 and for the writing and Shakespeare tests at key stage 3 because it is impossible to calculate a value of Cronbach's alpha for a test consisting of just one item.

The tests of mathematics, as might be expected, are more reliable. The reliability of the overall scores in mathematics at key stage 2 (obtained by adding the scores in the two written papers and the mental arithmetic test) has been 0.97 for several years. At key stage 3, the tests for mathematics are 'tiered'; there are two papers (one allowing the use of calculators and the other not) and each paper covers a band of just three levels (3–5, 4–6, 5–7) in addition to a mental mathematics test. This tiering was introduced in order to increase the reliability of the assessment, because, provided a student is entered for a tier that includes the level corresponding to their true score, then a tiered test is, in effect, a longer test, in that it allows more items to be asked that are directly relevant to the candidate's abilities. Of course the danger with a tiered approach is that if the student is entered for an incorrect tier (i.e. one that does not include the level corresponding to the student's true score) then the score obtained is likely to be highly unreliable, being based on only a very small number of items relevant to the student's abilities. Despite the tiering, the scores for the key stage 3 tests appear to be significantly less reliable than those at key stage 2, although part, if not all, of this is due to the fact that with tiered tests, the range of the true scores and therefore of the observed scores, is reduced. In other words, even if the 'noise' remains the same, the ratio of the signal to signal plus noise is reduced when the signal is smaller (e.g. four-fifths is less than five-sixths). The average reliability for each of the mathematics written papers at key stage 3 has been around 0.89 since 2000, which suggests that the reliability of the overall score is around 0.94.

The tests for science, as might be expected, appear to be more reliable than those for English but less than those for mathematics. At key stage 2, the reliability of the overall score across the two science papers has been around 0.92 since 2003, and at key stage 3, around 0.96 for the lower tier, and 0.94 for the upper tier.

Using the formula for the standard error of measurement described above, we can estimate that in the key stage 2 reading test, a student with a true score at the national mean on the test (64%) would receive a score between 58 and 70 just over two-thirds of the time (the 68% margin) and between 52 and 76 most of the time (the 96% margin). In mathematics, the two intervals are 65 to 73 and 62 to 76, while in science they are 57 to 63 and 53 to 67 (the confidence intervals for the science tests are smaller than those for the mathematics tests, because although the tests are less reliable, the performance of the students is less variable in science, so the standard error of measurement is smaller). At key stage 3 an average student would get a score between 38% and 56% on the reading test two-thirds of the time, and between 31% and 64% most of the time (i.e. 96% margin). In both mathematics and science at key stage 3, the width of the 68% and 96% margins are 7 and 10 percentage points respectively.

It is important to realize that these estimates of reliability are likely to be significant over-estimates, for three reasons:

1   Sources of errors not accounted for by Cronbach alpha, such as marker severity, or student inconsistency, have not been included.

2   Tests consisting of a single item, such as the writing test in English, have been omitted, and these are likely to be less reliable than those discussed above (both because the marking is less reliable, and because with a small number of questions, the particular selection of questions can significantly impact an individual's score).

3   The effect of entering a student for an inappropriate tier in mathematics and science has been ignored.

Nevertheless, the evidence is that the reliability of national curriculum assessments compares well to other similar tests. Despite this, however, even with highly reliable tests, there is a significant margin of error. Our purpose in highlighting this is not to criticize the tests – as noted earlier, given the amount of testing time available, it seems to us that these tests are as good as they can be, at least in terms of reliability. Rather our purpose is to highlight that we think it would be helpful if margins of error were routinely reported alongside assessment results, as they are currently with opinion poll data. While most people would have no clue how a margin of error is calculated for an opinion poll, they know that if one candidate is polling 47% of the vote and the other 50%, but the margin of error is 3%, the result is 'too close to call'. In the same way, we hope that reporting margins of error for test scores would lead to more informed use of these scores by key stakeholders. This is particularly important when the scores are reported in terms of grades or bands.

Reliability and classification

As well as information on the reliability of scores, the AERA/APA/NCME standards also require test producers to provide additional information on score accuracy, especially when used to classify individuals or groups into performance regions or other bands on a score scale. For example, if users of test scores understand the idea of standard error of measurement, then they are likely to be aware that the true score of a student receiving 70 on a particular test is on balance likely to be higher than that of a student scoring 69, but that there is a real chance that the student given 69 actually has a higher true score than a student given 70. However, if the students are then classified into bands, with scores of 70 and over being awarded an A, and those between 60 and 69 being awarded a B, then there is a real danger that the student awarded an A is regarded as in some way qualitatively better than the student awarded a B. If the danger with scores is spurious precision, then the danger with grades is spurious accuracy (Wiliam, 2000). A crucial criterion for effective communication to assessment users, therefore, is that the way that unreliability is reported should relate to how the assessment scores are reported and used.

Four studies serve to illustrate the importance of this criterion. The first is a study by Please (1971) in which he explored the impact of unreliability on the grades candidates were awarded in Advanced level examinations of the General Certificate of Education (often just called A-level examinations) using simulated scores. At that time, scores were reported on a 7-grade scale: A, B, C, D, E, O (signifying a pass at ordinary, rather than advanced level) and U (ungraded). He found that when the reliability of the examination was 0.85, for approximately 50% of candidates, their true scores and their observed scores were different enough to result in a different grade. In other words, 50% of students were 'wrongly graded'. Even when the reliability was 0.95, the proportion wrongly graded was 30%. The reason for this, of course, is that when one wants to allocate students to one of seven grades on the basis of a single test, the score boundaries are quite close to each other, so many students are close to a grade boundary, where a small difference in observed and true scores can result in different observed and true grades.

The second is a study by Rogosa (1999) of standardized tests used in the state of California. This shows that even for tests with apparently high indices of reliability, the chances of a candidate being misclassified are high enough to lead to serious consequences for many candidates. His results were expressed in terms of percentiles, a measure of position in the rank order of all candidates. If a candidate is on (say) the 40th percentile this means that 40% of all candidates have marks at or below the mark achieved by that candidate. His results showed, for example, that in Grade 9 mathematics there is only a 57% probability that candidates whose 'true score' would put them in the middle of the rank order of candidates, that is, on the 50th percentile, will actually be classified as somewhere within the range 40th to 60th percentile, so that the other 43% of candidates will be misclassified by over 10 percentile points. For those under-classified, this could lead to a requirement to repeat a grade or to attend a summer school. It could also result in assignment to a lower track in school, which would probably prejudice future achievement. Of the three sources of error listed above, this study explored the effects of the first only, that is, error due to the limited sample of all possible questions.

The third study has provided results that are more detailed and comprehensive. Gardner and Cowan (2000) report an analysis of the 11-plus selection examination in Northern Ireland, where each candidate sits two parallel forms of test with each covering English, mathematics and science. They were able to examine both the internal consistency of each test and the consistency between them. Results are reported on a six-grade scale and each selective (grammar) school admits its applicants on the basis of their grade, starting with the highest, and working down the grades until all the places are filled. Their analysis shows that if one expects to infer a candidate's true grade from the reported grade and one wants to be correct in this inference 95% of the time, then for a candidate in a middle grade one can say only that the true score lies somewhere between the highest and the lowest grades (the '95% confidence interval' thus ranges from the lowest to the highest grade). For a candidate just in the highest grade the true score may be anywhere within the top four grades; given that this is the 95% confidence interval, 5% of students will be misclassified by an even greater margin. Of course, for students close to the threshold, as noted above, even a small misclassification can lead to the wrong decision. Given that approximately 7,000 candidates secure selective places, it is likely that around 3,000 will be misclassified to the extent that either secures or denies acceptance of their entry to grammar school due to the unreliability of the test. This study reflects the effects of all three possible sources of error described above.

The fourth source of evidence was provided by an analysis carried out by Wiliam (2001) of the tests used for assessing students in England at ages 7, 11 and 14 respectively (the end of the first three 'key stages' of education respectively). The analysis followed the same basic model used by Please in the study cited above. The true scores of a number of students (in this case 10,000) were simulated and for each true score, an observed score was obtained by adding a random error to the true score, the size of the errors being varied to simulate the results of tests with different reliability. In order to allocate students to levels, it was assumed that a number of cut-scores would be specified on the mark scale, that these would be equally spaced, and that the lowest cut-score would be at 25% of the available marks, and the highest at 75% of the available marks, since tests are less reliable at the extremes of the score range. At the time, national curriculum assessment allocated students to one of four levels at the end of key stage 1, six levels at the end of key stage 2 and eight levels at the end of key stage 3. The results of this simulation are shown in Table 15.2.

As would be expected, the greater the precision (that is, the more different levels into which students are to be classified as they move from KS1 to KS3) the lower the accuracy, since with more levels, a student will, on average, be closer to a level boundary, and therefore a smaller amount of error would result in their being awarded a level different from that indicated by their true score. What is also clear is that although the proportion of misclassifications declines steadily as the reliability of a test increases, the improvement is rather modest.

Table 15.2 Impact of test reliability on mis-classifications in national curriculum tests

		\multicolumn{8}{c}{Reliability}							
		0.60	0.65	0.70	0.75	0.80	0.85	0.90	0.95
KS1	4	27	25	23	21	19	17	14	10
KS2	6	44	42	40	36	32	27	23	16
KS3	8	55	53	50	46	43	38	32	24

Since the publication of Wiliam's estimates, a number of critiques have appeared. Some of these have simply asserted, without any evidence, that Wiliam's estimates are incorrect. In his evidence to the House of Commons Children Schools and Families Committee's inquiry on Testing and Assessment, Jon Coles, Director of 14–19 Reform at the Department for Children, Schools and Families (DCSF) said:

> I simply do not accept that there is anything approaching that degree of error in the grading of qualifications, such as GCSEs and A-levels. The OECD has examined the matter at some length and has concluded that we have the most carefully and appropriately regulated exam system in the world ... I can say to you without a shadow of a doubt – I am absolutely convinced – that there is nothing like a 30% error rate in GCSEs and A-levels. (House of Commons Children Schools and Families Committee, 2008: 26)

Quite what is meant by 'error' here, is of course, not clear, but it could be that as a result of the widespread belief in the United Kingdom that only the first of the three threats to reliability outlined above are properly matters of reliability, these remarks are intended to describe only misclassification due to marker variability. As noted above, the inconsistency of a candidate's performance from one occasion to another, and from one version of the assessment to another, is widely seen as a problem for the candidate rather than any indication of the limitation of the assessment. If the candiate might have done better on a different occasion, or with a different selection of items, then that is seen as 'the luck of the draw'. In the words of a representative of one of the largest examining bodies, 'I don't think that is a valid misclassification. That is just what happens' (Hayes, in Ofqual, 2009: 8).

Other critiques have rightly pointed out that the national curriculum assessment no longer attempts to classify students into as many levels as was the case when it was first introduced. In English, students are classified into four levels at key stage 2 and six at key stage 3, and just four levels in mathematics, and in the higher tier of science at key stage 3, with five levels for the lower tier science at key stage 3. It is also the case that the tests are more reliable than they were at the time of Wiliam's original simulations. A more recent evaluation of the reliability of national curriculum assessments at key stage 2, using a range of methods, including the simulation method used by Wiliam, suggests that the level of misclassification at key stage 2 – students awarded different levels from those associated with their true score – is probably around 10% for mathematics, 12% for science and 15% for English (He, Hayes and Wiliam, 2011). However, like the estimates discussed above, these are likely to be under-estimates of the real extent of misclassification, since these are all based on an internal consistency approach to reliability.

We can make tests more reliable by improving the items included in the tests and by making the marking more consistent, but in general the effect of such changes is small. There are only two ways of achieving a significant increase in the reliability of a test: make the scope of the test narrower so you ask more questions on fewer topics (thus introducing a greater degree of construct under-representation), or make the test longer so you ask more questions on all of the topics.

Unfortunately, lengthening a test does not increase the reliability very much. A doubling of the length of the key stage 3 reading test would increase the reliability from 0.85 to 0.92, and it would require a test six times as long to match the reliability of the mathematics test at the same key stage.

Now it seems unlikely that even the most radical proponents of schools' tests would countenance the sorts of increases in testing time that would be necessary to reduce misclassification to a level where it was not significant (e.g. less than one student in each class). Fortunately, there is another way of increasing the effective length of a test, without increasing testing time, and that is through the routine use of the information that teachers collect on their students as a routine part of their classroom activities (Black and Wiliam, 2007).

Assessment results generated by teachers are able to address a broader range of aspects of a subject than timed written tests, which, by their nature, assess only what can be assessed in timed written tests. There is therefore the potential for teacher-produced tests to tackle some issues of construct under-representation, although it should be noted that it is likely that this will take a great deal of professional development (Black et al., 2011) and external support (Stanley et al., 2009).

However there is a real concern that using teachers' own results as part of national assessment will introduce a degree of construct-irrelevant variance, whether caused by systematic differences in leniency and severity between teachers, or the fact that teachers may take into account construct-irrelevant factors, such as effort and classroom behaviour, in determining a level that is intended to denote a student's achievement. A number of methods of reducing this form of construct-irrelevant variance have been proposed in the past. Some, such as having teachers meet together to share student work exemplifying particular standards, and making adjustments where necessary (sometimes called 'moderation') are undoubtedly valuable professional development activities, but have been questioned on the grounds of cost and effectiveness. Others, such as using 'matrix' sampling of student work to define an 'envelope' of student scores that the teacher can award would certainly be effective in standardizing scores across a system, but may rely on assumptions that may not be met in practice (such as assuming that students will attempt to do their best on tests that have only an indirect impact on their scores). What does seem unarguable is that, while we should seek to increase the reliability of high-stakes assessments as much as we can, for example, by involving the teachers more in the process, there will always be a need for the users of assessment information to have clear guidance on how to interpret the information they are given, not least in terms of its reliability.

Reliability for formative assessments

Given the theme of many of the chapters in this book, one issue that arises from the foregoing discussion is whether the same kinds of arguments can be made for formative assessment. Messick's definition of validity cited above centres on 'the adequacy and appropriateness of inferences and actions based on test scores or other modes of assessment' (Messick, 1989: 13). As suggested by Wiliam and Black (1996), for summative purposes it is the inferences that are most important, while for formative purposes, it is the actions that are most important. Black and Wiliam (2009) defined formative assessment as follows:

> Practice in a classroom is formative to the extent that evidence about student achievement is elicited, interpreted, and used by teachers, learners, or their peers, to make decisions about the next steps in instruction that are likely to be better, or better founded, than the decisions they would have taken in the absence of the evidence that was elicited. (2009: 9)

From this perspective, formative assessment is reliable to the extent that the assessment processes being used generate evidence that consistently lead to better, or better founded decisions, which turns out to be a less restrictive condition than is needed for summative assessment.

For a summative assessment to be reliable, the construct-irrelevant variance due to random factors must be minimized, because we want differences in scores to represent differences in the constructs being measured, in order that we can make different inferences about individuals. For a formative assessment, this matters less. The same assessment process, administered by different teachers, might result in different evidence of achievement, which jeopardizes the summative function, but as long as the instructional decisions based on this evidence are equally appropriate, they can be different from one teacher to another. This was summed up by Wiliam and Black (1996) as follows:

> As noted above, summative and formative functions are, for the purpose of this discussion, characterized as the end of a continuum along which assessment can be located. At one extreme (the formative) the problems of creating shared meanings beyond the immediate setting are ignored; assessments are evaluated by the extent to which they provide a basis for successful action. At the other extreme (the summative) shared meanings are much more important, and the considerable distortions and undesirable consequences that arise are often justified by appeal to the need to create consistency of interpretation. Presenting this argument somewhat starkly, when formative functions are paramount, meanings are often validated by their consequences, and when summative functions are paramount, consequences are validated by meanings. (1996: 544)

Conclusion

This chapter has argued that reliability is best thought of as an aspect of validity, specifically as the random component of construct-irrelevant variance. Treating reliability in this way explains the apparent paradox that reliability is both a pre-condition for validity, and in tension with it. Improving reliability reduces one source of construct-irrelevant variance, but generally at the expense of increasing construct under-representation, although the interactions between these can be extraordinarily complex.

The issues discussed here are clearly of great importance and ought to be understood by both designers of assessment systems and by users of test results. One arena in which this has importance is the use of assessment results within schools as guidance for students and decisions about them. The fact that teachers may be unaware of the limited reliability of their own tests and other assessments is thus a serious issue. Where assessment results are used for decisions beyond schools, knowledge of reliability is also important. The fact that, at least for public examinations in the UK, reliability is neither researched nor discussed, is a serious weakness. Data on reliability must be taken into account in designing test systems for optimum 'trade-off' between the various constraints and criteria that determine dependability. In the absence of such data, optimum design is hardly possible because it is not possible to evaluate fully alternative design possibilities. As emphasized at the beginning of this chapter, this absence is also serious because all users can be seriously misled. For example, decisions that have an important effect on a student's future may be taken by placing more trust in a test score than in other evidence about that student, when such trust is not warranted.

Overall, one consequence of the absence of reliability data is that most teachers, the public in general, and policy makers in particular do not understand or attend to test reliability as an issue and some are indeed reluctant to promote research into reliability because of a fear that it will undermine public confidence in examinations. Of course, it may well do so to an unreasonable degree where the media and the public generally do not understand concepts of uncertainty and error in data. A debate that promotes the development of such understanding is long overdue.

References

American Psychological Association, American Educational Research Association, & National Council on Measurement in Education (1985) *Standards for Educational and Psychological Testing* (3rd edn). Washington, DC: American Psychological Association.

Black, P.J. (1963) 'Examinations and the teaching of science', *Bulletin of the Institute of Physics and the Physical Society*, 14: 202–3.

Black, P., and Wiliam, D. (2002) *Standards in Public Examinations*. London, UK: King's College London Department of Education and Professional Studies.

Black, P. and Wiliam, D. (2007) 'Large-scale assessment systems: design principles drawn from international comparisons', *Measurement: Interdisciplinary Research and Perspectives*, 5(1): 1–53.

Black, P. J., and Wiliam, D. (2009) 'Developing the theory of formative assessment', *Educational Assessment, Evaluation and Accountability*, 21(1), 5–31.

Black, P., Harrison, C., Hodgen, J., Marshall, B. and Serret, N. (2011) 'Can teachers' summative assessments produce dependable results and also enhance classroom learning?', *Assessment in Education: Principles, Policy and Practice*, 18.

Camara, W.J. and Lane, S. (2006) 'A historical perspective and current views on the Standards for Educational and Psychological Testing', *Educational Measurement: Issues and Practice*, 25(3): 35–45.

Cortina, J.M. (1993) 'What is coefficient alpha? An examination of theory and applications', *Journal of Applied Psychology*, 78(1), 98–104.

Frisbie, D.A. (1988) 'Reliability of scores from teacher-made tests', *Educational Measurement: Issues and Practice*, 7(1): 25–35.

Gardner, J. and Cowan, P. (2000) *Testing the Test: A Study of the Reliability and Validity of the Northern Ireland Transfer Procedure Test in Enabling the Selection of Pupils for Grammar School Places*. Belfast, UK: Queen's University of Belfast Graduate School of Education.

He, Q., Hayes, M., and Wiliam, D. (2011) *Classification Accuracy in Results from KS2 National Curriculum Tests*. Coventry: Office of Qualifications and Examinations Regulation.

House of Commons Children Schools and Families Committee (2008) *Testing and Assessment. Third Report of Session 2007–08, Volume I: Report, Together with Formal Minutes* (Vol. HC 169–I). London, UK: The Stationery Office.

Linn, R.L. and Baker, E. L. (1996) 'Can performance-based student assessment be psychometrically sound?', in J.B. Baron and D.P. Wolf (eds), *Performance-based Assessment – Challenges and Possibilities: 95th Yearbook of the National Society for the Study of Education Part 1*. Chicago, IL: National Society for the Study of Education. Vol. 95(1), pp. 84–103.

Messick, S. (1989) 'Validity', in R. L. Linn (ed.), *Educational Measurement* (3rd edn). Washington, DC: American Council on Education/Macmillan. pp. 13–103.

Newton, P. (2009) 'The reliability of results from national curriculum testing in England', *Educational Research*, 51(2): 181–212.

Office of Qualifications and Examinations Regulation (2009) *The Reliability Programme: Technical Seminar Report*, 7 October 2009 (Vol. Ofqual/09/4638). Coventry, UK: Office of Qualifications and Examinations Regulation.

Office of Qualifications and Examinations Regulation (2010) 'Reliability', 22 October. Available at: http://www.ofqual.gov.uk/research-and-statistics/research-reports/92–articles/20-reliability#reports (accessed 18 December 2010).

Please, N.W. (1971) 'Estimation of the proportion of examination candidates who are wrongly graded', *British Journal of Mathematical and Statistical Psychology*, 24: 230–8.

Rogosa, D. (1999) *Accuracy of Individual Scores Expressed in Percentile Ranks: Classical Test Theory Calculations*. Stanford, CA: Stanford University.

Rogosa, D. (2002) *Irrelevance of Reliability Coefficients to Accountability Systems: Statistical Disconnect in Kane-Staiger 'Volatility in School Test Scores'*. Stanford, CA: Stanford University.

Stanley, G., MacCann, R., Gardner, J., Reynolds, L. and Wild, I. (2009) *Review of Teacher Assessment: Evidence of What Works Best and Issues for Development*. London, UK: Qualifications and Curriculum Authority.

Starch, D. and Elliott, E.C. (1912) 'Reliability of grading high school work in English', *School Review*, 20: 442–57.

Wiliam, D. (2000) 'The meanings and consequence of educational assessments', *Critical Quarterly*, 42(1): 105–27.

Wiliam, D. (2001) 'Reliability, validity and all that jazz', *Education 3–13*, 29(3): 17–21.

Wiliam, D. and Black, P. J. (1996) 'Meanings and cosequences: a basis for distinguishing formative and summative functions of assessment?', *British Educational Research Journal*, 22(5), 537–48.

Chapter 16

Validity, Purpose and the Recycling of Results from Educational Assessments

Paul E. Newton

Introduction

> We believe that using national test and exam data for sev-
> eral purposes is a strength. One of the core principles for
> efficient use of data in government should be 'collect once,
> use more than once', and this is the case. (A statement
> from England's Office for Standards in Education (Ofsted),
> recorded in House of Commons Children, Schools and
> Families Committee, 2008, see Appendix 2, p. 15)

The intention of this chapter is to interrogate the value-for-money
principle embodied in the above quotation: 'collect once, use more
than once'. Educational assessment is expensive to do well, especially
when it involves testing national or state cohorts. So the principle is
surely a no-brainer: the more results from educational assessments
can be recycled, the higher the value-for-money achieved. It requires
an additional caveat, of course: the test needs to be of a satisfactory
quality; which, in the lexicon of educational assessment, means that
it needs to be 'valid'. But, as long as the test is valid, there follows a
moral obligation to use its results for as many purposes as possible.

Although the principle seems indisputable, at a general level, there
are important issues of detail to interrogate; especially the validity
caveat. The intention of this chapter is to warn against crude conceptions of validity, which might tempt the unwary user into recycling

results inappropriately, that is, into using them for too many purposes. To understand how to recycle results responsibly, a more sophisticated conception of validity is required.

A naïve argument for recycling

A naïve argument for recycling educational assessment results (e.g. from a test of attainment within an area of learning like primary school mathematics) might go something like this:

1 The validity of any test is judged relative to its purpose.
2 The purpose of an educational test is to certify how much of its curriculum each student has mastered.
3 The validity of an educational test is, therefore, judged in terms of alignment between the content of the curriculum and the content of the test, which is known as content validity.[1]
4 If the test is content valid, then it will be capable of identifying, with accuracy, the extent to which the curriculum has been mastered.
5 If the test is content valid, and its results are therefore accurate and trustworthy, then we have no reason not to put them to all sorts of uses.
6 Indeed, for reasons of value-for-money, we have a moral obligation to put them to as many uses as possible.

According to this logic, the primary technical issue for debate is whether or not the test content provides a sufficiently good sample, or representation of the curriculum area studied. If so, then we have a licence to use, and to reuse, results. If not, then the results should not really be used at all; certainly not where the stakes of inaccurate assessment are high.

To some extent, this *is* a straw man argument. My intention is not to criticize any particular individual, or organization, for advocating it. Instead, my intention is educative: to introduce the reader to some central tenets of modern validity theory; and, thereby, to help prevent them from falling for the seductively persuasive logic of the naïve argument. Because there is a clear logic to this argument and it does sound persuasive! Yet, there are at least three major errors contained within its premises, which render it unsound:

1 Validity is not a property of tests, per se, and certainly not an absolute, once-and-for-always property.

2   Validity, even for a curriculum-based test, concerns *far more* than alignment between test content and curriculum content.

3   The idea of 'certificating learning' misses the really important point about test purposes.

Correcting errors in the argument

Correcting these errors leads to a far more sophisticated view of validity and of the accuracy of results from educational assessments. This, in turn, helps to clarify requirements for responsible recycling.

Validity is not a property of tests

Although the concept of validity has been central to educational assessment since the early 1920s (e.g. NADER, 1921), its meaning is still contentious (see Lissitz, 2009). Most commentators would agree, however, that it is incorrect to speak of the validity of a test; as though, once validated, a test is valid for all test takers, for all testing contexts and for all time. In stark contrast, it is widely recognized that – for a given test – results may be more or less accurate, depending upon:

- the way in which the test process is administered;
- the particular group of students tested;
- the circumstances under which students are tested;
- and so on.

If, for example, guidelines for administering a test are not followed then we cannot expect results to reflect attainment accurately. If students have more time than specified, or if they are not prevented from copying from each other, or if their performances are rated by untrained markers, etc., then validity cannot be assured.

Likewise, if a test is administered under unusual circumstances, it is likely to function differently. Results from a test administered during the afternoon of a World Cup final, or a Super Bowl, might well be suspect, if a large number of those assessed were distracted by events. Equally, a test administered under high-stakes circumstances might function differently from a test administered under low stakes; and it might even function differently for different sub-groups of students (increased anxiety being a motivator for some, inflating their scores, and a distracter for others, deflating theirs).

Similarly, a test that provides a good measure of a proficiency, trait or characteristic for certain groups of students might deliver a poor measure of the same 'construct' for other groups. A test of everyday numeracy might work well for native test takers, but poorly for recent immigrants; if, for example, the latter lacked familiarity with the everyday contexts utilized despite possessing the underlying numeracy skills.

From a technical perspective, validity is often described in terms of the accuracy of results from educational assessments. So, rather than being a property of *tests*, per se, validity is better understood as a property of a *set of results* from a given test that has been administered in a certain way to a particular group of students under certain circumstances (and so on). In fact, many would go a step further, defining validity as a property of the *interpretation* and *use* of results.

By way of example, validation, for a Year 6 mathematics test, might involve establishing grounds for the following argument: If the Year 6 mathematics test is administered to Year 6 students, under examination conditions and conventional circumstances, then we may legitimately interpret results in terms of a level of mathematics attainment for each student, and be reasonably confident in the accuracy of those conclusions.

The essential point, here, is that: if, for a particular administration of a test, the set of parameters *does not* hold for some reason, then it cannot necessarily be assumed that results will be interpretable as intended. For instance, results from a written test of critical thinking – designed and validated for native speakers of English – are likely to be less accurate for students who do not speak English fluently. If the negative impact of test format upon performance was large enough then the argument for interpreting their test results in terms of critical thinking ability might turn out to be insufficiently strong.

In summary, the 'one test: one validity' assumption is simply wrong. So there could be no one-off, absolute, universal licence for using test results for any purpose under the sun.

Validity concerns far more than alignment

It used to be widely accepted that different tests were validated in different ways. So if you wanted to investigate the quality of an occupational selection test, then you would simply need to examine its predictive (or 'criterion') validity, that is how well the test predicted performance in a certain occupational role. Likewise, if you wanted to investigate the quality of an educational test, a test of attainment within a curriculum area, then you would simply need to examine its content validity, that is how well the test sampled the curriculum.

Contrary to the conclusion of the previous section, if it *were* possible to validate an educational test purely on the basis of test content, then this would seem to revitalize the 'one test: one validity' claim. If a test contains a representative sample of content then it contains a representative sample of content, period. It always will do, for all test-takers, as long as the curriculum stays the same. The idea that validity can be established through a simple analysis of test content is fraught with problems, though.

Content analysis tells only part of the story concerning the interpretation of results from educational assessments. A test of science reasoning, for example, can be undermined by the use of unduly familiar content; turning it into a test of *knowledge of*, rather than *reasoning with*, the phenomena of science. So, content that seems to be appropriate for assessing science reasoning might actually fail to assess it in practice: students might pass the test on the basis of their general knowledge rather than on the basis of their ability to reason scientifically. In an exactly similar fashion, the use of unduly unfamiliar, confusing, or poorly presented content can undermine an assessment by introducing inappropriate barriers to successful performance. This time, students may fail not because they lack the necessary ability to reason scientifically but because something else about the test distracts them. The content of the test may sample the curriculum effectively, but the way in which it is presented may undermine this. If so, then results will be affected by factors beyond those that the test was intended to assess, that is 'construct-irrelevant variance' will be introduced into the results.[2]

Essentially, what needs to be established, through validation, is that higher scores indicate higher levels of the construct and lower scores indicate lower levels; where the 'construct' is the proficiency, trait or characteristic that is supposedly being assessed. In short, tests aim to assess constructs, and constructs are at the heart of validation activity. This is why commentators now tend to elevate construct validity to a central location within validity theory, such that all validity evidence (from content analyses, to reliability statistics or prediction studies) is ultimately interpretable as evidence of construct validity. This is the 'unified' conception of validity (e.g. Messick, 1989) which contrasts with the view that different kinds of test need to be judged by reference to different standards of validity. Construct validity is now the over-arching standard against which all educational and psychological assessments are judged.

Although constructs, like 'mathematics attainment', may be given meaning with reference to specific curricula, they are conceptually quite distinct from them. A construct is a rough-and-ready summary description of a proficiency, trait or characteristic, which is used to aid the interpretation of test results. From this perspective, even the name given to the construct needs to be part of a validation exercise.

Imagine, for example, a curriculum that led to a qualification in 'science'. The qualification title suggests that the construct 'science attainment' has been assessed. While content validation might look simply at alignment between the science examination and the science curriculum, construct validation ought to go beyond this to consider the interpretation of curriculum itself. Does it really stand up to the label 'science' as far as interested stakeholders and users of results are concerned? What if a substantial proportion of the curriculum was given over to geology, psychology, sociology? Would the aggregate still legitimately be interpreted as 'science'? What if the curriculum actually contained only psychology and sociology? What then? These are broader questions of construct validity that are fundamental to the correct interpretation of results from educational assessments. As Cronbach put it: 'Questions of construct validity become pertinent the moment a finding is put into words' (Cronbach, 1988:13).

As a final example of why content validity is woefully inadequate as a basis for establishing the proper interpretation of results from educational assessments, consider alternative approaches to combining results across components of an assessment. Imagine, for instance, that students learned how to play five instruments during a period of instruction in music. At the end of the period they were assessed on their practical performance skills, for each of the five instruments separately, with each performance rated on a 10-point scale. How might a single, overall result for music be derived? One solution would be to add the five separate scores to derive a total mark for music. Another would be to award students the highest mark attained across all five instruments. Yet another might be to pass only those students who achieved a minimum threshold score on all five instruments. Why might one of these approaches be chosen over another? Once again, we need to think in terms of constructs, not simply content. If we wished to assess 'musical virtuosity' we might opt for the second solution. If we wished to assess a general 'aptitude for musical performance' we might prefer the first solution. If we needed reassurance that students had attained a 'minimum musical competence' across all of the instruments that they had been taught, then we might opt for the third solution. Of course, in each case, the assessed content is exactly the same – performance on each of the five instruments – so there is no distinction to be drawn in terms of the outmoded conception of content validity. Yet, simply by changing the method of aggregation, we change the interpretation of results, that is, the construct that is supposedly being assessed.

Again, the 'one test: one validity' assumption is simply wrong.

The idea of 'certificating learning' misses the point

The mistaken view that validity is reducible to alignment between curriculum and assessment resonates strongly with our final red herring. It is not at all uncommon to hear 'certification' described as the 'primary purpose' of educational assessment – especially for school-leaving certificates, where it seems self-evident that their primary purpose must be the certification of the learning that has occurred during the years of compulsory education (see Newton, 2007). Ironically, though, the very idea of 'certificating learning' misses the really important point about test purposes; indeed, it obscures that point.

The certification of learning manages to muddy the water by appearing to constitute an important purpose, whilst actually not referring to any useful purpose at all; where a 'useful' purpose is a purpose for which results are used. For educational assessment, perhaps more so than for other branches of assessment, it is tempting to think that assessment is an end in itself: as though it were somehow of some abstract, academic interest to know how much of a particular curriculum a student had mastered; or, perhaps, as though the only point of the assessment were to represent a stick with which those who failed would ultimately be beaten.

What is entirely missed, from this perspective, is the fact that results from educational assessments – just like results from all other assessments – are produced in order to be used. They may be used immediately or they may be used only some way down the line. But they are produced in order to be used. And they are used to make decisions; decisions that would otherwise be made less intelligently, on the basis of less information. Furthermore, rather than there being a single purpose that dominates educational assessment (the certification of learning), results from educational assessments are used for all sorts of purposes, that is for making all sorts of decisions.

National curriculum testing in England provides an excellent illustration of the multiple purposes for which results are used. From the mid-1990s onwards, 11-year-old pupils were tested, at the end of their second 'key stage' of the national curriculum, in three subject areas (English, mathematics and science) and were awarded a national curriculum level in each. By the end of the first decade of the 2000s, results from these tests had acquired all sorts of uses, including the following, in no particular order:

1 **Screening** – teachers used pupils' subject results to decide which pupils might require further diagnostic testing for Special Educational Needs statements/provision.

2 **Transfer** – on transfer to secondary school, teachers used pupils' subject results to identify the general educational needs of the new intake.

3 **Placement** – more specifically, secondary school teachers used pupils' subject results to decide which set or stream to locate them within.

4 **Formative** – primary school teachers used subject results (for individual questions and groups of questions), aggregated to the class-level, to decide where their teaching had been effective and ineffective, for remedial action with subsequent teaching groups.

5 **Social evaluation** – pupils used test results to judge their own social standing within peer groups.

6 **Student monitoring** – teachers used pupils' subject results to decide whether they had made satisfactory progress since the last formal assessment.

7 **Target setting** – national and authority officials, school managers and teachers used results, at all levels of aggregation, to set attainment targets for authorities, schools, teachers and pupils, respectively.

8 **Reward** – school managers used results, aggregated to class- and school-level (within subjects), to identify high performance, and to promote and financially reward staff; parents decided whether or not to reward individual pupils on similar bases.

9 **Institution monitoring** – officials, managers and parents used results, aggregated to school-level (within and across subjects) and compared against earlier results, to identify the 'value-added' by primary schools and, therefore, to decide which schools were the most and least effective.

10 **Resource allocation** – officials used results, aggregated to the school-level (within and across subjects), to justify the allocation of resources to under-performing schools and to justify 'light touch' inspection for high-performing schools.

11 **Organizational intervention** – officials used results, aggregated to the school-level (across subjects), to justify the closure of failing schools.

12 **Programme evaluation** – researchers used results, at all levels of aggregation, to investigate factors associated with successful teaching and schooling.

13 **School choice** – parents used results, aggregated to the school-level (within and across subjects), to identify the schools most likely to educate their children effectively.

14 **System monitoring** – policy makers used results, aggregated to the school-level (within subjects), to proclaim the success of their educational policies and as the basis for further policy decisions.

15 **Comparability** – examining boards used results, aggregated across students entered for their own examinations, to establish comparability of standards across those examinations and across examining boards.

16 **Valuation** – estate agents used results, aggregated to school-level, to gauge appropriate catchment-area premiums.

No doubt results were also used for purposes not identified above, either officially or unofficially (see also Mansell, 2007: 6).

So we seem to have returned to where we started, the principle of value-for-money: 'collect once, use more than once'. But we now know that the naïve argument for recycling results from educational assessments is unsatisfactory. It is not the case that an educational test, once content validated, can legitimately be used for any purpose under the sun. A more sophisticated argument is required. It is not simply the case that changes in administration conditions, type of students assessed, context of assessment (etc.) may necessitate re-validation; validation needs to be undertaken anew for each distinct use of results.

Responsible recycling of results

One way of understanding the claim that each distinct use of results needs to be validated separately is to think of each use in terms of a specific construct: the construct that, if assessed accurately, would allow the relevant decision to be made correctly. To do so, we need to think outside the box of traditional educational assessment.

Traditionally, we define that which is assessed by an end-of-course, curriculum-based assessment in terms of an 'attainment' construct, like 'mathematics attainment'. If, for example, we needed to decide whether a student had made satisfactory progress since their last mathematics test, we would certainly want to interpret both current and previous test results in terms of a traditional conception of 'mathematics attainment'. We might draw an inference along the following lines: we can be reasonably confident that our student – who fell at the 79th percentile last time, with a level 4, and at the 85th percentile this time, with a level 6 – has genuinely made good progress, in both absolute and relative terms; that is, as well as having attained a higher level of mathematics attainment than previously, her mathematics attainment is also higher than previously, relative to her peers.

But what about an alternative use of results, say, placement? In making a placement decision we are concluding, on the basis of the test result, that a student will make better educational progress if located in one mathematics set rather than in another (i.e. they will, perhaps for a range of reasons, be better suited to the teaching and learning environment within that set). In an important sense, then, the construct interpretation that requires validation, in relation to this alternative use of results, is subtly different, even though exactly the same set of results is being used. Instead of 'attainment', per se, the construct underlying the placement decision is more like 'readiness' for studying mathematics within one of a number of sets.

Providing a validation argument for this alternative use of results would therefore go significantly beyond a traditional validation exercise (which provided grounds for interpreting results purely in terms of 'mathematics attainment'). It would need to provide grounds for interpreting (the same set of) results in terms of 'readiness' for one set rather than another, where current level of attainment might constitute only an aspect of this broader construct.

The point might appear confusingly subtle, with the placement example, but it becomes far more stark when results are aggregated across pupils in a class, or across subjects within a school. For example, when results, aggregated to the school-level, are used by parents, to make decisions on where to educate their children, we need to identify quite clearly how results are being interpreted and used. When primary schools are compared with each other, in terms of their aggregated school-level results, averaged across three subject areas, what interpretations of those results are being made? Or, from a slightly different perspective, what is the construct that, if assessed accurately, would enable parents to make good decisions about where to educate their children? Presumably, we must be implicating constructs like 'school effectiveness' whereby an effective school will be better at educating pupils than an ineffective one. If so, then a validation exercise, for this particular use of test results (school choice), would need to establish grounds for interpreting aggregated school-level results, averaged across three subject areas, in terms of the construct 'school effectiveness'.

From this angle, it should be clear that a validation exercise which focused upon each individual test in isolation, in terms of the particular attainment construct that it was originally designed to assess, would be woefully inadequate as a basis for justifying the use of results for a purpose as distant (from the test itself) as school choice. This distant use of results needs to be evaluated in terms of a significantly broader construct: not 'mathematics attainment' or 'science attainment' but 'school effectiveness'. And this, no doubt, will be a far more complicated task to undertake.

This brings us to the most important conclusion of the chapter: while the argument for interpreting outcomes from a certain assessment in terms of a certain construct (supporting one use of results) might be very strong, that does not mean that the argument for interpreting outcomes from exactly the same assessment in terms of a different construct (supporting another use of results) will be equally strong. It might, for instance, turn out to be entirely valid to use results from a test of English as the basis for making a placement decision (interpreting results in terms of 'readiness'); but entirely invalid to use results from exactly the same test as the basis for making a screening decision (interpreting results in terms of 'dyslexia risk').

Responsible test design

It is fair to say that educational assessments, especially end-of-course, curriculum-based assessments, are traditionally designed to be interpreted straightforwardly in terms of attainment constructs. So a school science test will typically be designed to assess a variant of 'science attainment' which will relate to the learning outcomes of a particular science curriculum. In a sense (the 'certification of learning' sense), this is natural and appropriate. However, where results are intended to serve a specific purpose or, more likely, purposes, then these purposes need to be considered explicitly at the design stage too.

If, for example, an end-of-school leaving examination in geography were intended to be used as a selection instrument, for entry to a higher level course in geography, then the interpretation of results would need to depart somewhat from the traditional attainment-based conception. That is, instead of results being interpreted purely in terms of school-level 'geography attainment' they would need to be interpreted in terms of a construct like 'geography aptitude' for college-level study.

Importantly, if the test had been designed to be interpreted primarily in terms of (current) attainment then an interpretation in terms of future (aptitude) would inevitably be less accurate. Correspondingly, whenever the traditional approach to designing educational assessments is followed, interpretations of results in terms of alternative constructs ('readiness', 'aptitude' and so on) are going to be correspondingly less accurate. By way of example, while we might be fairly confident that a student with grade B has attained higher (in school-level geography) than a student with grade C, we may be somewhat less confident that they have a lower aptitude (for college-level study). In short, the results were designed to be interpreted in terms of attainment; so, if we interpret them in terms of aptitude, then we are more likely to make mistakes. This is not to say that we should never interpret the results in terms of aptitude; simply that we should recognize that our conclusions will be correspondingly less accurate if we do so. Ideally, even at the design stage, a separate validation exercise should have been conducted to determine exactly how accurately conclusions concerning aptitude, as opposed to attainment, could be drawn.

This raises an uncomfortable question for the educational assessment designer. On the one hand, the principle 'the assessment tail must never wag the curriculum dog' seems to have acquired the status of a biblical commandment. Yet, on the other, if results from educational assessments are specifically intended to serve multiple purposes, then assessment design compromises will probably need to be made. For example, it might be necessary to make an educational assessment slightly less good, as a measure of current attainment, to make it slightly better as a measure of future aptitude; thereby optimizing the use of results for both purposes. If this were to reduce alignment between curriculum and assessment then this bitter pill might just have to be swallowed. After all, as we have already made clear, validity is far more than alignment. So, from time to time, the assessment tail may have to exert a significant force on the curriculum dog ... whether it actually wags it (whether the taught curriculum actually suffers in consequence) is ultimately up to teachers and learners to negotiate.

Conclusion

It is easy to fall into the trap of thinking that satisfactory alignment between curriculum and assessment (content validity) provides a licence to use results from a given educational assessment for any purpose under the sun. However, since validity is not a property of tests, per se, and since validity concerns far more than alignment, this view is simply mistaken.

Instead, a separate licence is required for each distinct use to which results are put. The licence is still grounded in validity, but in a modern conception which emphasizes the centrality of constructs. Indeed, it may be helpful to think of different uses to which results are put requiring the interpretation of results in terms of different constructs. This would mean that results from curriculum-based, educational assessments need to be interpreted not simply in terms

LIBRARY, UNIVERSITY OF CHESTER

of attainment constructs, but also in terms of far broader constructs, like 'readiness', 'aptitude', 'school effectiveness', and so on.

Responsible recycling of results requires the licence provided by a sound validity argument, for each construct and use of results separately. If there are 16 separate uses to which a particular set of results are put, then 16 separate validity arguments will need to be developed. Certain uses will undoubtedly be less valid than others, perhaps even to the extent of invalidity.

Finally, responsible test design means paying due attention to the possibility, or likelihood, of multiple uses of results, from the outset. Tough decisions on design optimization may need to be made. Ideally, the assessment tail should not wag the curriculum dog. Sometimes, though, it may be right to put up with a little canine vibration for the greater assessment good.

Notes

1 Part of sampling 'the right stuff' (to ensure content validity) is the related requirement of sampling 'enough of' the right stuff (to ensure reliability).
2 Contrast this with 'construct-relevant variance' – the variation between student results that can be attributed to genuine differences between them in the proficiency, trait or characteristic that you want to assess – which, from a technical perspective, is the only kind of variance you really want to see.
3 Very many more references could have been cited to identify and explicate positions adopted in this chapter. For insight into where these ideas may have developed from, please consult Messick (1989) and Kane (2006).

References[3]

Cronbach, L.J. (1988) 'Five perspectives on validity argument', in H. Wainer and H.I. Braun (eds) *Test Validity*. Hillsdale, NJ: Erlbaum. pp. 3–17.

House of Commons Children, Schools and Families Committee (2008) *Testing and Assessment: Government and Ofsted Responses to the Committee's Third Report of Session 2007–08. Fifth Special Report of Session 2007–08*. London: The Stationery Office Limited.

Kane, M. (2006) 'Validation' in R.L. Brennan (ed.), *Educational Measurement* (4th edn). Washington, DC: American Council on Education/Praeger. pp.17–64.

Lissitz, R.W. (2009) (ed.) *The Concept of Validity: Revisions, New Directions and Applications*. Charlotte, NC: Information Age Publishing.

Mansell, W. (2007) *Education by Numbers: The Tyranny of Testing*. London: Politicos Publishing.

Messick, S. (1989) 'Validity', in R.L. Linn (ed.) *Educational Measurement* (3rd edn). New York: American Council on Education/Macmillan. pp.13–103.

NADER (1921) 'National Association of Directors of Educational Research: Report of the Subcommittee on Statistical Methods of the Standardization Committee (Tentative)', *Journal of Educational Research*, 4(1): 75–80.

Newton, P.E. (2007) 'Clarifying the purposes of educational assessment', *Assessment in Education: Principles, Policy and Practice*, 14(2): 149–70.

Concluding Remarks

Chapter 17

Assessment for Learning: A Compelling Conceptualization

John Gardner

Introduction

At a seminar in 1998, hosted by the Nuffield Foundation at their London headquarters, the Assessment Reform Group launched the Black and Wiliam review pamphlet *Inside the Black Box* (Black and Wiliam, 1998b). The review itself, and the pamphlet, immediately attracted critical acclaim and have continued to enjoy significant impact on assessment thinking throughout the UK and further afield to the present day. However, one moment in the event sticks out clearly in my memory. After the main presentation, a senior educational policy maker stood up and declared that he had heard it all before; we had nothing new to offer. Indicating, with a glance at his watch, that he had commitments elsewhere he promptly left the seminar before the discussion proper got underway. My immediate urge was to rush after him and say 'Yes, you are absolutely right! But it seems to us that, powerful as it might be, formative assessment is actually off the schools' and policy-makers' radar! Surely we need to do something quite urgently if we are to reap the benefits we know are there?' I resisted the urge and instead a year later, at the same venue and with the same sponsors, we injected the urgency we all felt was needed. We launched the pamphlet *Assessment for Learning: Beyond the Black Box* (ARG, 1999). This pamphlet deliberately and directly challenged official complacency and inertia.

Thirteen years on, the Assessment Reform Group has recorded an impressive list of dissemination successes and official endorsements of assessment for learning from, for example, the Scottish and Welsh governments, the curriculum and assessment agencies of England, Scotland, Wales and Northern Ireland, and from overseas jurisdictions as diverse as Hong Kong and the Canadian province of Alberta. However, in contrast to the situation in Scotland, Wales and Northern Ireland the policy agenda in England remains hamstrung by an accountability agenda which is driving assessment policy. Despite many authoritative, research-based criticisms since 2006, the year of the first edition of this book, I am disappointed to record that schools in England are still being evaluated on the basis of the performance of their students on external assessments. The use of the controversial 'league table', which purports to indicate the relative quality of education in English schools continues unchanged, though abandoned in the three other jurisdictions as divisive and not fit for purpose, that is, forcing schools through competition to raise standards. What it does instead is to increase the emphasis on 'teaching to the test' as schools focus on raising their students' performance in external tests and assessments. There is evidence that the richness of the delivered curriculum suffers and that the pedagogic techniques associated with assessment for learning are neglected.

Paradoxically, assessment for learning's central message, prompted by the research review of Paul Black and Dylan Wiliam (1998a) and disseminated vigorously by the Assessment Reform Group, is that overall standards and individual performance may be improved by actually emphasizing formative assessment techniques such as student self-assessment, negotiation of learning goals and feedback to identify next steps. This message is now strongly established in schools across the UK, though the quality and effectiveness of its implementation is quite another question.

Much progress has therefore been made since the first edition was published, but let me return for a moment to the observations made by our disappointed seminar guest above. I readily concede that the principles and processes of assessment for learning are not novel in any real sense; indeed they have a fairly lengthy pedigree in curriculum and assessment developments in the UK. I could reflect on Harry Black's work with teachers in the early 1980s (Black, 1986) or I could cite the work by Wynne Harlen that led to the publication of professional development materials under the title *Match and Mismatch* (Harlen et al., 1977), to illustrate the point. Such sources would be in keeping with the book's primary focus on schools but I will illustrate the breadth of recognition of the principles we espouse with an example from post-compulsory (vocational) education. The quotation that follows could conceivably have appeared at any time in the last 13 years since the publication of *Inside the Black Box* (Black and Wiliam, 1998b) and the subsequent Assessment Reform Group outputs: *Assessment for Learning:*

Beyond the Black Box (ARG, 1999); *Assessment for Learning: 10 Principles* (ARG, 2002a) and *Testing, Motivation and Learning* (ARG, 2002b).

However, the quotation I reproduce below was actually written in 1986 by Richard Pring as part of an analysis of developments in vocational curricula, initially sponsored by the 1979 publication of the Department of Education and Science's Further Education Unit's *A Basis for Choice*. He argued that a number of implications for assessment had begun to emerge in the wake of the various initiatives in post-compulsory qualifications and summarized them as follows:

> First, *what* had to be assessed was different. A curriculum that stresses personal development, social awareness, cooperative learning, problem solving, is seeking to assess different qualities from those assessed in traditional forms of examination. Secondly, *the purpose of assessment was different.* The main purpose of assessment was the diagnosis of learning needs with a view to promoting the process of learning. It is difficult to provide well-informed guidance, and consequent negotiation of further learning experiences, without some assessment of what the students know or can do. Therefore, it was recommended that the assessment should be part of a continuous, formative profile of the experiences and achievements of the student. Furthermore, it was envisaged that this profile would be the basis of regular teacher/student discussion and guidance of educational progress. The radical difference lies not only in the content of what is taught but also in the processes of learning and thus the demands upon assessment. In its Resources Sheet ... the Joint Board [City and Guilds of London Institute and the Business and Technician Education Council] says:

> 'If the individual student is to be enabled to make the most of his/her programme, the quality of the assessment system and its link with supportive guidance will be critical. Most of the assessing will be formative; that is, a regular feedback on performance to the students from all those involved ... '

> Assessment is thus tied to guidance, negotiation, and the assumption of responsibility for one's own learning. (Pring, 1986:13–14, emphases in original)

There are many such examples, over time, of the acceptance that the classroom assessment techniques comprising assessment for learning are broadly 'good things' to do. However, the specific intention of this book has been to ground this 'goodness' in a credible argument that draws its authority and explanatory power from sound empirical and theoretical contexts. The central arguments have emerged in various ways throughout the chapters, using research evidence and theory to explain and support the points made. We have attempted to address the specific education-related aspects of assessment for learning, and complementary aspects of summative assessment, but clearly there are many more contextual issues that have a bearing on practice, policy and indeed perception. There are many challenges still remaining for assessment researchers and practitioners, but specifically for policymakers, and in our final pamphlet as a group (ARG, 2009) we drew attention to these. I have summarized three below:

1 Putting effective in-class assessment into practice system-wide;
2 Enhancing confidence in tests and examinations;
3 Justifying the costs of assessment.

Putting effective in-class assessment into practice system-wide

Effective use of formative assessment in English schools is considered to be patchy among teachers, who generally appear to have a strong idealistic commitment to the thinking behind formative assessment concepts but struggle to put them into practice in the face of competing pressures on their time and priorities. This contrasts with the situation in other countries of the UK. These have reduced some of the critical pressures by rejecting whole cohort testing, as the basis of accountability, and have promoted assessment for learning through rather different kinds of development programmes. For example, the extension of a Thinking Skills and Assessment for Learning development programme in Wales is based on close partnership between civil servants, local authorities and schools, as well as local and national networking to encourage adaptation and spread good practice. Something similar has been effected in Northern Ireland where thinking skills and assessment for learning are firmly embedded in a radical new curriculum. In Scotland, the Assessment is for Learning (AifL) programme has been succeeded by the Curriculum for Excellence programme which has re-affirmed the importance of AfL. As a result, there are high levels of commitment and engagement amongst teachers and learners.

Enhancing confidence in tests and examinations

Assessment data, for the most part based on pupil performance in tests and examinations, are now used in an extraordinary variety of ways, underpinning not just judgements of pupils' progress, but helping to measure the performance of their teachers, schools and the nation's education system as a whole, among other uses. These uses can have far-reaching consequences for those being judged by the data. An important question that must continue to be asked is: how reliable is this data? Research presented in this book strongly suggests that we should treat test results with caution. A second important question relates to the validity of tests and examinations: do they measure the aspects of education which society feels it is important to measure? A third issue relates to the impact of publishing information on pupils' test and examination scores. The underpinning accountability agenda lost ground in Scotland, Northern Ireland and Wales and is now largely an English phenomenon, at least in the context of public rankings of schools and their pupils' performances on national tests. Side-effects include the often excessive and inequitable focus of many schools on pupils whose results may be key to a school hitting particular achievement targets; the repetition involved in months of focusing on what is tested and on test practice, which also serves to narrow the curriculum; and the consequent undermining of professional autonomy and morale among teachers. Despite the great volume of material cataloguing these educational side-effects, and the lack of confidence in the reliability and validity of the tests and examinations used, this system persists.

Justifying the costs of assessment

Extraordinary sums of money are now devoted to assessment systems in the UK and the key question is whether these resources could be better spent. In 2005, the consultants PricewaterhouseCoopers published a report (PWC, 2005) based on an investigation carried out in late 2003, which estimated the annual total cost of the English examinations system as £610 million. This total consisted of £370 million which was spent by schools, colleges, awarding bodies and the Qualifications and Curriculum Authority on direct examination costs, and a further £240 million estimated as the cost in terms of staff time in running examination activity in schools and colleges. In Northern Ireland there is a statutory requirement for diagnostic testing of all children in their last four years of primary education and figures released for this (see Gardner, 2010) suggest that in such a small jurisdiction this testing cost over £830,000 for 2009–10, not counting teacher time and disruption to class teaching. A report, in 2009, for the examinations regulators for England, Wales and Northern Ireland (Ofqual, 2009) collated the incomes of 12 leading awarding bodies covering these countries for the three years to 2007.

These figures gave an average yearly expenditure of £659.3 million, an increase of 15% over the previous two years. We believe that considerable proportions of this money could be better spent on assessments that support learning.

There are many more challenges for the education system but I will finish off with the example I used in the first edition, of how one small community espoused assessment for learning; an example that continues to inspire me today.

Assessment for learning: a compelling conceptualization

Any book covering the practice, theory and policy relating to a given educational concept might conceivably claim to provide a comprehensive analysis of that concept. We do not make such a claim for this book on assessment for learning because the extent of existing knowledge and understanding of such a complex process and set of techniques is still in its early stages. We might claim, however, to have assembled an authoritative account of what is known today, however inadequate the extent of this knowledge and understanding might be. Drawing as it does on the work of many researchers and practitioners, as well as our own, this is not an unreasonable claim. We will leave this for others to judge. What we can say categorically about assessment for learning, however, is that it is more often than not a fundamental element of any successful learning context.

Throughout all of the text in this book, therefore, the aim has been to offer what we hope is a 'compelling conceptualization' (Fullan, 2004: 43) of assessment as a process that exists primarily to serve learning. A deep appreciation of this concept was brought home to me very clearly in a presentation I attended on assessment for learning in 2004. The presenters were two teachers, Margo Aksalnik and Bev Hill, from a Rankin Inlet school in the Nunuvut Territory, a new province established in northern Canada in 1999. The main illustration in the talk was of the national symbol of the Inuit people, the Inukshuk. An Inukshuk is a person-like construction of medium-sized rocks, which has been used by the Inuit people for millennia as a means of guiding wayfarers in the treeless and landmark-less expanses of northern Canada. Their various uses include giving directions to good fishing waters or simply reassuring the wayfarer that others have passed the same way, and that they are on the right path. A reproduction of the illustrative model used by the two teachers is presented in Figure 17.1.

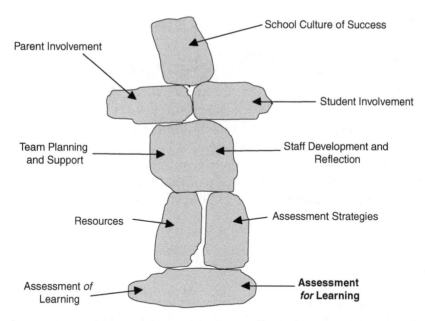

School Culture of Success

Parent Involvement

Student Involvement

Team Planning
and Support

Staff Development and
Reflection

Resources

Assessment Strategies

Assessment *of*
Learning

**Assessment
for Learning**

Figure 17.1   An Inukshuk guide to successful education (after Aksalnik and Hill, 2004)

As can be seen, they placed assessment for learning squarely in the set of main ingredients designed to create a school with a culture of success. The other elements included teachers, their planning of the learning activities, their teaching and assessment strategies, their capacity to reflect about their own and their students' learning, and the resources they bring to the learning environment. Outside of the classroom, additional elements include professional development and team support for the teachers while outside of the school, the positive involvement of parents adds to the recipe for success.

It is arguable that other aspects of a successful school could be found to populate the Inukshuk's frame – successful sporting programmes or a students' council, for example. No doubt they and other features of successful schools are also somewhere within the model, but the community-based context in which the two teachers introduced assessment for learning to their school dispelled any notion that its inclusion in the Inukshuk was either whimsical or contrived for the event (a seminar on assessment for learning on Vancouver Island). They recounted that: 'The Elders met to consider these new approaches and had the concept of assessment for learning explained to them. They then came up with a word to identify the dynamic – the resonance – between teaching, learning and assessment.' (Aksalnik and Hill, 2004)

This new word, in the Inuktitut language of the Inuits, is:

$$\Delta c C \triangleright \sigma d c n \sigma^{q_b}$$

i   li   ta   u   ni   ku   li   ri   ni   q

and is written in Roman form as Illitaunikuliriniq (or in sound form: ee-lee-tau-nee-qu-lee-ree-nee-kay).

Most non-Inuit educationalists will have difficulty articulating this word but they will not fail to empathize with the assessment for learning aspirations of this small community in Canada's frozen north.

References

Aksalnik, M. and Hill, B. (2004) Oral presentation to 'Making Connections', Assessment for Learning Symposium, Vancouver Island, Classroom Connections, Courtenay, July.

ARG (1999) *Assessment for Learning: Beyond the Black Box*. University of Cambridge: Assessment Reform Group.

ARG (2002a) *Assessment for Learning: 10 Principles*. University of Cambridge: Assessment Reform Group.

ARG (2002b) *Testing, Motivation and Learning*. University of Cambridge: Assessment Reform Group.

ARG (2009) *Assessment in Schools: Fit for Purpose?*, available at www.tlrp.org/pub/documents/assessment.pdf

Black, H. (1986) 'Assessment for learning', in D.J. Nuttall (ed.), *Assessing Educational Achievement*. London: Falmer. pp. 7–18.

Black, P. and Wiliam, D. (1998a) 'Assessment and classroom learning', *Assessment in Education*, 5: 7–71.

Black, P. and Wiliam, D. (1998b) *Inside the Black Box: Raising Standards through Classroom Assessment*. London: King's College (see also *Phi Delta Kappan*, 80: 139–48).

Fullan, M., Bertani, A. and Quinn, J. (2004) 'New lessons for districtwide reform', *Educational Leadership*, April: 42–6.

Gardner, J. (2010) Report from the Working Group on the InCAS Errors of October 2009, Department of Education for Northern Ireland, available at: www.deni.gov.uk/incas_working_group_report.pdf

Harlen, W., Darwin, A. and Murphy, M. (1977) *Leader's Guide: Match and Mismatch Raising Questions and Match and Mismatch Finding Answers*. Edinburgh: Oliver and Boyd.

Ofqual, Welsh Assembly Government, Council for Curriculum, Examination and Assessment (2009) *Annual Qualifications Market Report, 2009*. Ofqual.

Pring, R. (1986) 'The developing 14–18 curriculum and changes in assessment', in T. Staden and P. Preece (eds), *Issues in Assessment, Perpectives 23*. Exeter: University of Exeter. pp. 12–21.

PricewaterhouseCoopers (PWC) (2005) *Financial Modelling of the English Exams System* 2003–4.

Name Index

Subject Index

978-1-84860-616-6

978-1-84920-030-1

978-1-84920-114-8

978-1-84860-713-2

978-1-84920-076-9

978-1-84920-126-1

978-1-84920-078-3

Find out more about these titles and our wide range
of books for education students and practitioners at
www.sagepub.co.uk/education

EXCITING EDUCATION TEXTS FROM SAGE